917.30

W9-DAO-148

Hunt, Gaillard

Life in America
one hundred years
ago

$10.00

90
96
98

LIFE IN AMERICA
ONE HUNDRED YEARS AGO

Corner House Publishers

SOCIAL SCIENCE REPRINTS

General Editor MAURICE FILLER

EDITOR'S PREFACE

❦   ❦

First published in 1914 exactly 100 years after the United States and England signed the peace treaty that concluded the War of 1812, *Life In America One Hundred Years Ago* provides a fascinating look at the Republic in its still formative period. Badly divided by the recent War with England but united in their optimistic vision of the future, the American people set about healing their political wounds and building their fortunes large and small. Gaillard Hunt, scholar and historian, vividly portrays the nature of early 19th century American life. His primary concern is the quality of that life. What were ordinary Americans concerned with in 1814? What did they wear and how did they spend their time? What was the position of women? of religion? of sports? How did they educate their children? What were the feelings of the American people toward their leaders little more than thirty years after the Revolution? The author discusses these aspects of life along with the status of medicine, hospitals, transportation and virtually all aspects of life during this period. Highly readable, richly illustrated, filled with illuminating information, Mr. Hunt's study has long been used as a valued picture of the social life of the United States on the eve of the Industrial Revolution.

LIFE IN AMERICA ONE HUNDRED YEARS AGO

BY

GAILLARD HUNT, Litt.D., LL.D.

ILLUSTRATED

CORNER HOUSE PUBLISHERS
WILLIAMSTOWN, MASSACHUSETTS 01267
1976

FIRST PUBLISHED 1914

SECOND PRINTING 1976

BY

CORNER HOUSE PUBLISHERS

ISBN 0-87928-023-9

RAR3276

Printed in the United States of America

TO

RIDGELY HUNT

MY ELDEST BROTHER AND KINDEST FRIEND

I DEDICATE THIS BOOK AS A TOKEN

OF MY AFFECTION AND GRATITUDE

CONTENTS

ILLUSTRATIONS

PREFACE

THIS book was written at the request of the Committee of One Hundred to celebrate one hundred years of peace between Great Britain and the United States at the city of Washington, and is a contribution to that celebration. It is a sketch, drawn in outline, of life and manners in the United States in the year when peace was made with Great Britain, and this nation started upon a career of separate, independent national development. I have suggested some of the causes of the development, and have portrayed the character of the people in a general way. I hope I have been able to communicate some of the atmosphere of the time to my narrative. It was an invigorating atmosphere, full of life and inspiration to those who breathed it. We must believe that it was, for if it had not been we should not now rank among the great nations.

While I write these lines the minds of all Americans are occupied with fearful thoughts of the war in Europe. The ebb and flow of the tide of battle are watched anxiously from day to day, and we are wondering helplessly what will be the eventual outcome. We are conscious that changes in civilization, the nature of which human knowledge and human experience cannot foretell, are now preparing. At this

period of dreadful uncertainty in the European outlook our minds may turn with satisfaction to the con-
templation of that time, one hundred years ago,
when England and the United States made a treaty
which recited that they wished to be at peace with
one another. The progress of the spirit of peace between the two nations during the century which has
ensued is a fact which we can accept with full knowledge that it has been of benefit to mankind. Yet it
has grown with the strength of the nations. They are
of more equal strength now than they were when the
peace was first made. Nor has the friendship been
due to absence of rivalry and to separation from each
other. On the contrary, we are rivals in every branch
of human effort, and the whole length of a boundary
of each touches a boundary of the other. Yet so
amicable have the relations between Canada and the
United States been for the past century that it requires an effort of memory to recall any differences
that have arisen. One can walk across the boundary
line without realizing that he has passed from domestic to foreign territory, except as he is reminded of it
by the existence of a custom-house. The most populous portions of the United States and Canada are
separated by the Great Lakes, and the traveler may
sail them from end to end and see no sign to suggest
that they are not a highway reserved exclusively for
peaceful voyaging. Unfriendly feelings must have a
starved existence when all the outward signs are of
amity and good-will. The treaty of peace of 1815
had a far-reaching consequence in that simple agreement made on April 28, 1817, by Richard Rush, act-

PREFACE

ing for the American government, and Charles Bagot, acting for Great Britain, which recites that each government may have only one small vessel, with one small cannon upon it, on each lake, and that "All other armed vessels on these lakes shall be forthwith dismantled, and no other vessels of war shall be there built or armed."

GAILLARD HUNT.

WASHINGTON, D. C., *October 9, 1914.*

LIFE IN AMERICA
ONE HUNDRED YEARS AGO

LIFE IN AMERICA ONE HUNDRED YEARS AGO

I

PEACE

THE treaty of peace which terminated the second war between the United States and Great Britain was signed at Ghent by the American and British envoys on December 24, 1814; and on the 26th Henry Carroll, one of the secretaries to the American envoys, started for Washington with a copy of the treaty, going by way of England, where he met the British sloop of war *Favorite*, on which he sailed from Plymouth for New York, January 2, 1815. On the same ship with him was Anthony St. Jno. Baker, secretary to the British negotiators, also carrying a copy of the treaty and clothed with authority to ratify it with the American government. To insure safe delivery of the precious document a second messenger had been sent by the American envoys on a ship bound for Chesapeake Bay, but he arrived two days after Mr. Carroll, and consequently brought no news. The *Favorite* was spoken off Sandy Hook on Friday evening,

1

February 10th, by the British ship *Tenedos*, having been thirty-eight days in crossing. She came up the Bay the following day, and Carroll landed at the Battery at eight o'clock on Saturday evening and went directly to the City Hotel on Broadway near Cedar Street. The news which he carried swept before him, and within twenty minutes after he had landed lower Broadway was illuminated, and men paraded up and down the street with lighted candles in their hands, shouting that peace had come. At noon of Sunday Carroll left New York by post-chaise for Washington. He passed through Philadelphia just twelve hours later and reached Washington shortly after dark on Tuesday. This was fast traveling, for the distance was two hundred and ten miles by the road he took. When the treaty was ratified a few days later a copy was sent to New York by express, going from Washington to Philadelphia in fourteen hours and from Philadelphia to New York in nine hours, making twenty-three hours for the whole distance; but this was by relays, and was considered a notable feat.

As late as Sunday, February 12th, there was no inkling in Washington that Carroll had reached American shores, nor of the news he bore; but on Monday evening a rumor of the facts was abroad and threw the city into a tremor of excitement. It had come by express from Baltimore, and there was doubt of its truth, for people feared lest it might be a report started by speculators in stocks. Early the following evening, however, Mr. Carroll's post-chaise, drawn by four horses, came lumbering through Bladensburg,

2

on past the ruined Capitol and down Pennsylvania Avenue, following for this part of the journey the same road that Ross and Cockburn's men had traveled when they had entered and sacked the city the summer before. It was a clear, cold night, but Pennsylvania Avenue was deep with mud, for it had been raining all the previous week. So the chaise plunged and splashed on in the darkness, until it came to the house where Carroll's chief, James Monroe, the Secretary of State, lived. As soon as Carroll's coach had been recognized it was known that the rumor of the previous day was true, and a crowd of cheering men and boys followed him as he drove through the city. Their enthusiasm was partly due to an error on their part, for they thought the peace had been brought about in consequence of the battle of New Orleans. On February 4th the city had been illuminated in honor of that victory, and on February 11th rockets had been set off to celebrate the evacuation of Louisiana by the British army. The treaty of peace had been signed before these things occurred, but the news coming soon afterward was inextricably interwoven in the popular mind with this final triumph of American arms.

As soon as Secretary Monroe had received the treaty from Carroll they went down the street together to show it to President Madison.

The President was not occupying the White House at the time. The walls of that structure were standing in unimpaired strength, but they were defaced and blackened by the fire with which the enemy had sought to destroy it four months before. While the work of rebuilding was in progress he was living in the private residence which Col. John Tayloe had generously placed at his disposal. It stood, and still stands, at the corner of New York Avenue and Eighteenth Street, and is a unique example of the genius as an architect of Dr. William Thornton. There is a large circular hall on the first floor from which a broad staircase winds upward for three flights. The rooms are large and cheerful, with bay-windows and curved walls; and to obtain these lines of beauty in the interior the outer walls are several-sided, and the house has always been known as the "Octagon House." The dining-room is on the right of the front door as you enter, and the large drawing-room is on the opposite side; and here, if he followed his custom, the President was sitting, conversing with his wife and members of his household, when Secretary Monroe and Mr. Carroll were announced. Of course, they were talking of peace, and they made no secret of their hope that it would come soon.

In truth, everybody was tired of the war. It had worn itself out without either side conquering. The American navy had won glorious victories. General Jackson had annihilated the British army at New Orleans. The disgrace of Detroit and Bladensburg had in a measure been wiped out. The contest could now be closed with honor, and it was expedient to close it. As a matter of fact, none of the concrete causes which had brought it on now existed. They had arisen in consequence of the war between France and England and our neutral position. But France and England were now at

THE OCTAGON HOUSE

Occupied by President Madison after the burning of the White House in 1814

peace, we were not neutral any longer, and there were no neutral rights to infringe upon. There were no war orders, no decrees against our vessels, no seizures, no searches for contraband, no paper blockades, no impressments of American seamen. We could keep on fighting, if we chose to do so, over the abstract question of whether England had had a right to do these things and would have a right to do them again. For the present they were not being done, and we had fought because they had been done, and not because England had asserted a right to do them. As for the question of expediency, the American government had no desire to stand against the undivided land and naval forces of England, fresh from their victories over France.

The greatest disappointment of the war had been the attitude of many of the people at home. Speaking broadly, the South had supported the war; the new West had supported it better than the South; in the Middle States there was much opposition to it, and the East had opposed it bitterly. At this very moment five leading citizens of New England, sent as delegates from the convention which had met at Hartford early in January to formulate measures against the war policy of the administration, were on their way to Washington, bearing grievances and threats against the federal government.

Although the President earnestly desired peace, the last advices from the commissioners at Ghent had discouraged his hopes of obtaining it until there had been more fighting. He and his envoys thought the British envoys were purposely delaying the negotiations, believing that New Orleans and the mouth of the Mississippi would soon fall into their hands. They demanded as a basis of peace that each country should retain in its possession such territory as it might hold when the war should close. As late as October 19th the American commissioners had been instructed not to yield to the British demands. After further discussion they had been dropped, and at the same time the American commissioners withdrew their insistence that the treaty contain a clause in which Great Britain should expressly abandon the right of impressing into her service American seamen of British origin. So both commissioners having withdrawn the demands which caused contention, there was nothing to do but to write a treaty which declared that the two countries, having been at war, now desired to be at peace. The rest of the document was detail and a postponement of minor questions in dispute. The Federalists ridiculed the treaty as soon as they saw it, and most historians have dealt with it in the same spirit; but time has justified it, for the points of difference between the two countries on which it was silent have since been settled peacefully.

The President did not hesitate to accept the treaty, and it was no sooner in his hands than he announced his satisfaction with it. He was not a demonstrative man, and it is not recorded that he uttered any unusual expressions of pleasure when he knew that the war was over; but it was different with his wife. Dolly Madison radiated good nature, and her happiness was irrepressible. There are several accounts of what took place at the Octagon House that night, when the

PEACE

President told his wife that peace had come, which may be incorrect in the fact but are undoubtedly true in the impression they convey. It is said that she announced the fact to all the house by shouting, "Peace!" that some one rang the dinner-bell and shouted, "Peace!" that Miss Sally Coles, a cousin of Mrs. Madison's, who was living with them, went to the head of the basement stairs, where the negro servants were crowded, and shouted, "Peace!" that they took up the cry. Presently guests began to arrive, and the house was thronged with people who had one word upon their tongues—"Peace."

II

WHEN Mrs. Madison's dinner-bell rang in honor of peace it was not known that it was ringing out an old order and ringing in a new; that a turning-point in the destiny of the country had been reached; and that it was now for the first time fairly starting on a career, separate, independent, and its own. The days of ascendancy and control of its fathers were over. They had passed off the stage or were limping useless upon it. The Declaration of Independence had been signed thirty-eight years before, and only six of the signers survived—Jefferson, John Adams, Charles Carroll of Carrollton, William Floyd, and William Ellery. All were permanently retired from participation in public affairs except Ellery, who held the inconspicuous office of Collector of Customs at Newport. Elbridge Gerry, who died November 14, 1814, being at the time the Vice-President, was the last signer to hold an important office. None of the leading military characters of the Revolution was in the public eye except Timothy Pickering, who was playing an unpatriotic part. Nicholas Gilman, of New Hampshire, who died May 2d, 1815, and Rufus King, of New York, were the only members of the in surgery and mechanics, in navigation and agriculture, nay, even in mathematics, we find this distinction. Everywhere there is a class of men who cling with fondness to whatever is ancient, and who, even when convinced by overpowering reasons that innovation would be beneficial, consent to it with many misgivings and forebodings. We find also everywhere another class of men, sanguine in hope, bold in speculation, always pressing forward, quick to discern the imperfections of whatever exists, disposed to think lightly of the risks and inconveniences which attend improvements and disposed to give every change credit for being an improvement.

Thus it was that while the country was yet struggling in the meshes of its old customs there had arisen naturally a political party composed of men who remembered their origin and the origin of their institutions, who sympathized with England and who hated France. They wished to cultivate England's good will, and only stopped short of a desire to be in political subjection to her again, but in reality they were still in mental subjection to her. A French party was formed also, composed of radicals who looked with intense interest and sympathy upon her revolution as fully in line with our own, who remembered the alliance with sentimental feelings, who hated England because of the cruel incidents of the war. As the death-struggle of England and Napoleon grew fiercer the enthusiasm of the English and French parties in this country cooled, for both combatants treated American rights with that indifference which the rights of the feeble commonly receive. Moreover, few Americans went so far as to sympathize with a foreign nation against their own. The contemptuous treatment we received revealed our feeble-

Congress then sitting who had served in the Continental Congress.

It was twenty-seven years since the Constitution had been framed, and eleven of the forty-one members who attended the last sitting of the convention were alive. Except the President, only two of them were now men of influence—Charles Pinckney, who was powerful with the Republicans of South Carolina, and Rufus King, who had a following among the moderate Federalists of the East. Jared Ingersoll, of Philadelphia, had recently been defeated for the vice-presidency, but his influence hardly extended beyond the circle of lawyers and aristocrats among whom he moved. Gouverneur Morris, old and ill-tempered, was cursing the administration's policy, but he had no audience. As the membership of the Cabinet had changed it had shifted steadily away from the old order. Albert Gallatin, the Secretary of the Treasury, who had participated in the Revolution and the adoption of the Constitution, was succeeded by George W. Campbell, who gave way to Alexander H. Dallas, and he to William H. Crawford, and none of these had been in public service until after the Constitution was adopted. Dallas and then Crawford had taken over the War Department, after William H. Eustis and John Armstrong, both officers in the Army of the Revolution, had successively retired. William Pinkney and Richard Rush, the Attorneys-General, were too young to have seen Revolutionary service; so was Benjamin W. Crowninshield, who succeeded William Jones, a Revolutionary soldier, at the head of the Navy Department. When Madison left the Presidency in 1817 he and James Monroe, his Secretary of State, were the only members of the administration who had been in public life when the new government was started.

In Congress there had been a revolution, and the power had passed into the hands of the young men, who controlled the House of Representatives—Henry Clay, the Speaker from 1811 up to 1814, aged in the latter year only thirty-seven; Langdon Cheves, his successor, of the same age; John C. Calhoun, the Chairman of the Committee of Foreign Affairs, and William Lowndes, the Chairman of the Committee of Ways and Means, both aged thirty-two; Felix Grundy, aged thirty-seven, and a few others who accepted their leadership.

The people had been slow to break away from old conditions, for habits of thought are not easily nor quickly changed. One hundred years ago there was not a man in America over thirty-eight years of age, of American birth, who had not been born a colonial Englishman. There was not a grown-up man of American parentage whose parents had not been born the subjects of a king, and nearly all had been born the subjects of the British king. The people had been brought up as colonists and had been stamped with the characteristics of colonists when their minds were in the plastic state. The Revolution had obliterated the stamp for a time, but in the quiet of peace it had begun to reappear, and many Americans began to look at things as they had been accustomed to look at them in earlier days. Each man concerned himself with his immediate surroundings and the

political entity of which he and his forefathers had been a part. This had been the colony and was now the state. He took an interest, too, in the affairs of Europe. For a century and a half he and his ancestors had resided in a European dependency, and during all of that time European politics had been of direct concern to him. He was not yet used to his own national government, which had taken the place of the European government. It was an experiment which he regarded critically, with a feeling of aloofness and without affection. France and Englan[d] then monopolized the European stage, and it is n[ot] strange that they should have taken up a great d[eal] of the attention of Americans. One country they [had] been accustomed to think of as the mother cou[ntry] and until recently they had called it "home." [The] other had been their traditional enemy, against [whom] their forefathers had waged war almost contin[ually]. Recently she had fought with them when th[ey] rebelled against the mother country. The u[...] of cleavage between those whose minds cli[ng to the] past and who take their lessons from its [...] and those who put the past behind them [...] upon the present and the hopes of the fut[ure ...] parent. Macaulay's description is as a[pplicable to] parties in America as it is to parties i[n England:]

In one sense, indeed, the distinction which [was ob-] vious [in 1641 in England] had always existed [and will always] exist. For it has its origin in diversities of [temper, of under-] standing, and of interest, which are found [in all societies, and] which will be found till the human mind c[eases to be drawn in] opposite directions by the charm of habit [and the charm of] novelty. Not only in politics, but in litera[ture ...]

ness as it had not been revealed before. It appeared that we had grown in size, but not in strength.

Two serving-men in Shakespeare's "Coriolanus" are arguing against peace:

"Ay," says one, "and it makes men hate one another."

"Reason," says the other: "because they then less need one another."

It is undoubtedly true that in the long interval of peace after the revolution the different sections, states, and parties of the country, not having the need of one another plainly before their eyes, drifted into a selfish rivalry and opposition to one another which engendered bad feeling and closely bordered upon the land of hate.

A new generation of men who had never themselves known colonial dependence came to the rescue. They pushed the old leaders aside and led the country, all unprepared and disunited as it was, into the war, and there it was more united than it had been in peace, and soon the English and the French parties disappeared. Factional opposition to the war itself, however, became more dangerous; and, of course, the personal jealousies and antagonisms which arose among the military rivals were communicated to their followers and created bad feeling. The passions of the factions had reached the critical stage when the peace came. The people were united in approving that, at any rate. They were worn out with domestic quarrels and glad to readjust themselves to new conditions. The foreign parties were dead; the conduct of France and England had killed them. So was the issue upon which the people had split so bitterly—of whether the war should be waged. There was no European aggression to fear; the European peace had settled that. Old points of difference being dead, there was a season when the new points were developing, but were not yet plainly obvious—a season of calm between storms and of uninterrupted development of material strength. The signing of the Declaration of Independence had marked the beginning of the nation; the signing of the Treaty of Ghent marked the beginning of its vigorous young manhood.

III

THE LAND

WHEN an American spoke of his country a hundred years ago he always spoke of it in the plural number, having it in his mind as a union of separate sovereign states. He had not yet grasped the fact that he was a citizen of a continental nation. When he bounded the United States he bounded the territory of 1783 and nearly always left out Louisiana, although that enormous domain had been added to the United States thirteen years before. When the question of buying it was under discussion in the House of Representatives in 1802 one of the members, Roger Griswold, of Connecticut, truly said that the framers of the Constitution had never looked forward to an addition to the Union of new territory so large that it would overbalance the old territory. Nor had the citizens of the old states looked forward to it, and they did not understand it. That they were beginning to do so was an important circumstance in showing that the consciousness of the national destiny had awakened. Already the more advanced teachers were telling their scholars that all the territory under the federal government might be properly included in the term the United States.

The boundaries of the territory of 1783 were commonly understood to be New Brunswick on the northeast, Canada on the north, the Atlantic Ocean on the southeast, the Spanish possessions of East and West Florida on the south, the Mississippi River on the west; but the northeastern boundary line was not yet drawn, and there was dispute with Spain over the extent of the Floridas. The area was ordinarily computed as being 1,000,000 square miles, about 1,400 miles from the northern to the southern boundary, about 1,400 miles across in the northern and about 700 miles in the southern part. Of the boundaries of Louisiana all was uncertainty. The eastern limit was put down as the Mississippi River, "which," said the geographers, "separates it from the United States and West Florida," but they did not agree about the other boundaries. One said it was bounded on the south by the Gulf of Mexico, on the west by New Mexico and unknown lands, on the north by lands still possessed by the Indians. Another gave the southern boundary as New Orleans, the western as New Mexico, the northern as "the unknown regions." A more detailed description of the western boundary was New Mexico and a "ridge of mountains generally denominated the Shining Mountains, which divide the western waters of the Mississippi from those that flow into the Pacific Ocean." It was generally believed that some part of it extended to the Pacific Ocean. The area was computed as being more than a million square miles, but how much more no one cared to guess. The real area of the original territory was only 827,844 square miles, and of Louisiana 1,171,931, but our concern is to know what the people thought it was rather than what it was.

In 1815 there was no land-hunger in America. If there had been any before the purchase of Louisiana the unexpected acquisition of that vast expanse had more than satisfied it. It was not until a generation later, when a Southern party which desired to increase its political power by increasing the territory which it could control arose, that the appetite for more land became a craving with a part of the people. It is true that the Floridas were desired; not, however, for their terrritory so much as because they were in the way of the orderly progress of the commerce and population of the United States and were a menace to our peace. The symmetry of the sea-coast was destroyed by this foreign peninsula between the ocean and the Gulf. As soon as Louisiana was acquired the fate of the Floridas was sealed. Already the government had taken steps to buy them from Spain, and five years later the sale was consummated.

The United States was divided territorially into eighteen states and four territories. Vermont had been admitted in 1791, Kentucky in 1792, Tennessee in 1796, Ohio in 1802, Louisiana in 1812. The organized territories were Indiana, Illinois, Michigan, Missouri, and Mississippi. Maine was a district of Massachusetts till 1820. Wisconsin was included in Illinois until 1818, when Illinois became a state, and Wisconsin was attached to Michigan. Missouri took in everything north and west of the state of Louisiana. The area of the whole country was understood to be about 2,000,000 square miles, the extreme length from north to south 1,500 miles, the extreme breadth from east to west 2,000 miles. The inhabitants proudly said that it was the largest country in the civilized world except Russia. The great size and unknown extent furnished food for their imagination; and now that their attention was concentrated on their own affairs they began to see the vision of the future and to indulge in bold and expansive hopes. That they were well governed was recognized by foreigners. "Humanly speaking," said one of them, "no circumstance *can* prevent these United States from becoming eventually, and at no distant period, a great and powerful nation, influencing and controlling the other sovereignties of the world."

From every old community in the East adventurous young men went forth to explore and conquer the unknown country stretching toward the "Shining Mountains," and to every old community came back the stories of its wonders. The people fed upon wonders, and, not unnaturally, came to believe that their own wisdom and energy had accomplished things which the favors of nature alone had produced.

"The United States," says the *Easy Grammar of Geography*, published in 1818, compressing all the virtues of the nation into two sentences, "are celebrated for the excellence of their Constitution, which provides for political liberty and individual security. The inhabitants are justly famed for their ardent love of freedom, for their hospitality and industry, and for the great attention they pay to agriculture and commerce."

IV

THE PEOPLE

THE census of 1810 showed that there were then 7,239,903 inhabitants in the United States, including Louisiana, of whom 1,191,364 were negro slaves. By 1815 the whole population was more than 8,000,000. For the first ten years of national existence (from 1790 to 1800) it had increased by 2,000,000; for the second (1800 to 1810) by 3,500,000; that is to say, by 34½ per cent. for the first ten years and 36¼ per cent. for the second decade. By 1830 it was 12,866,020; by 1860, 31,443,321, and it is now about 94,000,000. The most sanguine prophets did not prognosticate so rapid an increase.

It was customary to divide the population ethnologically into three great classes: Europeans and their descendants, Africans and their descendants, and Indians. The Europeans were of English, Dutch, German, French, Irish, Scotch, Swedish, Swiss, and Welsh stock. New England and the South, so far as its white population was concerned, were inhabited almost exclusively by English descendants. One-fourth of the population of Pennsylvania were Germans, of whom there were many also in New Jersey and New York. There were descendants of French Protestants in New York and South Carolina and

French Catholics in the new state of Louisiana. There were Dutch in New York, New Jersey, and Pennsylvania; Irish in New York, Pennsylvania, New Jersey, and Kentucky; a few Scotch in New Hampshire, New York, New Jersey, and North Carolina; Swedes in New Jersey, Pennsylvania, and Maryland; Swiss in Indiana Territory; and Welsh in New York and Pennsylvania. The Germans in Pennsylvania spoke their own language among themselves, but most of them knew English. Many of the French in Louisiana spoke only French. Speaking generally, however, the universal language was English, the predominant ancestry was English, the predominant customs and habits were English, modified by environment. The most populous state in the Union was still Virginia, with 974,622 people; but New York had moved up from the third place, which it had occupied in 1790, and was now close to Virginia, having a population of 959,949. Pennsylvania was third, with 810,091. The population of Virginia had grown in ten years by more than 200,000 people, but it had only gained 31,860 whites, and in the same period New York had gained 372,999 whites, and was now the most populous state in the number of white inhabitants. Massachusetts was the fourth state, with 472,040 people. It had gained 50,000 people in ten years. Kentucky had jumped from 73,677 to 406,511, and Ohio from 42,156 to 230,760. South Carolina had 415,110, having gained nearly 70,000 in ten years, but of these only 17,946 were white; and in the same time New Jersey, with 245,562 in 1800, had gained 34,000, nearly all of whom were white. It was plain that the old Southern states were losing their supremacy, the movement of population being to the North and the West.

Of the 1,200,000 slaves in the country only 418 were in New England. The so-called Middle States had 147,737, but this included 11,502 in Maryland, where slavery was still lawful. There were 15,017 in New York, 10,851 in New Jersey, 795 in Pennsylvania, 4,177 in Delaware, and 5,393 in the District of Columbia. All the rest of the slaves were in the South, including Kentucky and Tennessee. They were dying out in the North, where slavery was no longer lawful.

The Indian population had become unimportant in the East. A number of the Iroquois, or Six Nations, remained on their lands in the western part of New York. Wyandots, Delawares, and Shawanese had small areas of land in Indiana and Illinois. In Michigan and the Northwest territories there were many Indians, chiefly Chippewas. The Creeks, Cherokees, Choctaws, and Chickasaws occupied some of the most fertile portions of Georgia, Alabama, Mississippi, and Tennessee; but their power had been broken in the recent war, and already it was decreed that they must emigrate to the wilderness west of the Mississippi. It was estimated that there were still between 70,000 and 80,000 Indians east of the Mississippi. In the Western territory there were supposed to be 80,000 more.

The densest population was in Massachusetts, where the average was 65 people to the square mile; in New York State were 20, and only 14 in Virginia. In Illinois, Indiana, Michigan, Missouri, and the far

Western territory there were more square miles than there were people.

There were few large cities. New York was the largest, with 96,373 inhabitants, having passed Philadelphia, which had been the largest until recently and now had 92,247. The third city was Baltimore, with 46,555; Boston came next, with 33,250; then Charleston, with 27,711. New Orleans (17,242), Salem (12,615), and Providence (10,071) were the only other cities having more than 10,000 inhabitants. There were ten other cities which had more than 5,000. The whole population in cities of over 5,000 inhabitants was 406,731, only 6 per cent. of the whole. The proportion of city population increased steadily thereafter, and is now more than 40 per cent. of the whole. The figures are enough by themselves to show that the people were nearly all farmers. Many of them had a fear of the cities, born of ignorance and the free play of their imagination, and thought them to be centers of luxury and sin, places of gaiety and pleasures which turned the heads of girls, made them worldly, and tempted them to their fall, and where young men were led into dissipation, vice, and crime. The influence of the cities was not extensive. People traveled little, and comparatively few of them resorted to the cities often. The dependence upon them did not spread far, and their population subsisted upon the country immediately around them. The newspapers were published in the cities and were generally read, but they did not contain reports of those phases of life which lure the light-minded and viciously inclined.

THE PEOPLE

In the country each family was an independency. It provided nearly all the food it consumed, spun its own thread, and made much of its own cloth. There was exchange at the mill, and sales were made to obtain money for hats, shoes, metal ware, agricultural tools, and a few luxuries, but in the main the household stood alone, and might be cut off from communication with the rest of the world for months at a time without inconvenience.

The average value of the land for the whole country was $10 an acre. The highest valuation was in Rhode Island, where it was $39 for the whole state. In the South, where there was extensive planting, it was $4 in Virginia, $2.50 in North Carolina, $8.00 in South Carolina, $2.50 in Georgia. In New York large tracts were held by individuals under ancient charters or by purchase at state sales, and they were rented out to farmers for payments partly in produce and partly in money, but the rents were low. These were the only tenant farmers, all the rest of the land being tilled by those who owned it. There were no vassals, except as the slaves of the South were vassals. Leaving them out, there were no large bodies of men dependent for their sustenance and welfare upon a few men and subject to be used by them to further their designs, and consequently there were no large bodies of men who felt the animosity which dependents feel toward those who have power over them. Here was a land where men were free politically and industrially. Diversification of industries and consequent complications in the national life were beginning to appear, but had not yet come.

23

There had always been some manufacturing in the country, and after independence it had been encouraged by protective laws. The second war with Great Britain gave it a sudden and irresistible impulse by the high prices which manufactured articles commanded and the suspension of the foreign trade, which eliminated competition. Manufacturing sprang up quickly, especially in New England and the Middle States, and in the aggregate employed many persons. It was estimated in 1815 that the cotton and woolen manufactures, which were by far the largest and most important, employed in all about 200,000 persons, about 20,000 of whom were men, the rest being women and children and boys under seventeen years of age. Much of the manufacturing was carried on in families, however, the machinery used being simple and inexpensive. This was the case especially with cotton, wool, and flax. Two-thirds of the clothing and house linen of the inhabitants who did not live in cities was of family manufacture. In 1820, after the impulse to manufacturing had become settled, the largest number of persons employed in one district in manufacturing was in Huntingdon District, Pennsylvania, where 390, distributed through nine establishments, were engaged in making bar iron. The largest number in one locality in New England was 150 to 250 persons employed in making window-glass in three glass-works—two in Boston and one in Chelmsford. The country was far behind England in the use of machinery in manufactures. Steam iron-works were erected in Baltimore in 1814; but the motive power for all other manufactures was water or hand, whereas steam was already extensively in use in English factories. Great aggregations of capital, large establishments operated by expensive machinery, populous communities composed almost exclusively of factory workers, were unknown. So insignificant was the factory population when considered with reference to the whole that it need not be taken into account in forming a conception of the national life.

The school-book from which I quoted in the last chapter spoke of the devotion of the people to commerce as well as agriculture. Such was the case on the seaboard, especially in New England, and the shippers and seafaring men were an important although not a numerous part of the population. During the war some of the sailors had found employment in the navy, and many on privateers, and after the peace they went back to the merchantmen; but some of the capital which had been in the shipping had shifted permanently to manufactures. The commerce, except when it was interrupted by the war, was greater with Great Britain than it was with all other countries combined; but when the Spanish colonies in South America revolted it was believed that commerce with them would soon become the most important of all. An American authority (John Bristed), writing in 1818 on "The Resources of the United States," said "the greatest commercial benefit resulting from the emancipation of Spanish America would be the formation of a navigable passage across the Isthmus of Panama, the junction of the Atlantic and Pacific oceans. The expense of such an undertaking would not exceed three or four millions, sterling, and Great

Britain could not more profitably employ twenty or thirty thousand of her distressed laborers than in executing such a task, under the superintendence of competent engineers."

The idea was not new, but no one seriously advanced the proposition that the United States should build the canal.

V

OURSELVES AS OTHERS SAW US

THERE was little knowledge of the United States in foreign countries in 1815, and not much interest. The American Revolution had come when liberty was the fashion in Europe, when it was discussed by popular writers and talked of in drawing-rooms; and, with France as our ally, our struggle had arrested the attention of the civilized world; but the painful struggle of the new nation to stand alone afterward was not an inspiring spectacle, and received little notice. It was not generally believed that we would stand alone long. The cause of popular liberty had suffered serious discredit because it had assumed a hideous form in the French Revolution, and the pendulum had swung back to orthodox monarchical ideas of government. Moreover, the affairs of Europeans were in a crisis and engrossed their minds. Our second war with England received meager attention even in England itself, and still less on the Continent. Contemporaneous historians barely gave it a paragraph, and there were many intelligent Englishmen who had never heard of Andrew Jackson even after the battle of New Orleans. Such demand for information about the country and its people as existed was supplied by a few publications of travelers who told their experiences and impressions. Naturally, the narratives were disparaging, for the roughness of life and the hardships of travel put the tourists in bad humor. It is to be remarked, also, that the people of one nation are commonly prejudiced against other nations and that travelers are apt to belittle all nations but their own. Foreigners were not more unfair to Americans than Americans were to foreigners. The opportunities for observation of the travelers must also be remembered when we read their opinions. Some of them told of what they saw from the stage-coaches and learned from their fellow-passengers and at the taverns of the road, and knew nothing more. A dance held in the public room of an inn they recorded as a good example of the amusements of the people, and the drunkenness which was common among the frequenters of a place whose chief business was the sale of liquor was cited as an illustration of their habits. Thus one writer, Thomas Ashe, an Englishman, said that bigotry was the characteristic of the people in the Northeastern states; that society in the South was in a shameful state of degeneracy; that the people were turbulent, abandoned Christians, unnatural fathers, and treacherous friends; that there was no eloquence among the public men; and so forth. His observations were valueless because they contained hardly a trace of truth. Parkinson, another Englishman, wrote more discriminatingly, but hardly less severely. We were avaricious and unscrupulous, he said, and no transaction brought discredit on a man unless he lost money by it. This judgment was expressed by most commentators.

Isaac Candler, an Englishman who was pleasantly entertained on his travels and wrote sympathetically, said we were less sober than the people of the Continent, and about on a level in this respect with the Irish. Profanity prevailed to a shocking extent. Gambling was extensively practised, especially in the South, and dueling was more frequent and engaged in for less cause than in any country of Europe. The women were remarkably virtuous. The people were sociable, even to the point of familiarity, and were fond of asking questions. In the South they were irritable and quick to quarrel. Hospitality was a prevalent virtue, and the manners were generally agreeable.

Of course, the Englishmen took notice of the peculiar use of many words or expressions in America— of *clever* for *worthy* or *obliging*, of *smart* for *clever*, of *I guess* for *I suppose*, of *elegant* for *excellent*, of *I reckon* for *I think* or *I guess*, and similar colloquialisms; but several critics declared the mass of the people spoke better English than the mass of Englishmen, and that nowhere was anything heard as bad as the whine of Suffolk, the chipping of words of Yorkshire, and the guttural of Newcastle. Americans did not find an *h* at the beginning of words where it did not exist nor overlook it when it was there. The common pronunciation was that of educated Londoners. They were poor conversationalists, however, and inattentive to details. They had no taste in architecture and ornamentation, but the women dressed becomingly.

Perhaps the severest of all the critics, because there

was so much of truth in his criticisms, was Felix de Beaujour, a cultivated Frenchman who made a painstaking study of the country. Philadelphia, he said, was not only remarkable for the regularity of its streets, but for the cleanliness of the houses. New York wore a smiling aspect and was like a continental town; Boston and Baltimore were like English towns; Charleston, Norfolk, and New Orleans resembled the towns of the West Indies. Of the new capital, Washington, all he could say was that it resembled "those Russian towns traced in the deserts of Tartary, in whose inclosures we behold nothing but naked fields and a few glimpses of houses." As for national character, the Americans were a mixture of people sprung from so many different nations that thus far they had none. They had as much vanity as the oldest nations in Europe. The latter boasted of what they had done and the Americans of what they could do. They had no habits of their own. In the Northern states they were bold and enterprising, in the Middle states light and inconstant, in the South heedless and lazy. "A Bostonian would go in search of his fortune to the bottom of hell; a Virginian would not go across the road to seek it." In the North one found English manners; in the Middle region a thousand shades had colored English manners; in the South the manners were those of West-Indians. The planter's life was a continual scene of indolence and dissipation. Horse-racing and cock-fighting were his outdoor sports, gaming and drinking his diversions indoors. In the interior west of the Alleghanies manners were simpler and purer than in other parts. Gain

VIEW OF NEW YORK BAY FROM THE BATTERY, 1822

was the subject of conversation among all men and the level of all their actions. There was no country in the world where there was less generosity of sentiment, less charm of life. Everything was sacrificed to interest. All disinterested acts, all talents purely agreeable, were looked upon with contempt. An unbridled love of money was the spring of the Republic. Everything favored a vile cupidity. Bankruptcy in the commercial towns was often the shortest and surest road to fortune. In the country and the villages good and upright characters were as common in the United States as they were elsewhere; but high-spirited and lofty souls, great and noble characters, were rarer. The people had, however, a love of liberty, were industrious, and had high regard for the laws. The women were better than the men. They were beautiful until they were twenty-five years old, when their forms changed, and by the time they were thirty their charms had disappeared. They enjoyed great liberty till they married. Then they buried themselves in their families and appeared to live only for them. As wives they were faithful and thrifty and had none of the vices, but all of the virtues, of their husbands. The social life was joyless and monotonous. He thought the Americans were called upon to act a great part in the world, if they did not make their appearance on the stage too soon. The danger was that they might become the victims of their own dissensions and dissolve before they had formed into the body of a nation. Mongaret, another Frenchman, confirmed the general opinion that the Southerners were more dissipated than the Northerners, and more fond of gaming. He, also, thought the women pretty and amiable. Montule, also a French traveler, agreed on this point. He especially remarked the love of pleasure of the people of Louisiana and the deplorable frequency there of duels engaged in for insufficient cause. A careful estimate was made by Mackenzie, a Scotchman. He thought that the people of New England were inquisitive, that the descendants of the Dutch especially were avaricious, that the laboring - classes were better dressed and more independent than those of England, but the genteeler classes were more slovenly. The women were handsome, but not so healthy in appearance as the English, and their beauty was short-lived. The people of the Northern states were plain, honest, and industrious; the planters were lazy and self-indulgent. There was a deep prejudice between the people of the sections. Tobacco was used to excess by all classes, and they were generally addicted to dram-drinking. They carried the spirit of independence to an extreme and lacked courtesy. There was a dead-level of intelligence in the United States, the gradation of intellect which existed in England being unknown. The laborer was more intelligent than his brother in Europe; but the middle classes were not so well informed.

A few German and one or two Italian and Spanish travelers recorded their impressions, but they are unimportant. On certain points the foreigners were agreed, and these must be taken as being American characteristics palpable to outsiders. We were domestic in our tastes and fond of family life. Our women were beautiful and good. We were inquisitive; we were inordinately devoted to making money; we were too fond of strong drink; we were too fond of gambling; we were industrious in the North, but lazy in the South; intelligence was well diffused among us, but we produced few great characters; we neglected the light and agreeable things of life. They were fond of quoting this remark: "American theory is at least two centuries in advance of American practice."

As for the country itself, those who passed over it hardly saw more than the landscape and generally underestimated the fertility of the soil, while they appreciated the wonderful scenery.

As I have said, liberty was not the fashion for the moment, so the American government came in for condemnation because it had not power enough, especially in the executive branch. The general verdict was that the President ought to be given greater permanency of office, that there was an excess of liberty, the people being all and the government nothing. The elections were thought to be too frequent. As a consequence the Representatives were too dependent on their constituents and too local in their policy. Moreover, the constituencies were kept in an incessant turmoil of corrupting electioneering. The Union was in danger of breaking, because of the growth of sectional feeling engendered by the existence of slavery in one part. The West, too, when it became powerful would probably separate from the East.

3

VI

WHEN we came to judge ourselves Northerners and Southerners were prejudiced in their estimate of one another, and they then constituted the two great divisions of the people, the new West not yet having formed into a separate group. Southerners had no sympathy with the hard frugality of the North. Having slaves for laborers, large holdings of land by individuals, and a climate without a long, rigorous winter, frugality was not necessary with them. They found the leveling of classes of the North disagreeable, being accustomed to an aristocratic organization of society with a recognized higher class. They were fond of saying that there were few gentlemen in the North, and they used the word "gentlemen" in the same sense that Englishmen used it. They superintended their farms or engaged in professional pursuits, and the interests of a commercial people and of farmers who worked their own land seemed petty to them. In short, they thought themselves superior to their Northern neighbors. These remarks apply to the ruling class of Southerners, who owned the property and shaped the destiny of their part of the country. The poorer classes had no power, but they, too, disliked the Northerners. They knew very little about them and commonly associated them in

34

their minds with the Yankee peddlers who came among them occasionally and cheated them. The Southerners were often men of affairs, but they were seldom writers, and the product of their printing-presses was small. The result is that the record of their opinions is meager.

The home of the writers was then, as it is now, New England, and an investigator has not far to go to learn what they thought of themselves and of all other Americans. Even the most cautious and fair among them were outspoken in their reprobation of slavery and the effect it had upon the people of the South, making them lazy and arrogant, causing them to pursue pleasure too eagerly, thus encouraging gaming and conviviality, giving a tone to their character which placed them at a disadvantage when they were compared with the people of the North. Coming to more specific judgment, they found the planters of Maryland imperious and proud, "an almost necessary consequence of slave-keeping," but hospitable, with manners as polished as those of English country gentlemen, and generally of liberal education. The Virginians west of the Blue Ridge were industrious and temperate; east of the mountains the great planters were hospitable and of independent spirit, but idle and intemperate in their habits, and the lower orders were ignorant and abject. Here there was great disparity of fortunes and intellectual acquirements. The North-Carolinians were hospitable, but had no taste for learning, and temperance and industry could not be reckoned among their virtues. Among the lower classes the barbarous custom of rough-and-tumble fighting prevailed, as it did in the rest of the South and the West and in a less degree in the wilder portions of all the states, when the adversaries bit, scratched, and kicked as well as punched each other, and tried to blind each other by the horrible practice of "gouging," which consisted of forcing a man's eyes out of their sockets with the knuckles. This practice excited a great deal of comment, but the extent to which it prevailed has probably been exaggerated. North Carolina was said to be remarkable for the early marriages of some of its citizens, grandmothers not more than twenty-seven years old being occasionally met with. In South Carolina the fertility of the soil made the acquisition of wealth easy. Many people were rich and addicted to convivial pleasures and licentiousness. They were naturally quick and vivacious, but lacked enterprise and perseverance. They were open-handed in giving, highly polished, and well educated. The women lacked the bloom of the North, but had an engaging softness and delicacy of appearance and manners and were possessed of polite and elegant accomplishments. Charleston was famous for the gaiety and conviviality of the inhabitants, and many families there made a great display of wealth and taste. The Georgians were generally pronounced to be lazy, a result of the hot climate. Of Louisiana little was known; but the peculiar population, in which people of French origin predominated, was looked upon as essentially foreign and not yet within the circle of American life.

Of the character of the people of New England the highest opinions were entertained; and justly, although they came from New England men. There, they said, the people were nearly all of English descent, and the English language had been preserved pure and free from the corruptions which had crept into it in the Middle States, where the proportion of foreign-born residents was so large. The population were mostly of the middle class and escaped the vices of the rich and the sufferings of the poor. They were hardy and independent, and so jealous of their liberties that they were often the victims of imaginary grievances and groudless suspicions against the government. They were accused of impertinent inquisitiveness, but it was really only a form of their desire for knowledge. It was true that they were frugal in their personal expenses; but they were liberal in expenditures for public purposes. Especially were the people of Connecticut fortunate, for the individual holdings of land were small. There was a degree of political tranquillity in that state greater than in any other. They enjoyed as perfect independence and equality as any people in the world. But the state scandalized the country by the number of divorces it granted. They were the consequence of a law passed in 1667 permitting divorce for three years' wilful desertion by the husband or the wife. Many were arranged by mutual understanding. The immigrants who were building up the new West came largely from New England, so it could appropriately be called a nursery of men. As for the women, they were educated in housewifery, assiduous in household employments, and occupied their leisure hours in reading books of useful information.

The people of the Middle States presented variations which made it difficult to characterize them as a whole. In New York the Dutch descendants were noted for their conservatism and refusal to adopt improvements in agriculture. The large landholders lived like Englishmen. There were many New England people, and the most prevalent characteristics were those of New England. New York City had a social life as agreeable as any on the Continent. Already the turbulence and corruption of its elections were remarked upon. In Pennsylvania the population came from so many sources that general remarks could not be applied to it. The people were for the most part plain, frugal, and industrious, these being the qualities of the Germans to a notable degree. There had been a great deal of enterprise displayed, and much over-trading in consequence, with ruinous results. Of New Jersey there was a general verdict that the people were industrious, but paid little attention to education. The western part of the state traded with Philadelphia, and East Jersey with New York, so that manners in the former were like those of Philadelphia and in the latter like those of New York.

As for the people of the new states and the West, they were like the people of the states from which they had come. Kentuckians resembled Virginians; Tennesseeans, North-Carolinians; and the settlers in Ohio were like the people of Connecticut.

The hard judgment which the people of the two sections rendered of each other was due to the presence of slavery in one section.

VII

A MAN'S BODY AT AUCTION

AS this is a true picture of our country one hundred years ago, a chapter on slavery must be written; but the task is not so repulsive as it would be if we were considering slavery in America forty years later, when intelligent and well-meaning men were extolling it as a beneficent institution and trying to make it national in scope. In 1815 it was considered everywhere to be a local problem. It had existed in all of the colonies at the time of the Revolution; but each of the Northern states had abolished it by a gradual process, the first being Massachusetts and Pennsylvania in 1780 and the last New Jersey in 1804. Thereafter it existed only in the Southern states, including Delaware, and the few slaves still remaining in the Northern states were a negligible quantity. Nobody in the South defended it. The greatest apostle it had at a later period, John C. Calhoun, had already entered upon his public career, being one of the leaders of the House, but no word of defense of slavery came from him until some years later. George Mason's denunciation of it in the federal convention of 1787 was a correct statement of Southern sentiment then and for many years afterward. "Slavery discourages arts and manufactures," he said. "The poor despise

39

labor when performed by slaves. They prevent the immigration of whites, who really enrich and strengthen a country. They produce the most pernicious effect on manners. Every master of slaves is born a petty tyrant. They bring the judgment of Heaven on a country. As nations cannot be rewarded or punished in the next world, they must be in this. By an inevitable chain of causes and effects Providence punishes national sins by national calamities." There is not much to add to this sweeping paragraph from a Virginia planter and slaveholder.

As for the negroes themselves, they were better off as slaves in America than they had been as savages in Africa, and none of them wished to be sent back. Their morals were lax, their education was neglected, and their religious practices were crude; but in all these respects they were far in advance of their fathers and brothers on the Gold Coast. So far as food, medical attendance, clothing, and the amount of work exacted of them were concerned, speaking generally, they fared as well as the lowest class of free laborers. Again speaking generally, they had no feeling of animosity toward their masters. Although the masters sat in deathly fear that they would mutiny, subsequent events showed that there was never any real danger from this source. For the most part they were treated humanely and even indulgently. If the planter lived on his plantation he did not allow the overseer to ill-use them. The house-servants nearly always experienced kindness, and between them and their masters and mistresses there were strong ties of affection. Public opinion strongly reprobated

A MAN'S BODY AT AUCTION

cruelty to the slaves. The laws recognized them as having some of the rights of men. Under the national law five negroes were equal to three whites in computing the representation in the Lower House of Congress. In the states very severe laws existed designed to keep them in subjection; but the laws protected them also. The masters had no power of life and death over them, and could be punished for excessive cruelty. Nevertheless, individual cases of cruelty from the coarser members of society and those having charge of the slaves of others were common. But above all other cruel things that they had to endure was the cruel fact that they were slaves. Kind treatment, affection, improvement in mental, material, and moral condition, easy work—none of these things could cause them to forget, even for an instant, that they were bought, bred, and sold like brutes, and that they were men. Nor could any circumstance of expediency and the knowledge that they were not responsible for the imposition of the iniquity, nor any appeals to history and the Gospel, cause the owners to forget that it was a wrong for one man to hold another in bondage. These owners were proud of their record in the Revolution; they regarded themselves as peculiarly the guardians of freedom; they were orthodox in their religious views and believed that the earth was made especially for man. They held the sentiment which Walt Whitman wrote sixty years later:

A man's body at auction (For before the war I often go to the slave mart and watch the sale).
I help the auctioneer, the sloven does not half know his business. Gentlemen, look on this wonder:

Whatever the bid of the bidders they cannot be high enough for it.

For it the globe lay preparing quintillions of years without one animal or plant.

For it the revolving cycles truly and steadily roll'd.

The old President had been the master mind of the convention which framed the Constitution and had contended against any recognition in it of slavery, and the word, if not the fact, was excluded. He had agreed then with George Mason's views which I have quoted, and he never changed his mind. Henry Clay, also born in Virginia and a citizen of a Southern state, already the leader of a great party, denounced slavery boldly. David Ramsay, of South Carolina, published his history of the United States in 1818, in which he said that slavery produced idleness, which was the parent of every vice, and, while it caused a few men to grow rich, depressed the community to a low station in the scale of national greatness. "Unhappy are the people," he said, "where the original decree of Heaven that man should eat his bread in the sweat of his brow is by any means whatever generally eluded."

These are examples which could be multiplied indefinitely. Instances of the defense of slavery at this time cannot be found, for there are none.

But if everybody disapproved of the institution, why was it continued? The answer is that no good plan for getting rid of it was proposed and none could be devised. If the negroes were freed they must be removed, because they were a permanently inferior race which could not fuse with the white race. There

must come a complete readjustment of society, and
problems worse than slavery would arise. The slaves
represented the chief property of the South. Who was
to pay for them if they ceased to be property? The
expense would be tremendous and the free states
showed no desire to share it. A hundred ways of freeing them were discussed, but none seemed practicable. Moreover, there were a great many people who
did not want them freed. They did not approve of
slavery morally or theoretically, but they preferred
it to the prospects which freedom opened. So when
emancipation projects came to the issue public opinion would not support them.

Mason, Madison, and Clay, were slaveholders.
So were John Gaillard, the Vice-President; James
Monroe, the Secretary of State; and George W.
Campbell, the Secretary of the Treasury. Gaillard
was president *pro tempore* of the Senate; Clay was
speaker of the House till his place was taken in June
of 1814 by Langdon Cheves, of South Carolina, another slaveholder. The leaders of the House were
Calhoun, William Lowndes, and Felix Grundy, all
slaveholders. William H. Crawford, of Georgia, was
Minister to France; Thomas Sumter, Jr., of South
Carolina, to Portugal; two of the four representatives of the United States to foreign powers were
slaveholders. The proportion was about what it had
been since the beginning of the government. Three
of the four Presidents, two of the five Vice-Presidents,
fourteen of the twenty-six Presidents of the Senate,
five of the ten Speakers of the House, had been slaveholders. Up to the time of Lincoln's election in 1861,

a period of seventy-two years, the President's chair was occupied by a slaveholder for fifty years—two-thirds of the time.

Surely, then, if we believe that the United States advanced in those years, we must believe that there was something of good in the institution under which those who governed it while it advanced were born and reared. That good can be stated in a word. It was the companion of the evils of the system. As George Mason said, every man born a master of slaves was born a petty tyrant; and as Ramsay said, he was born to idleness and to wealth without laboring for it. Thus there arose a class of men accustomed to exercise authority over others from their infancy, having time to study and to undertake public affairs, having the power and prestige of wealth—in short, a governing class. The President was one of them. He held his first public office when he was twenty-five years old, and thereafter was almost continuously in the service of the state or the nation for more than forty years. Beyond conducting the large farm which he inherited from his father, he followed no gainful employment. Another was William Lowdnes. A few weeks after he was married, when he was only twenty years old, his wife's father advised her to learn to keep the plantation books, so that she could take charge of her husband's affairs. "Before many years," said he, "Lowndes will undoubtedly be called to public life." He entered the state legislature when he was twenty-four years old and remained in public affairs until a few months before his untimely death at the age of forty.

That country was fortunate which had in its gov-

44

ernment men like Madison and Lowndes. It was not to be expected that many of their colleagues should be their peers—that there should be many as profound scholars of government as Madison or as effective legislators as Lowndes—but they had worthy associates in John Marshall, the Chief Justice; James Monroe; James Barbour, Senator from Virginia; Felix Grundy, Representative from Tennessee; William Gaston and Nathaniel Macon, Representatives from North Carolina; Calhoun; Clay; Cheves; and many others, all Southern slaveholders.

One influence that operated to produce men of this type was the high character of the mothers who bore them and the wives who ruled their homes. Among the wealthy ruling class the side of slavery which the women saw developed their compassion and unselfishness. They were the ones who improved the negroes' morals, taught them religion, and attended to their bodily welfare. Before marriage their lives were idle enough, but their pleasures were innocent. They married early and had large families. They did not cultivate their minds by much book learning, but their characters were developed by their duties and responsibilities. Like Mrs. Lowndes, some of them managed the business affairs of their plantations, and most of them had large households with many domestic servants, and dispensed a lavish hospitality. The men might be coarse among men, but their homes were refined. Among the pernicious effects that slavery had on manners was an increasing number of mulattoes. Sensuality among the lower-minded men degraded the morals of the negro women;

45

and at the same time, removing the white women from dangers from these men, left them to live in an atmosphere of purity. The men associated the women of their order with their higher and better ideas, domestic pleasures, charitableness, religion and virtue. Although the society was idle and wealthy, it was remarkably free from domestic scandals.

The institution depressed the mass of the people in the community, but elevated individuals. Taking it with its evil and its good—and the evil far outweighed the good—it must be recognized that it played an important part in forming the national character and shaping the national destiny.

It created a fundamentally different civilization from that of the North. Here was the strange spectacle of a country one-half of which based its prosperity on slave labor and the other half of which owed its advancement to free labor. Antagonism was certain to arise. The *Farmer's Almanac* for 1814, printed in Boston, had these remarks to make for the month of November:

It has been said that we cannot live without the corn, rice, etc., of the Southern planter; but the fact is if we cultivate our land as we ought we shall have abundance of breadstuff, and there will be no need of depending upon the labor of the poor and miserable slaves of the South for our maintenance.

If the farmers felt so strongly on the subject, it was plain that the seeds of disunion sentiments because of opposition to slavery were already planted. They had not yet, however, appeared aboveground. It was only a few years since the Northern states had emancipated their slaves, and it was believed the

Southern states would, one after the other, follow the example. At any rate, there was no belief that slavery would spread. It was regarded strictly as a state institution and each Southern state might abolish it, as each Northern state, acting by itself, had done. This was the feeling in 1815, and whatever dissatisfaction on the part of any faction existed with the Union was not then based upon the existence or non-existence of slavery.

VIII

COACH AND SLOOP

NOW the people of the United States were more
nearly united after the Treaty of Ghent was
signed than they had been at any time since the close
of the Revolution, but they still looked at many things
which were really national from a sectional point of
view. Because the sections were so far away from
each other, and knew so little of each other, they were
jealous and were constantly playing for advantage.
One example of the feeling which, while it was diminishing and was not universal, was prevalent will suffice. Because the capital had been located on the
border of Virginia a writer said it was "calculated to
entail upon the state of Virginia the chief sway and
influence over all the rest of the Union, and to check
the career of the Northern and Middle states, whose
far superior capacities, both physical and moral, in
population, wealth, industry, and intelligence, would
eventually sink Virginia into the rank of a second-rate
sovereignty, if the seat of the national government were
on the Northern line and the Northern states were permitted to avail themselves of all their agricultural and
commercial advantages. Whereas now, the Virginians
having the seat of government within their own territory, made it the focus of their own political intrigues;

FROM A BOOKING-LIST

and by managing the people withindoors in the different states, they return nearly what members to Congress they please, and induce them to legislate in accordance with the scheme of Virginian policy; which never has been favorable to large and liberal views of commercial enterprise." Thus there was believed to be antagonism of interests between the sections, and consequent suspicion of motives and harsh accusations instead of friendly rivalry and emulation of members of the same family having common interests. It was inevitable that it should be so, however, when the people lived far apart and few could travel. Between New York and Philadelphia, the two chief cities, there was more travel than there was between any other two points in the country. Four stages started from either city for the other each day, or daily except Sundays. A "Pilot Stage" left every morning at five o'clock, and traveled the distance in from fourteen to sixteen hours. The fare was ten dollars, and seven passengers could be carried in summer. The "Commercial Stage," which went every day but Sunday, carried the same number. It left New York at seven in the morning, stopped at Trenton for the night, and reached Philadelphia at seven the following morning. The fare was six dollars. The "Mail Stage" charged ten dollars and carried only six passengers. It left New York at one o'clock every afternoon and arrived in Philadelphia at six the next morning. Carrying seven passengers at ten dollars fare for each, the "Expedition Stage" left New York daily at four o'clock in the afternoon, stopped at Bridgetown or Milton for the night, and arrived in Philadelphia the following afternoon. The stage office was at No. 1 Cortlandt Street, in New York, and the stages stopped in Philadelphia at the Mansion House, City Hotel, and Mail-Stage Office on South Third Street. They were ferried over the Hudson River at New York to and from Powles Hook, or Paulus's Hook, now Jersey City, from the foot of Cortlandt Street, by the steam ferry-boat. The boats ran every half-hour and the fare was 12 cents for a foot passenger, carriages being from 75 cents to $1.50. Between New York and Brooklyn there was a horse-boat running every fifteen minutes, the fare being 4 cents per passenger. By this boat the power which turned the paddle-wheel was made by two horses on a treadmill. The stage-coach fare did not include the road expenses. Breakfast cost 62½ cents; dinner, with table drink, 75 cents; supper and lodging, 87½ cents.

In addition to the stages were three steamboat routes between New York and Philadelphia. By one the boat left the north side of the Battery at New York at five o'clock in the morning, the passengers breakfasting at Elizabethtown, dining at Trenton, and arriving at Philadelphia in the evening. The fare was $8. By another the passenger left New York at ten in the morning, dined at Bridgetown or Milton, supped and lodged at Trenton, breakfasted at Bristol, arriving in Philadelphia at ten or eleven. The fare was $5.50. Yet another, charging the same fare, left New York at three o'clock in the afternoon, and reached Philadelphia at ten or eleven the following morning. The boats went by the sound and canal

BOSTON EXCHANGE COFFEE-HOUSE
This building was burned down in 1818

to Elizabethtown or New Brunswick, where stages carried the passengers to Trenton or Bristol, some thirty or forty miles, when they took another boat on the Delaware, arriving in Philadelphia at the wharf on the north side of Market Street. The Olive Branch Philadelphia Steamboat Line left New York at 7 A.M., went to Brunswick, stopping at Blazing Star Ferry and Perth Amboy on the way, and from Brunswick to Philadelphia, being due at eleven o'clock in the morning. Passengers breakfasted and dined on board and the land carriage was only twenty-five miles.

There was much travel between New York and Albany, the stage taking three days, but the steamboats, of which there were now several, only took twenty-four hours. Between New York and New Haven there was a good water route which Sound steamboats traveled in eighteen hours, the fare being $5. There was a stage between New York and Boston, leaving the City Hall in New York at six in the morning, going through Rye, Stamford, Norwalk, Fairfield, and New Haven, the first day; Hartford, Tolland, and Ashford the second day; Pomfret, Thompson, Douglass, Mendon, and Dedham, the third day; arriving at the Exchange Coffee House in Boston on the third night. The fare was $16. The fare by stage from New York to Baltimore was $18, and to Washington, $24.

The "Pilot Stage" from New York belonged to what was known as the "Philadelphia, Baltimore, and Washington City Lines," which had a continuous service between those cities. From Washington there was a popular line of stages to Richmond. It started

51

in the morning from Mr. Semmes's tavern in Georgetown, took up passengers at O'Neil's tavern, the
Franklin House, and Indian Queen Hotel in Washington, and arrived at the Bell tavern in Richmond in
twenty-four hours. The average time taken on the
main roads by the mail-stages, which were the fastest,
was, between the great commercial towns, 60 to 120
miles in twenty-four hours, by cross-roads 40 miles in
twenty-four hours. From this it can be seen that a
journey from Washington to Boston, which was 460
miles distant by stage, took a week, and that to go from
Washington to New Orleans, which, by the quickest
route through Richmond, Raleigh (N. C.), Columbia
(S. C.), Augusta (Ga.), and Mobile (Ala.), was 1,219
miles distant, must take nearly a month. There was
a post-road between Washington and New Orleans;
there was one even from Robbinstown on the northeast boundary in the province of Maine to St. Mary's
on the southeastern extremity, a distance of 1,733
miles. Of course, there was great variation in the
badness of the roads. Some of the main roads running out from the larger cities were fairly good in
summer, but the cross-roads were bad, and all of the
roads were bad part of the time. In many parts of
the country there were no regular stages and a traveler must use his own carriage and horses or hire them.
The easiest and quickest mode of travel was by horseback, and in some places it was the only way possible.

The expense of travel was considerable, as the fares
recited show. The meals varied much in price, but
were higher between New York and Philadelphia
than elsewhere. The average was about twenty-five

cents for each one, and the night's lodging cost about one dollar. Travelers incurred less danger from highwaymen than there was in England at this time; but a single rider ran great risk of being killed by Indians, unless he was in the well-populated part of the country. They seldom attacked a stage-coach, however, and on the frontier traveling was generally done in parties for protection.

The coaches were strongly built, the body being swung on strong leather straps for springs, but they were subjected to a tremendous strain, ploughing through deep mud, plunging into holes, bumping over rocks and stumps, and often they broke down. Although they were not swung high, there was weight on top and they sometimes overturned. There were few bridges over the streams and fording some of them was dangerous, and when the current was swollen a coach was sometimes swept down the stream and the passengers might be drowned. If a passenger were of a peaceful disposition he need fear no personal molestation; but if he were truculent he might have a fight at almost any stopping-place, for at the inns were many bullies and rowdies who preferred fighting to any other form of excitement.

The conversation on the road and in the inn parlors ranged over a variety of subjects, but it was quite sure after a time to come around to political affairs, where all met on common ground and in which all took an interest. Feeling strongly and drinking as they talked, a conversation often rose to a quarrel and ended in a fight. The inns on the line of travel were all bad, but especially so in the South, where there was so much entertaining of travelers in private houses that the innkeepers could hardly make a living.

For long distances and for transporting families, travel by sea was preferable to land travel, where it was possible. The vessels varied greatly in size, being sloops or schooners, but none were large. Few of them carried more than thirty passengers. They sailed at irregular intervals, according as they obtained their cargo and passengers. After the newspaper announced that a ship would sail she might wait a week or a month before she was ready. Her destination could not always be assured. For example, she would sail from Savannah "to an Eastern port (as may be most convenient to make)." It took about two weeks to sail from New York to Savannah; from New York to Charleston, about ten days; from Savannah to Charleston, from three to five days; from Charleston to Wilmington, North Carolina, about as long; from Philadelphia to Charleston, about ten days; from New York to Boston, about four days; from Norfolk to New York, not less than two days. The ships were tolerably well-fitted; but, of course, a voyage which included for the longer distances the doubling of Cape Hatteras was not undertaken for pleasure. From what has been written it is plain that only a small proportion of the people ever went far from home, and their means of communication by mail were proportionally difficult and expensive. To send a single letter not more than 30 miles cost 8 cents; over 30 and not more than 80 miles, 10 cents; over 80 and not more than 150 miles, 12½ cents; over 150 and not more than 400 miles, 18½ cents; over

WATERLOO INN. THE FIRST STAGE FROM BALTIMORE TO WASHINGTON

400 miles, 25 cents. For a double, triple, or quadruple letter, double, triple, or quadruple postage was charged. It cost 1 cent to send a single newspaper 100 miles, and 1½ cents above 100 miles. The charge for pamphlets and magazines was 1 cent per sheet (sixteen pages) for 50 miles; and 1½ cents for 50 to 100 miles; and 2 cents above 100 miles. Every one tried to avoid paying postage by sending letters by the hands of travelers.

A few boys of the wealthier classes were sent away from home to be educated; but even the great colleges were in the main local institutions. Princeton was the only one which had as many students from other states as it had from New Jersey, but they were principally from contiguous states. Some Southern boys were sent to Northern colleges, but no Northern boys were sent to be educated at the South. Thus the class of 1816 at Yale, which was typical, had 36 members from Connecticut, out of a total of 54; 7 from the contiguous state of Massachusetts; 3 from South Carolina; and 1 from Virginia.

Now, though each community was isolated, the isolation was irksome to the people, and they were bending their attention to the problem of how to overcome it. Stage lines were being multiplied, roads were being improved and new ones opened. Canals and internal improvements were being projected. There was an epidemic of steamboat construction. Beginning on the Hudson, the boats were now on the Delaware and Potomac; arrangements were being made to put them on the Mississippi and the Ohio, and to send them across the seas was seriously talked of. A great change in this respect had come over the spirit of the people in the last twenty-five years. In 1787 John Fitch's boat, which William Thornton had made to go successfully, had plied the Delaware, but the interest in it was so feeble that Thornton had thought it useless to take out patents. When Robert Fulton put very much the same boat on the Hudson in 1809 the public mind received it with enthusiasm and it was the mother of a flock which soon crowded the inland waters. But until steam should be applied to locomotion on land the utmost efforts to shorten distances must have very limited results. A horse was still as swift as a steamboat, and horses could not go long distances at a rapid rate. In 1814 John Stevens applied to the state of New Jersey for a charter for a railroad between New York and Philadephia, but it was not till fifteen years later that a locomotive ran. Travel in 1815 was still in a primitive state.

But the individuals in the isolated communities were close to one another in their relations, understood one another, and sympathized with one another. As people who followed the same occupation could not co-operate except in the same place, there was no class co-operation. The specialization which has been brought about by shortening of distances, encouraging minute divisions of labor, could not exist. As we have seen, the people were nearly all agriculturalists, and a farmer's occupations, interests, and knowledge must be diversified when he lives at home and supplies nearly all his own needs. The communities, too, were so small that the members were in constant personal association. If a man built a house he directed the operations himself, selected the materials himself, and if he was a proprietor and did not actually wield a hammer or saw, he himself employed those who did and paid them with his own hand. He saw the planting done, if he did not himself throw the seed; he dealt directly with those who bought the product of his land. He knew his neighbor. Benevolence and charity were personal. The poor, unfortunate, and distressed appealed to the well-to-do of their neighborhood and received assistance directly. In consequence of the individual intercourse there was no class antagonism. In reading the letters written at this period we are constantly reminded of the great breadth of interest of the individuals who wrote them—going from public affairs to the proper methods of shoeing horses; from classical literature to the best way of preparing lumber for building purposes. The many functions of a man's nature were exercised and his characteristics had room to develop. The civilization of steam and electricity has raised the general level of culture, but it may well be doubted whether it has not lessened the opportunities for the highest individual development. In 1815 men were not in constant and almost exclusive contact with others of the same class as themselves, doing the same things, having the same interests, and influencing one another to a general sameness; as one of Kingsley's characters put it, "rubbing off their angles against each other, and forming their characters, as you form shot, by shaking them together in a bag till they have polished each other into dullest uniformity."

Undoubtedly the world has grown since 1815, but the individual has withered.

IX

TURBANS AND PANTALOONS

ONE morning during the second session of the First Congress John Adams, the Vice-President, took a seat beside Charles Carroll of Carrollton before he called the Senate to order, and began to question him about his estate in Maryland. He persisted in speaking of it as an empire and in treating Carroll as if he were a baron; and he seemed to derive personal satisfaction from the fact that he presided over a body which contained several barons. William Maclay, a Senator from Pennsylvania, one of the earliest members of the Republican party, sat near by and heard Adams's remarks with disgust. He had been disgusted ever since the Senate had convened, however, for it had been more exercised over the question of the proper title to apply to the President than by any other subject. Adams and a majority of the Senate wanted him called "his Highness," or "his Mightiness," or by some other lofty designation, and had been saved from the blunder only by the disagreement of the House. If they had had their way something corresponding to a court circle might easily have been created. The resounding title of the head of the state would have encouraged the use of high-sounding titles by the lesser officials. These titles would have conferred prestige in private life, and public office would have been sought for that reason. A privileged class might have grown up.

Maclay and his followers were right in objecting to the introduction of undemocratic titles as dangerous to liberty. Nevertheless, John Adams and his group were not royalists. If there were any such in the country they were a few unimportant individuals, who supported their views in parlor conversations and did not dare to seek the public ear. Adams believed that dignity and authority should attach to office, and he liked the trappings of power, but he went no further. Charles Carroll voted with Maclay for the simple title for the President. Titles meant little to him and other large landholders and slaveowners of the South. They belonged to a class whose power and prestige were undisputed, and titles could add nothing to their supremacy.

It must be remarked, however, that, using the word "society" as meaning the more cultivated members of a community in their social relations to one another, their private intercourse and recreations, it has never been democratic in its constitution, nor admitted that all men are equal, and one hundred years ago it was less democratic than it is now. Here many of the forms and observances which had prevailed in the days of the king and a court circle lingered long after they had disappeared from public life. Congress might refuse to call the President his Highness or his Mightiness, but the ladies persisted in calling his wife "Lady" Washington. As late as 1815 they often spoke of Mrs. Madison as "her Majesty." As soon as the government gave the President a house to live in, nearly everybody called it "the Palace" or "the Great House," and when his wife held a reception they called it a "levee" or a "drawing-room."

In 1815 the head of society in America was generally held to be the President's wife, and the primacy of the White House began with the reign of Dolly Madison. When John Adams and his wife had moved into it in the first year of the century it was hardly finished and they disputed possession with the workmen. The city of Washington was in a state of chaos, and there was no society for Mrs. Adams to lead. During Jefferson's administration the house had a master, but no mistress. His daughter, Mrs. Randolph, was with him most of the time, and Mrs. Eppes, another daughter, part of the time, but he was an overshadowing personage, who dominated in every sphere, and the White House was his rather than theirs.

It was not fully furnished till Mrs. Madison and Benjamin H. Latrobe equipped it in 1809, spending eleven thousand dollars for the purpose. It cost three thousand dollars to furnish the great reception-room, known as the East Room. When they had finished their labors the interior of the house presented a pleasing appearance in harmony with the perfect taste of the exterior. When it was lighted up for Mrs. Madison's first reception in May, 1809, a thousand wax candles glittered from the chandeliers, and the scene was really beautiful. The house became the gathering-place for society in Washington, which was considered to be the best the country af-

THE CAPITOL IN 1814
Redrawn from an old print

THE WHITE HOUSE IN 1814. SOUTH FRONT
From a contemporaneous print

forded and was called "the first circle in the nation."
The mistress of the White House followed the customs of her time, and was neither above them nor below them. She dressed in the fashion and loved beautiful clothes. She played "loo" and other games of
cards for money, as other ladies of her class did, until
she entered the White House and felt that the example might be harmful. She painted her cheeks, which
was not considered to be a crime. She took snuff,
which was a common practise among women as well
as men. When she got old she remained the same
age for several years at a time.

To show what clothes a fine lady wore, a description of her costume on the day her husband was inaugurated may be ventured. At the reception after
the ceremonies she "was drest in a plain cambrick
dress with a very long train, plain round the neck
without any handkerchief, and a beautiful bonnet
of purple velvet, and white satin with white plumes."
In the evening at the inauguration ball she had on
"a pale buff-coloured velvet, made plain, with a very
long train, but not the least trimming—a beautiful
pearl necklace, earrings, and bracelet—her head-dress
was a turban of the same."

A few years later, in 1811, a visitor to the White
House said, "Her Majesty's appearance was truly
regal, dressed in a robe of plain satin, trimmed elab-
orately with ermine, a white velvet and satin turban,
with nodding ostrich plumes and a crescent in front,
gold chain and clasps around the waist and wrists."
To pursue the subject a little further, a young lady
who went to the peace ball given in Boston in

1815 in honor of the Treaty of Ghent must be quoted:

"I wore," she says, "a sheer dotted muslin skirt trimmed with three rows of plaited white satin an inch wide. The bodice of white satin was also trimmed with the same ribbon. I wore white lace round the neck, a bouquet, gold ornaments, chain, etc. My hair was arranged in braids, bandeau, and curls."

The admiration for oriental things was a dominant note and showed itself in the ugly turbans which Mrs. Madison and other ladies wore, but delicate Cashmere shawls, graceful tunics and mantles, were also the fashion. Some of the turbans were made of spangled muslin and others of bright-colored cloth, and from the center of a few glittered a precious stone. There was a passion for gems and jewelry. Women twined long gold chains about their necks four or five times. They wore bracelets, armlets, and earrings. Instead of the turban some wore drooping ostrich plumes in their hair, or bound it with ribbons or a narrow band of gold. It was the fashion to gather it at the back in a knot, as it appears in Greek statues, and this style was known as "turning up the hind hair close." In front it was often worn in curls or ringlets, and a few had it cut and curled tightly over the whole head. Wigs were coming into fashion for women, having passed out for men. A pleasing adaptation of the Greek costumes was affected. The gowns were cut low in the neck and a muslin ruff rose behind the head, but they hung in graceful, natural folds. Tight lacing was not in vogue, because the "round gown," as it was called, was gathered a short distance below the shoulders and did not show the lines of the waist. The gloves came up to the elbows, and the kid or silk slippers barely covered the toes and had no heels. In England at this time, when a fine lady went to court she wore an enormous dress puffed out with a thousand frills and flounces, but no especial costume was prescribed for the White House. The skirts of the older women trailed on the ground, but long trains, as we saw them at a later day, were not worn. The skirts of the girls barely reached to their ankles.

The costume for men was in a transition stage, and it was not until many years later that the fashion of a special uniform suit for evening wear came in. Pantaloons had been affected by the radicals of Paris during the French Revolution and had found their way to America, but here they never rose to political importance. By 1815 they had come into general use with the younger men, but the older ones adhered to breeches and long stockings. There was, therefore, great variety in the costumes of a gathering of men. Some wore square-skirted coats, and others a newer style of coat made of blue or green cloth with large gilt or pearl buttons, a high rolling collar, and long narrow tails reaching down to the calves. Beau Brummel had already introduced starch into the neckcloths of Europe, and the fashion had reached America. Shirt-collars were prodigiously high and reached to a man's ears. Some wore "pudding cravats" designed to make the chest look deep, but stocks were coming into use. A few old men still powdered their hair, but others parted it on the side and wore it cut long. A few fops had it curled.

There was general interest in the social life and everything else pertaining to the city of Washington. It had been deliberately planned and artificially made, instead of coming into existence naturally from the needs of the surrounding country or as a port for shipping. It was the common property of all the nation, and everybody had an opinion about it. It deserved little praise and received none. Foreigners and Americans made it a butt for their wit, and it is doubtful if any other city in the world was ever so peppered with epigrams.

Here are some of the criticisms taken at random from an inexhaustible supply. One of the early doggerel rhymes said that it was a place

Where the houses and kitchens are yet to be framed,
The trees to be felled, and the streets to be named.

In 1806 the poet, Tom Moore, called it

That fam'd metropolis where fancy sees
Squares in morasses, obelisques in trees.

A few years later the Abbé Carrea da Serra, Portuguese minister, whom President Madison called "the most enlightened and esteemed foreigner among us," said it was "the city of magnificent distances."

It was a sorry place to look at. The broad streets were unpaved and most of the houses were cheap and mean. The few public buildings were classic in design, but they were framed in a ragged waste. The parks existed only in the plan. Yet there was

AFTERNOON DRESS   WALKING-DRESS   PROMENADE DRESS   EVENING DRESS

an agreeable social life in the city, and a compact society was built up from the various elements. The high Federal officials were the dominant class. It is true that they embraced many degrees of culture and lack of culture, especially among the Senators and representatives. There is an account of a Western Senator who saw a pianoforte for the first time and was as curious concerning it as an Indian would have been, but other Senators powdered their hair, drank old Madeira, and quoted Horace. They were particular about being called upon, and had quarrels over precedence. There was a group of army and navy officers always in the city, and they were generally well-educated and entertaining companions. The stationary inhabitants comprised a few high officials, several hundred government clerks, who occupied a more important place in the city's life then than government clerks do now, a small diplomatic corps of not more than a dozen people, and a few wealthy landholders and resident families, chiefly in Georgetown, who had been on the scene when the government arrived and acted in some sort as hosts.

The society was held together by two generally accepted principles. One was that a man of high rank in the government service was entitled to privileges and prestige in private life, and the other was that a member of a family which had enjoyed social privileges for several generations had a vested right to their continuance. Every one was proud of the new country and esteemed it a privilege to associate with the officials who governed it. To attain public office

5   65

was then almost the only goal of an ambitious man. Wealth was powerful, as it has always been, and was sought after, but it was not by itself all-powerful, and to pursue it was not regarded as the sole business of life. Many people were getting rich, it is true, but the time of the mad race for money and the accumulation of vast fortunes had not arrived, being reserved for a later generation, when machinery, steam, quick locomotion, and instantaneous communication of intelligence produced combinations of interests and cooperation of effort, opened limitless markets, resulted in greatly increased production and fabulous profits. The industries in the isolated communities of 1815 were strictly circumscribed in extent and the profits were not large.

The respect which generally maintained for members of old families was a survival of the colonial times, the lingering of a habit which came from the days of privileged classes. It was supported by the agricultural foundation of society. Where nearly all men were farmers, one who had a large farm was a man of consequence. The stability of country life produced family cohesion and families were then a power in every direction. The history of New York, for instance, up to this time is concerned largely with the history of the relations between the Livingston and Clinton families; and in several Southern states a few rich families monopolized the public offices.

So an agreeable and well-selected society existed in Washington. It was a generation later, when the new West—where men had grown up unoppressed by

66

visible social restraints—came into control, that the doctrine of political equality was held to carry with it social equality and the removal of the barriers which had separated groups of people in private life. To be specific, the fabric of Washington society was destroyed when Andrew Jackson became President.

The days were not crowded in 1815, and leisure fostered social intercourse. Morning calls were paid, and the callers stayed long enough for rational conversation. When they gathered together their number was small enough to permit of general acquaintanceship. Even at the inauguration ball there were only four hundred people present. In the large cities there were occasionally as many at a public ball; but a private entertainment was considered to be a very large one if there were two hundred guests.

Men of standing in the community did not esteem the affairs of society to be unworthy of their attention. In 1802 Capt. Thomas Tingey, an officer of high standing in the navy; John Peter Van Ness, lately a representative in Congress; Samuel Harrison Smith, founder of the *National Intelligencer*; Dr. William Thornton, the first superintendent of the Patent Office and the designer of the Capitol, and several others of similar rank—organized the Washington Dancing Assembly, which continued in existence for many years and gave dancing-parties at short intervals during the winter season. There were similar organizations, managed by men of prominence, in all the large cities. The amusements of society were not left to the exclusive control of idle and frivolous people.

When Philadelphia ceased to be the capital some of the spirit which had made it the gayest and most luxurious city on the continent departed from it and the severity of the old Quaker life reasserted itself, but it was still an agreeable place to live in. Subscription dances or assemblies were begun there in 1749 by an association which, omitting the period of the Revolutionary War, has been giving them ever since, and is thus the oldest dancing organization in the United States.

There were a number of foreign dancing-masters in Philadelphia, as there were in other cities. They taught the cotillion, a lively French dance, executed by any number of couples performing evolutions or figures, as in the modern german, the *menuet de la cour*, the waltz,—which was new and was received with some doubts of its propriety—Highland reels, fancy jigs, which were not often seen in polite circles of society, and American country dances which were like our Virginia reel.

The Philadelphia assemblies began promptly at six o'clock and stopped at midnight. They were attended by the older people as well as the young men and girls, card-tables being always provided for those who did not care to dance. The difficulty of finding a suitable place for the assemblies was solved at this time by making use of the Mansion Hotel on Third Street.

It was some years before there was a hotel in Philadelphia in a building constructed for the purpose, the Mansion Hotel having been adapted from the large town house of the Binghams. The meals which

WALL STREET, CORNER OF BROAD STREET, SHOWING CUSTOM-HOUSE, FIRST PRESBYTERIAN
AND TRINITY CHURCHES

were served were typical of the best hotels. For breakfast there were tea and coffee, eggs, cold ham and beef, hot fish, sausage, beefsteak, broiled fowls, fried and stewed oysters, and preserved fruit. The supper was essentially the same as the breakfast, but for the dinner roasts of beef or turkey or mutton, game, vegetables, puddings and pies, and wine and liquors were added.

The greatest hotel in the country was the new City Hotel in New York, which had recently been erected on Broadway between Thames and Liberty streets. It was five stories high, contained seventy-eight rooms, and was regarded as a marvel of size and luxury. There was a large assembly-room where dancing-parties were held.

The society of New York was changing and already the commercial life of the city was rising to the top. The population was about one hundred thousand people. It had passed Philadelphia and was increasing in size at a tremendous rate. Wall Street was regarded as the typical street. The *Stranger's Guide-Book* for 1817 said:

In Wall Street, which commences at Broadway, crosses Pearl Street, and descends to the river, are situated the Banking-houses, Custom-houses, Insurance offices, Tontine Coffee-house, the offices of Exchange Brokers, and most other public mercantile officers. This is a very handsome, airy street. Towards the bottom, in the neighborhood of Pearl Street, and in front of the Coffee-house, the public sales by auction are conducted, which renders this quarter extremely busy, and gives a very favorable and correct idea of the extensive trade and commerce of New York.

Like Boston, New York had suffered from the embargo, but it recovered with startling rapidity, and business went forward so furiously that in a few years there was a reaction and a temporary business collapse. Notwithstanding the obvious commercial destiny of the city, the society was still aristocratic. Great families, such as the Livingstons, Clintons, Van Rensselaers, Schuylers, and Morrises, dominated politically and socially and even industrially. The social life was gay. A few Dutch customs—for instance, general visiting on New-year's day—prevailed and spread to other cities. Many private balls were given. The favorite dining-place for the men was the Tontine Coffee-house; the lounging-place for people of fashion in the warmer seasons was the beautiful Battery overlooking the Bay. There were as yet no men's social clubs, but a few popular shops, to a certain extent, took their place. A man could stroll into one of these, meet his friends, and linger for hours at a time. In Boston there were several shops which were as well known as meeting-places as clubs are now.

In spite of the presence of a Puritanical element there was almost as much entertaining in Boston as in New York. It had suffered severely during the war, as much of its wealth was in shipping, and it received the news of peace with wild rejoicing. There was a long emblematical procession, and a great oratorio was sung in the concert-hall. On the evening of February 24th there was a peace ball which everybody, including the gentry, attended. In spite of the general evenness of fortune among the people of New England, and the consequent democratic nature of the social life in Boston and other large towns, there

CITY HOTEL, BROADWAY, NEW YORK, 1812

was a perfectly clear dividing-line between the gentry and the common people.

The chief gathering-places for the society of the South were Baltimore and Annapolis for Maryland, Richmond and Norfolk for Virginia, Raleigh and Wilmington for North Carolina, Charleston for South Carolina, and Savannah for Georgia. New Orleans was a city by itself, deriving its prosperity from commerce and from the vicinity. It was as much French in its characteristics as if it had been in France.

One Southern city in particular stands out as having the characteristics of the others in an exaggerated degree. Charleston was then among the first five cities in the country in population, among the first three in the importance of its commerce, and without a rival in the lavishness of its hospitality and the luxurious life of the members of its ruling circle. Few families in this circle had less than twenty household servants, all had coaches and horses, and their servants wore family liveries. It is true that the servants played as much as they worked, that the coaches were not always in repair, and that the liveries were often shabby, but the masters lived like a landed nobility, were treated as a nobility, and often spoke of themselves as a nobility. Those who had their plantations near the coast were generally called the "low-country nobility." Writing some years later, John H. Hammond, Senator from South Carolina, said he wished his sons to be "South Carolina country gentlemen, the nearest to noblemen of any class in America." In colonial days some of the gentry had been in commerce, but as the civilization developed more and more upon a foundation of slavery all trade came to be looked down upon as an occupation unworthy of gentlemen. It fell almost exclusively into the hands of foreigners, while the Carolinians planted and went into the learned professions and public life. It was the custom for each of the wealthy families in Charleston to give a large ball every year. In February the races took place, when the Jockey Club ball was held, which was the most important social event of the year. The city was most famous, however, for the dinner parties given. There was a good market, so far as fish and game were concerned; at any rate, there was profusion; and gentlemen spent a great deal of money on their wines in those days. There was a circle of wits, of raconteurs, of cultivated conversationalists who gave attention to dinner-table accomplishments, who repeated one another's good jokes and epigrams, who prepared themselves for their contests of wit, and took pride in victory.

There were similar groups in other cities. The hours of leisure, which compelled social intercourse; the diversification of occupations and of acquaintances which gave a wide range to thoughts and interests; the continued familiarity with the classics which educated men were expected to maintain—all combined to produce good conversation and to cause it to be cultivated. The table talk was better than it can be in an age of hurry and of incessant employment at one thing. No one thought in those days of describing the qualities of a man without speaking of his colloquial parts.

A VIEW OF CHARLESTON
From a painting made in 1774

X

WOMEN

A RECENT commentator on American life has
observed that our political history is notably
free from the names of women; and he is correct.
The historian of the United States cannot begin his
work with an account of a wholesale flirtation, as
Herodotus, the father of history, began his; nor is he
called upon to discuss the wholesale divorces of a
monarch as a part of the history of a great crisis, as
an English historian must. It is true that a queen
as well as a king gave encouragement to Christopher
Columbus and sent him on the voyage which resulted
in the discovery of America, and that it was under
another queen, Elizabeth, that the first English settlements were made, but when we come to America
itself we find ourselves in a land where men have
been thus far in undisputed political possession. It
is necessary for our purpose to point out only one
reason why this is so. It is because there has never
been a permanent governing class in this country,
with a permanent society of officials and their families, in which, as a matter of course, the women
would be supreme. Whenever the same officials have
been in power for a long time, however, a society of
their own has begun, and there have been signs of

73

the influence of women in political affairs. Such a society was forming in 1815, when the same party had been in control of the national government for fifteen years. It grew in force during Monroe's term of eight years, which was a continuance of Madison's; and when three members of his Cabinet, Adams, Calhoun, and Crawford, were candidates to succeed him, each had a coterie of women followers in Washington, who exerted themselves to further the interests of their favorite. When Andrew Jackson, an outsider, became President, Washington society was strong enough to try a fall with him. He offended it by taking into his Cabinet the husband of a woman whom it would not recognize, and it compelled him to send the obnoxious couple beyond the seas and reorganize his administration. But soon the personnel of Washington society was changed, the circle was broken into pieces, its power was gone, and women's influence disappeared from national political life. That influence had been exerted indirectly, however, and a woman of polite breeding would have resented a charge that she meddled in public affairs. What she thought on the subject is illustrated by the remark of Mrs. Samuel Harrison Smith, a woman of unusual intelligence, to a Federalist whom she met a few hours after she had fled from Washington when the British invaded the city in 1814. He said the defeat of the Americans was an argument for a standing army, and Mrs. Smith replied that she had always understood that a standing army was an instrument of despotism; but, she added, "I am not competent to discuss such questions, sir." Mrs. Madison herself furnishes another illustration. She enjoyed the friendship of more public men than any other woman of her day, but there is no record anywhere of her views on public questions, or that she ever influenced the political views or actions of her husband, who was wholly devoted to her. We can, in fact, eliminate consideration of women in any other than their private relations when we consider the American women of a hundred years ago. "A female politician," said *The Female Friend*, a little book published in Baltimore in 1809 under the patronage of citizens of that city, Annapolis, Alexandria, Georgetown, and Washington —"a female politician is only less disgusting than a female infidel—but a female patriot is what Hannah More was and what every American woman should study to be."

So the women were domestic, and the home was the scene of their activity. The object of their education was to attract men, gain husbands, have homes, and manage families. Their teaching was entirely different from that of men. All boys who went beyond the merest rudiments must learn Latin and mathematics, but the girls learned neither, nor Greek, nor the sciences, except some geography, astronomy, and physics—or natural philosophy, as they called it. To give a girl the same course of study as a boy beyond the first reader would have been regarded as an absurdity. Addison's description, in the *Spectator*, of the accomplishments of an Englishwoman of high breeding in 1712, would have answered with some modifications for the daughter of a well-to-do family of America in 1815.

She sings, dances, plays on the lute and harpsichord, paints prettily, is a perfect mistress of the French tongue, and has made a considerable progress in Italian. She is, besides, excellently skilled in all domestic sciences, as preserving, pickling, pastry, making wines of fruits of our own growth, embroidering, and needlework of every kind.

The domestic sciences all of them were taught, whether they were rich or poor. When President Madison was inaugurated in 1809 he wore a suit of dark-brown cloth made of wool which had been carded, spun, and woven by Elizabeth Stevens Livingston, the daughter of Robert R. Livingston, of Clermont, and her accomplishments were not regarded as exceptional for a woman of her class.

All women were expected to learn to nurse the sick. Professional nurses were not readily obtainable and were ignorant and untrained, so it was the custom of women to nurse not only in their own families but in the families of their neighbors and friends. When the qualities of a woman were enumerated it was usual to speak of her skill and tenderness as a nurse.

Elementary as it was, the book education of women was far better than it had been in earlier days and was more generally diffused among them. Women wrote well, though their grandmothers had not been able to write at all. They read some books besides the Bible, and spoke better grammar. They wrote very good letters, although they were taught a stilted and unnatural style. Their choice of appropriate words seemed to be instinctive, their sentences were well constructed, and their meaning was clear.

The system of education fulfilled its object. According to report, the girls of North Carolina married at such an early age that grandmothers of twenty-seven years of age were often met with, but, as a matter of fact, early marrriages were usual in all the states. Even among the higher classes girls often married when they were thirteen. This was a new country and there were more men than women, so there were few old maids It was a farmer's country, productive land was plentiful, and it was easy to support a family, so from the early marriages came large numbers of children, often a dozen or more from one marriage. Widows married again if they were young; widowers married again whether they were young or old. It was the land of marriage.

To describe more particularly the position which "females," as the contemporaneous authors usually called women, occupied, it is necessary to reconstruct an archaic condition of society. Rousseau, writing his *Emilie* some years earlier, showed what he thought was the object of their education and training, and Americans generally were in accord with his view.

"The education of women," he said, "should be always relative to the men. To please, to be useful to us, to make us love and esteem them, to educate us when young and to take care of us when grown up, to advise, to console us, to render our lives easy and agreeable; these are the duties of women at all times."

Americans were a religious people, and the women, especially, were orthodox. They put human conduct to the touchstone of the rules laid down in the New Testament. They accepted the gospel according to

St. Paul without protest, even when he told them that they must learn in silence, with all subjection; that the head of every woman is the man; that woman is the glory of the man; that the man was not created for the woman, but the woman for the man; that she must be a keeper at home, good and obedient to her husband; that she must submit herself to her husband as to the Lord.

The books which were written for the guidance of young women and accepted by them quoted this passage from Milton:

> To whom thus Eve with perfect beauty adorn'd:
> "My Author and Disposer, what thou bidst
> Unargued I obey; so God ordains;
> God is thy law, thou mine: to know no more
> Is woman's happiest knowledge and her praise."

A standard author with them was Hannah More. She was quoted, remembered, emulated, and shamelessly imitated. Her philosophy was that of the men of her time. One of her ablest essays was on St. Paul; but, while she defended him from the charge that he opposed marriage, she did not defend his views on woman's subordination, because no one attacked them.

The books addressed to the women tell us what was expected of them. They were advised to cultivate the art of conversation so as to be pleasing. When a woman married she should resign all claims to general attention and concentrate herself upon her husband and her home. One author said, she must understand in the beginning "that there is an inequality in the sexes, and that for the economy of the world the men, who were to be the guardians and lawgivers, had not only the greater share of bodily strength bestowed on them, but those also of reason and resolution." She was told that unchastity was regarded as "superlatively criminal in women," but in men was "viewed in a far less disadvantageous light." Therefore, the woman who had an unfaithful husband should not expostulate with him, for that would drive him away, but should feign ignorance of his misconduct and by superior agreeableness and attractions win him back. She should never blazon forth her wrongs, for she would not have the public on her side. Separation from her husband should be her last resort. It was a terrible experiment, and made the wife responsible for all the vices the husband might fall into after separation. The great duty of woman was to contribute daily and hourly to the comfort of husband, parents, brothers and sisters, and other relations and friends, to form and improve the manners and dispositions of men by her society and example; to care for children and mold their minds. She was prescribed strong doses in reading, most of the books dealing with religion; but she could read *The Rambler*, *The Idler*, and *The Spectator*. Shakespeare was too coarse, but selections from his works were permitted. Byron must be avoided; but Young's *Night Thoughts*, Thomson's *Seasons*, Milton, Cowper, and Goldsmith were recommended. Moral essays, such as Mrs. Chapone's letters on the Government of the Temper, Knox's essays, and, of course, everything of the incomparable Hannah More, were considered the best things for her; but she was encouraged to read American history—Hutchinson's *History of Massachusetts*, Ramsay's *History of the Revolution*, and the *Proceedings* of the Massachusetts Historical Society being specified as suitable works. Of American biography there were the lives of Franklin and Washington. She was warned against novels, but might indulge herself with *The Vicar of Wakefield*, *Don Quixote*, and a few others. Life was a serious affair, and preparation for eternity should be made by reading serious, contemplative books, such as Dodd's *Reflections on Death* and his *Thoughts in Prison*, Taylor's *Holy Living and Dying*, and Littleton's *Dialogues of the Dead*. I am not writing a humorous parody on the education of a young lady, but am faithfully transcribing the titles of the books which those who directed her reading placed in her hands. She accepted these books submissively; nay, she even accepted books in which Dean Swift's letter to a very young lady on her marriage was printed, paraphrased, or plagiarized. The Dean informed the "very young lady": "The grand affair of your life will be to gain and preserve the friendship and esteem of your husband," and admonished her that love is "that ridiculous passion which has no being but in play-books and romances." Of course, the latter remark she did not believe, but it is surprising that she consented to listen to insults like these: "As little respect as I have for the generality of your sex," etc., and concerning their fondness for fine clothes:

So your sex employs more thought, memory, and application to be fools, than would serve to make them wise and useful. When I reflect on this, I cannot conceive you to be human creatures, but a sort of species hardly a degree above a monkey; which has more diverting tricks than any of you; is an animal less mischievous and expensive; might in time be a tolerable critic in velvet and brocade, and, for aught I know, would equally become them.

I doubt whether many women took Swift seriously or read the *Dialogues of the Dead* when the teacher's eye was not upon them. I doubt if they cared much what men thought their positions ought to be, because they knew what it really was; and they were willing that men might have the word of sovereignty as long as they had the fact. Mary Wollstonecraft might protest to the utmost, but they were content "rather to be short-lived queens than labor to attain the sober pleasures that arise from equality." Their condition compared favorably with that of the women of other countries. As we saw in another chapter, foreign observers spoke of them admiringly, remarking upon their beauty, industry, and faithfulness in marriage. As yet there was no class of rich, worldly, pleasure-loving women, living in an atmosphere of vacuity and immorality, such as Hannah More and her contemporaries directed their denunciations against. There were fast women of fashion, of course, but they were not numerous enough to constitute a class in any part of the country. The majority fitted Hannah More's description, being—

Those women who bless, dignify, and truly adorn society. The painter, indeed, does not make his fortune by their sitting to him; the jeweler is neither brought into vogue by furnishing their diamonds, nor undone by not being paid for them; the prosperity of the milliner does not depend on affixing their name to a cap or a colour; the poet does not celebrate them; the novelist does not dedicate to them; but they possess the affection of their

6   81

husbands, the attachment of their children, the esteem of the wise and good, and, above all, they possess *His* favour "whom to know is life eternal."

We are not to suppose that there were no whispers of rebellion from the women against their subjection. Those who were not "short-lived queens," not busy wives and mothers, whose hopes of sovereignty were waning or gone, murmured against an order of things which left them derelicts, but there were very few of them.

Mary Wollstonecraft had published her *Vindication of the Rights of Women in England* in 1791, and it had been republished in an American edition at Philadelphia in 1794. There were a few American writers who followed in her train and wrote on woman's rights and wrongs, but they had an audience of insignificant proportions. Miss Wollstonecraft's plea was for a liberal human education for women, and against a system which, she said, was designed to make them alluring mistresses rather than rational wives and companions of men. She was pitiless in her arraignment of women for their complacency in their degradation, and of men for their selfishness in forming women only with reference to themselves. In her power of penetration and logical presentation it is probable that none of the myriad women writers who have treated the same subject since her day have surpassed her. I cannot find that she was much read in America, nor heeded at all. She had no school here. Her immoral life and tragic death in 1797 had furnished a concrete argument against her philosophy, which negatived her teachings. At this

time her daughter was illustrating their effect by her
unlawful union with the poet Shelley.

Americans practised marriage freely, but the habit
of unmarrying had not been acquired and divorce
was not a national evil. The social life of the country
existed without this scandal to furnish food for conversation. In 1811 Thomas Law, an eccentric Englishman, whose real residence was in Washington,
established a legal residence in Vermont so as to obtain a divorce from his wife, Elizabeth Parke Custis,
a granddaughter of Mrs. Washington. They had
been leaders of the society of the capital, and their
separation and marital differences had caused a social
commotion. This was probably the first instance of
a divorce in the society of the city, and it stood alone
for many years. Regular divorce laws were a novelty
in the country. In South Carolina a divorce had never
been granted. In New York for a hundred years before the Revolution there had been no divorces. That
state had no law on the subject until 1787, when the
courts of chancery were authorized to pronounce decrees from the bonds of matrimony for adultery alone;
but the legislature might do so also; and the law remained thus for many years. Generally speaking,
the states in which English customs held most tena-
ciously were very strict in their reasons for divorce,
and those which applied rules of their own were more
free. Louisiana had the liberal laws of the *code Na-
poléon*. Divorce was still exclusively a function of
the legislatures in Delaware, Kentucky, and Maryland. In Georgia the legislature might allow divorce
by a two-thirds vote of each house, after the cause

had been tried and a verdict given in a court of justice. In the other states it was a function of the courts, and the causes for allowing it extended to intolerable ill-usage, wilful desertion, and habitual drunkenness. In Connecticut it might be granted even for misconduct permanently destroying the happiness of the person applying for the divorce; and there conditions were regarded as discreditable, and it was charged that divorces were obtained by collusion of married people. But whatever the laws were, they were rarely invoked.

We have no way of judging of the extent of marital infidelity. It was considered to be less of a crime on the part of the husband than of the wife, and undoubtedly there were many unfaithful husbands, and very few unfaithful wives. Heavy penalties for adultery—whipping, branding, fining, imprisonment, and, in several New England States, wearing the letter A sewed upon the sleeve of the outer garment, "of color contrary to their clothes," had prevailed under colonial laws, but they had given way to less drastic enactments. The punishment in Virginia at this time was a fine of only twenty dollars. As a matter of fact, however, the law was seldom executed for this offense. When punishment was inflicted upon a man it usually came in the form of death by the hand of the dishonored husband, a lawless retribution of which public opinion approved.

XI

PLAYS AND SONGS

A PEOPLE in the first flush of young manhood,
glorying in its vigor, delighting in the struggle
of life, restless, immature, with an uncontrollable impulse for action—such a people as the Americans
were in 1815—has not reached the stage when it can
pause to cultivate art or appreciate it. There was
some classic architecture exemplified by the work of
William Thornton upon the Capitol, a few good
painters, especially of portraits, like the Peales, John
Trumbull, Gilbert Stuart, and Washington Allston,
and a very few who carved in marble and wood, like
William Rush. An association for promoting the
fine arts, chartered in New York in 1808, was lan-
guishing, but was revived in 1816 as the American
Academy of Fine Arts. The Pennsylvania Academy
of Fine Arts in Philadelphia, chartered in 1806, and
the Society of Artists of the United States, organized
in that city in 1810, were barely alive, but they too
took on some vigor a few years later under a new
name. These and a few other similar struggling organizations served to make all the plainer the fact
that America was not then a home for art. That must
wait for populous cities, a cultured, traveled class,
the patronage of settled wealth, leisure, and what

may be called the contemplative stage of national life.

But there was a general desire for amusement, and one form which it took was a fondness for the play. The more cultured people went to the theater freely and there was no prejudice against it among the Irish immigrants; but the middle classes of English origin had an inherited fear of it as a dangerous excitement to the imagination and productive of immoral conduct. To state the matter by religions—and nearly everybody was religious—Episcopalians and Roman Catholics went to the play without misgivings, but Presbyterians, Methodists, and Baptists had a feeling that they ought to be disciplined for going, and Quakers did not dare to go. It was believed that seven-tenths of the people were opposed to the theater, but those of the seven-tenths who went, notwithstanding, and the remainder were sufficient in numbers to support it in all the cities and towns. The actors were English or Irish, except in New Orleans, where they were French. Not a prominent actor on the stage in 1815 was an American.

In 1811, on the night after Christmas, there was a terrible fire in the theater at Richmond, when it was crowded with a holiday audience. Seventy people, nearly all occupants of the boxes, were burned or trampled to death, those in the pit and gallery escaping unharmed. It was the popular belief that the tragedy was a punishment of God for attending a play. The legislature of the state forbade all public amusements for four months. Later a church was erected on the spot where the theater had stood, to

propitiate divine justice. Throughout the country
the disaster made a deep impression, and it was not
until 1818 that the drama was revived in Richmond,
when a new theater was built by James H. Caldwell,
who had already erected theaters in several other
Southern cities.

In Massachusetts all theatrical performances were
unlawful till 1793, when an act was passed permitting
them, but in 1799 Connecticut passed a law which
closed the theater at Hartford. The law had been
evaded in Boston, and when the ban was lifted the
Federal Street Theater, a handsome playhouse, was
opened with appropriate ceremonies. A gold medal,
offered as a prize for the best poetical prologue, was
won by Thomas Paine, the son of Robert Treat Paine,
a signer of the Declaration of Independence; but soon
afterward Thomas petitioned the legislature for permission to change his Christian name to that which
his father bore, so that he might not have the same
name as the hated infidel who had written the *Age
of Reason*. Paine's prologue was a poem characteristic of the taste of the day. It began with a description of the drama in Athens, passed on to Rome, spoke
of the dark ages, and then introduced Albion and
Shakespeare. Next, it was natural to say of the
Muse:

> Long has she cast a fondly wistful eye
> On the pure climate of the Western sky,

and presently to land her in Boston.

In protest against the new playhouse another poet
offered a prologue running thus:

If alien vices here unknown before
Come, shameless, to pollute Columbia's shore,
If here profan'd Religion's sacred name
Be dressed in ridicule and marked with shame—

and much more to the same affect. Such was the opposition to the play that a committee of substantial citizens of New York refused one hundred dollars offered for the poor of the city, because it came from the manager of a theater. One peculiar custom prevailed which justified some of the strictures against the theater. A number of the proscenium boxes in the large playhouses were given up to the prostitutes. There they sat together in a conspicuous part of the house, decked out in all their professional finery and blandishments. It was a shameless spectacle, which friends as well as foes of the stage protested against, but which was not abolished till some years later. As for the players themselves, they set no worse examples than actors have always done. There was a goodly proportion of blackguards among them, and some of them died of drink. Divorces were very rare, but elopements occurred. A few moved in the circles of good society and became worthy members of their communities. All seemed to take kindly to the new country, and most of those who came over to join the several good American companies never returned to England. There was no difficulty in recruiting the companies, the profession having discovered, as an American manager expressed it, that "a continent existed oversea, called America, where some of the people were white, spoke English, and went to see plays." Many of the actors came from provincial boards, not yet having won a London reputation, but there were several who would have done credit to any stage. Thomas Abthorpe Cooper, a tragedian of merit; Mrs. Oldmixon; Mr. and Mrs. Darley; Mr. and Mrs. Hodgkinson; Mr. and Mrs. Hallam; Mrs. Merry, and Mrs. Whitlock, a member of the famous Kemble family, a sister of Mrs. Siddons and possessed of similar talents; and John E. Harwood, who married Miss Bache, a granddaughter of Benjamin Franklin—were some of the players who were deservedly popular. The first great actor to come over was George Frederick Cooke, in 1811, but he was shattered from dissipation and died soon afterward. He was followed by Joseph George Holman, an actor of equal merit. Companies did not travel regularly, but they moved from one city to another at intervals, and their personnel changed constantly. Stars traveled alone and played with different companies. Thus a playgoer in a large city saw all the chief actors in the course of two or three seasons.

In some of the theaters there were good orchestras. At the Philadelphia Theater the conductor was Alexander Reinagle, who played the harpsichord in the orchestra. The conductor in New York was James Hewitt, a musician of attainments hardly less than Reinagle's. Many of the musicians were foreigners of decayed fortune — at New York, for instance, a French nobleman who had fled from Paris during the Revolution, a French army officer who had made an unfortunate marriage, and a refugee from the slave insurrection at Santo Domingo.

LIFE IN AMERICA ONE HUNDRED YEARS AGO

A theater comprised the pit, where people of all sorts sat on benches, paying for their tickets from fifty to seventy-five cents; above this pit was a tier or sometimes two tiers of boxes patronized by wealthy and fashionable people who paid at least a dollar for a seat. Above the boxes was the gallery, where the rabble went, paying twenty-five cents each for admission. The theater built in Philadelphia on Chestnut Street in 1792 was, until it was burned in 1820, probably the best in the country. The auditorium was semicircular, and there were two complete rows of boxes besides the pit and gallery. The Boston theater, also a fine one, had a square auditorium, only one row of boxes, and held 500 people. In New York a theater had been built on Chatham Street opposite the park. It had seats for 2,500 people and was the largest in the country. It was lighted by many lamps and candles in brackets. There was a great ornamental chandelier suspended from the ceiling, and the grease from the tallow candles dripped upon people in the pit who were sitting under it. In Washington there was a good theater which had been opened in 1800.

The bill offered at a theater must please many different tastes, for there were no folk-theaters. Rich and poor, high and low, went to the same performance. The play bill of the Richmond theater on the night of the fire is typical. Placide, whose benefit it was, was a well-known actor-manager and afterward played at the theater at Charleston:

VIEW OF CITY HALL, PARK THEATER, AND CHATHAM STREET, 1822

———— ▬ ————

MR. PLACIDE'S BENEFIT

WILL CERTAINLY TAKE PLACE ON

THURSDAY NEXT

WHEN WILL BE PRESENTED, AN ENTIRE NEW PLAY,
TRANSLATED FROM THE FRENCH OF DIDEROT,
BY A GENTLEMAN OF THIS CITY, CALLED

THE FATHER

OR

FAMILY FEUDS

[*The caste follows*]

AT THE END OF THE PLAY

A COMIC SONG . . . . By MR. WEST
A DANCE . . . . By MISS E. PLACIDE
SONG . . . . By MISS THOMAS
A HORNPIPE . . . . By MISS PLACIDE

TO WHICH WILL BE ADDED (FOR THE FIRST TIME HERE) THE
FAVORITE NEW PANTOMIME OF

RAYMOND AND AGNES:
OR, THE BLEEDING NUN

[*Follows the caste*]

A long "description of the principal scenes in the Pantomime" follows. Often, however, the after-piece was a farce.

The bill at Richmond shows that there was a fondness for foreign plays, but the public taste took a wide range. Shakespeare, Sheridan, translations and adaptations of the German playwright Augustus von Kotzebue, were regularly performed. There was a demand for American plays, and William Dunlap, the most prolific American playwright, produced among many others, "André," "The Glory of Columbia—her Yoemanry," and "The Soldier of '76." Mordecai M. Noah, afterward a conspicuous journalist, contributed "Marion, the Hero of Lake George," "Oh Yes, or the New Constitution," "The Siege of Yorktown"; William Joor, "The Battle of Eutaw Springs"; James N. Barker, "The Embargo, or What News?" and the "Indian Princess." The frontier play had not yet come into vogue, but the Indian play was performed. Dunlap had already dramatized the story of John Smith and Pocahontas and it served as a theme for plays of several other authors.

The audiences at the theaters often gave interesting exhibitions of the public mind. On the night of November 25, 1793, the anniversary of the day when the British had evacuated New York ten years before, there was a remarkable demonstration at the theater in the city. Citizen Genêt, the first envoy from republican France, had exchanged congratulatory addresses with Governor George Clinton in the course of the day. In the evening the theater was crowded to hear Murphy's play, "The Grecian Daughter,"

Mrs. Melmouth taking the leading part. In the boxes on one side of the stage sat the French naval officers, and on the other side the American officers, all in full uniform. The pit was filled with French sailors and American militiamen. As soon as the orchestra appeared the audience called for "Ça ira." The strains of that lively air, then the song of the Revolutionists, had hardly begun when the Frenchmen and then the Americans began to sing it.

> Ah! ça ira, ça ira, ça ira,
> Le peuple, en ce jours sans cesse répète ah!
> Ah! ça ira, ça ira, ça ira.
> Malgré mutins tout réussira
> Et nous allons chanter alleluia.
> Ah! ça ira, ça ira, ça ira!

It is not conceivable that the Americans sang all the French words, but a repetition of the first line was easy and served all essential purposes. Next came the "Marseillaise" sung with solemn enthusiasm while the audience stood up. Then came tumultuous shouts and counter-shouts of, "*Vivent les François,*" and "*Vivent les Américains.*" The curtain rose and the audience was silent. In the course of the play the Grecian daughter strikes to the earth the tyrant who is about to kill her father, and when this part was reached the applause became a mighty shout of approval. Old theater-goers, indulging in reminiscences many years afterward, declared that never had they witnessed a scene of such elevated enthusiasm as that which took place at the theater in New York on this night. Twenty-three years later no foreign cause could have aroused such fervor. The public temper had completely changed and "Ça ira" was already forgotten.

The relationship between the drama and music was, of course, intimate, and many of the actors were also singers.

There was no peculiarly American music, but, as Mr. Oscar G. Sonneck, the historian of American music, has remarked, there was no more reason why an American music should be made than there was for making an American language. The early settlers had their music when they came, and kept it. There was a phase of American life that was bombastic and pretentious in tone, which the people confused with the heroic, and the same audiences which liked the "Grecian Daughter" and Paine's prologue liked the heavy Presidents' marches, which were composed in honor of each of the Presidents and played on public occasions, and did service, to some extent, for national airs. Better than these, however, was the English hymn, "God Save the King," to which Americans adapted words of their own from the time of independence. As yet, however, no settled version had been accepted. In 1798 Joseph Hopkinson, the son of Francis Hopkinson, wrote the words of "Hail, Columbia," and they were set to the music of the President's march which Philip Phile had composed in Washington's honor. Probably more people knew the words in 1815 than know them now, for it was better suited to their poetic taste. Francis Scott Key's "Star-spangled Banner" was composed to commemorate an incident of the war of 1812, and sung to the air of an English drinking-song, which everybody knew. "Yankee Doodle" was there, come whence no one knew, and its authorship claimed by nobody, but liked by the gallery and pit, and many other patriotic songs with European airs which had become naturalized as American.

Of indigenous music there could be only that of the Indian. The white man liked to learn many things from him, especially his woodcraft and some of his methods of fighting, but never cared to learn his music. In fact, the tonal method was so different that it was not music at all to white ears.

But it was different with the music of the negroes. They had developed a local music full of harmony and beauty. It was made by welding their native chants upon the white man's hymns, lullabies, and folk-songs. They were more passionately fond of music than the whites.

Nevertheless, there was much music among the people. Many countrymen and working-people played the fiddle, the frontiersman, according to tradition, sometimes to frighten off the wolves. The boatman, sailing down the river with the breeze behind him, leaned against the tiller and fiddled a particular tune; travelers often carried a musical instrument with them. Monologues, partly recitative, partly sung, and partly played, being humorous descriptions of travels and adventures, were composed. The singing-school where hymn-singing was taught was common in New England, and the itinerant teacher of psalmody, with a pitch-pipe for his musical instrument, was frequently met with in the East. For the gentleman the "gentleman's flute" was then the fashion, and European travelers often remarked on the skill and taste with which the ladies played upon the harpsichord, pianoforte, guitar, or harp. Higher music flourished encouragingly. In New England many of the inhabitants still doubted whether any singing was not ungodly, unless it was of hymns; but concerts had been patronized by the more cultured people of Boston, and in 1815, on Washington's birthday, there was a great musical festival in honor of peace with England. An audience of over nine hundred persons gathered in King's Chapel at the corner of School and Tremont streets to listen to an oratorio. The chorus numbered nearly one hundred voices, all of them male but ten, and nearly all Americans. Already there were piano-makers in that city, and a musical journal, *The Euterpiad*, was published in 1820. There had been concerts in Boston for many years, and this was true of all the chief cities of the country. All of them had musical societies. In Charleston the St. Cecelia Society was giving concerts, having been organized for that purpose as early as 1762. Here, as in Europe, the concerts usually closed with a ball, and in course of time to give the ball became the chief business of the St. Cecelia Society and usurped the place of the concert; but this was after the time of which we are writing. The concerts were both vocal and instrumental, and the audience listened to Haydn, Pleyel, Davaux, Corelli, Karl Stamitz, Handel, and other standard composers. The composers in America were not many, but they were respectable. William Billings, Andrew Law, and Oliver Holden were Americans who had devoted themselves chiefly to psalmody, and Francis Hopkinson to secular music. Among the emigrants who had settled in the country were several men known to musical history—besides Alexander Reinagle and James Hewitt, Benjamin Carr, Joseph Gehot, and Gottlieb Graupner.

As the theater existed in every city or town, the union of music and acting was a natural development. Up to 1800 many English operas had been performed, and opera went forward rapidly after that. By 1815 every city had made its acquaintance. Baltimore had seen French opera in 1791, and, beginning in 1810, it was regularly performed in New Orleans, whence it made its way experimentally into other cities.

7

XII

COMMON PEOPLE

ONLY an insignificant proportion of the population of the United States lived in cities in 1815, and a very small proportion worked in factories or mills. Universal manhood suffrage did not exist and very few laborers could vote, so there was no legislation in the interest of labor. There was no labor problem, and socialism was unheard of. With a scattered population extensive combinations of laborers were impossible. The working-day was from twelve to fifteen hours long, and it was not till ten years later that a movement was started to shorten the day to ten hours, the motive back of it being humane, but not political. There was no legal restriction on the employment of women and children, and they constituted a majority of the employees in the factories. There the discipline was what the employers chose to make it, and in some instances it included the use of the whip upon the women and children to urge them to work. Work began at half past four in the morning in some mills. In New England the hands were taxed by the employers for the support of the churches, and continued absence from church services on Sunday was punished by dismissal. The wages of the men operatives were from sixty-five to seventy cents a day. There were a few societies of mechanics for benevolent purposes—of journeymen shipwrights and of house carpenters in New York, for example. Occasionally there were mutinies in the factories, and in 1802 some sailors in New York made a demonstration, paraded the streets with a band of music, recruited their ranks from other sailors, and demanded an increase in their wages from ten dollars a month to fourteen dollars. There was no popular sympathy with them; they were put down with a strong hand, and the leaders were lodged in jail. Organized strikes were unknown. Some of the cities regulated the work and pay for a few services. In New York chimney-sweeps were allowed to work in winter only from six o'clock in the morning till four in the afternoon, and in the summer from five in the morning till six in the evening, and no boys under eleven years of age could be employed. The price for sweeping the chimney of a high house was fixed at 44 cents. Porters using a wheelbarrow might charge 12½ cents for taking a load half a mile, and 25 cents for more than half a mile and less than a mile. For a load carried by hand-barrow the charge was nearly twice as much, and by handcart 18 cents for half a mile and 31 cents up to a mile. By cart and horse the charge was 12½ cents for taking a bale of cotton, barrel of oil or potash, box of Havana sugar, or 100 feet of lumber a distance less than two miles, and one-third more for every additional half-mile. For the same distance 31 cents was the charge for a hogshead of beer or molasses containing 60 to 90 gallons; 37½ cents for a load of bricks or earthware over 1,000 pounds in weight, or a pipe of brandy; 50 cents for a load of furniture; $1.00 for a load of loose hay; $5 for every cable whole shot above 15 inches in circumference. Hacking coaches and carriages could charge, for less than a mile, 25 cents per passenger, and 50 cents for any distance within the lamp-and-watch district above a mile; for conveying one or more passengers on a tour, $1 or $2.50; to Kingsbridge and back, keeping the carriage all day, $5.

There was no specialization in the trades. The apprentice system prevailed, and the boy who was bound out learned everything about the trade—in shoemaking, for example, from the tanning of the leather to finishing the shoe. The apprentice lived with his employer, ate at his table, slept under his roof, and was subject to his discipline outside of the workshop as well as in it.

Generally speaking, the wages were high and there was a brisk demand for workmen. As industries were localized, there was a considerable variation in the wages in the different sections. In Massachusetts, where the pay was good, horseshoers received 90 cents a day and found themselves, or 45 cents with board and lodging; ship carpenters, $1.25 a day, boarding themselves; common laborers from 50 cents to $1.50. In the South much of the labor was performed by negroes hired out by their owners, and the wages were about $6 a month with board. Boathands on the Mississippi were paid as much as $1 a day with board; laborers on the public roads $1 to $1.25 a day, with board. The board always included a daily allowance of whisky or rum. Much of the skilled labor in Pennsylvania was performed by redemptioners, the wages going to those who had been at the charge of bringing the workmen from Europe. There was competition to get workmen for extensive city improvements, and a city government often advertised for laborers in the newspapers of other cities. Working on the streets were many Irish immigrants.

The chief element among the immigrants was Irish, but the great tide of immigration had not begun, the number admitted each year averaging 5,000. The inducements that the country offered were becoming known to the working classes of Europe, however. Guides for immigrants were being issued, telling of conditions in America, the wages offered and the cost of living. The wages were fully double those paid in England and four times as much as those paid in France, and the working-man was under none of the compulsions to work and pay taxes which harassed him in European countries. He was free to work for any employer he chose, and to travel. If he had no property he paid no direct taxes. The cost of living was much less than in Europe, bread being one-third less than in any part of England, and beef, mutton, pork, and poultry one-half the price that prevailed in London. The same proportions maintained in groceries, and house rent and fuel even near New York were as low as they were in any part of Europe. Fruit cost one-tenth as much as it did in England; beer, wine, spirits, furniture, and even farm implements were cheaper. Some of the city governments fixed the price and standard of bread. In New York it was 12½ cents for a full loaf weighing at least 38 2-53 ounces, and 6¼ cents for a half-loaf. If a man chose to board he could find a good boarding-house for less than two dollars a week.

The few people who employed household servants complained that it was hard to get them and that they were inefficient; and well-to-do foreigners thought it a hardship that they must not call them servants, but "help." They found them untrained, disrespectful, and disobedient. If they brought their servants with them they left their service almost immediately for more independent employment. Such household servants as there were were Irish immigrants, a few were farmers' daughters for whom it was a temporary employment only, many were free negroes, and some were redemptioners. In the South the servants were slaves, except a few white housekeepers, and here there was less complaint by employers and the supply was plentiful. Those in the South who did not own slaves hired the slaves of others as servants, and paid them less than the white servants received at the North. There the best women servants received about fifty dollars a year. The household of a well-to-do resident of Washington might comprise a white housekeeper, who was also a seamstress and made part of the clothing even for the man of the house, besides doing the clear starching and ironing, a colored cook, a waitress, and a chambermaid. The charge of insubordination was not made against servants alone, but against all members of the working class. They had abolished the word "master" and held themselves to be the equals of their employers.

The hired laborer on the farm did not constitute a class. He might be a young man filling in an interval before he should have a farm of his own, or perhaps a thriftless fellow deficient in enterprise who chose to live from hand to mouth and stay in one neighborhood. How an energetic and thrifty man could rise can be shown from a typical case. The man was thirty years old, married, and had three children. His father gave him $500 to begin the world with and he went to Ohio. He took a cargo of flour down the river to New Orleans and sold it, thereby increasing his capital to $900. Then he bought a farm of 250 acres of land, 65 acres being cleared, for $3,500. In a few years it was paid for and he was worth $7,000. The farm laborer received wages of from $8 per month in winter to $10 in summer, with board and lodging, living in the farmer's family and eating at his table. In the West the wages were higher. The hours of work were from sunrise to sunset. Usually the farmer and his family did all the work themselves, the boys going into the field as soon as they were strong enough, and the girls helping their mother in the house and the dairy. The household employments included spinning, weaving, knitting and sewing, making butter and cheese, stuffing sausages, salting meat, and preserving.

Entertainment was not wanting for them, and it often combined work and pleasure. There were quilting-parties, or "quiltings," as they were commonly called. "She was invited," says a farmer, "to Tabitha Twist's quilting, and my girls were left out of the list." Husking-bees and similar parties lightened the routine of life. The men liked rough sports, and in some parts of the country fought in a ring, with spectators, like prize-fighters. They attended horse-races and raced their own horses. They cultivated the trotting-horse and raced him under the saddle. They amused themselves with cock-fighting. They were good shots with the rifle and shotgun, and hunted a great deal. The boys were taught to shoot at an early age. They hunted foxes with hounds, following on foot or horseback. There were bowling-greens in many of the villages. They played cards and checkers and bought lottery tickets. Indulgence in strong drink was the curse of every class and every section, but the greatest curse to the working class. There was a coarse song in vogue among them, called "Nothing Like Grog," which shows the degradation of the tipplers. One verse of it will suffice:

> My father, when last I from Guinea
>   Returned with abundance of wealth,
> Cried, "Jack, never be such a ninny
>   To drink." Says I,"Father, your health."
> So I passed round the stuff; soon he twigg'd it,
>   And it set the old codger agog,
> And he swigg'd, and mother and sister and brother
> And I swigg'd, and all of us swigg'd
>   And swore there was nothing like grog.

The temperate men who would not drink rum or whisky drank cider. The women were sober, but many of them used snuff.

In every farm-house there was sure to be a Bible, bought usually from a peddler, and he purveyed lighter literature also, but the people who read seldom went much beyond the Bible and a few religious works.

All day they were too busy to read, and at night a tallow candle was not a good light for reading, so the story-teller came naturally into being to beguile the evening hours. Religion furnished them with mental excitement, and it was complained that when a revival was in progress the women neglected their household duties to attend the meetings. Strolling preachers came often and were regarded as a greater nuisance even than the peddlers. Quack doctors, too, robbed the credulous. "Here comes the famous Doctor Dolt," says the *Farmer's Almanac*, "with his skunk's grease and liverwort. A larnt man is the Doctor. Once he was a simple knight of the lapstone and pegging awl; but now he is blazoned on the first order of quack heraldry."

The people were normally superstitious. They believed in miraculous cures. In 1813 a man appeared in Vermont, who declared he could cure all diseases by prayer. Patients flocked to him by the thousands and his letters accumulated by the bushel. It was a common thing to dig for treasure, the hiding-place having been revealed to some one in a dream. As many people were prejudiced against banks, and as banks were, moreover, not accessible to all who saved money, much of it was hidden, a favorite hiding-place being a hole in the ground. A magic hazel wand was often used to locate an abandoned hoard. One who was born "with a veil over his face," as they termed it, or a caul, had supernatural gifts, and was apt to carry a talisman in the form of a small stone which did not differ in appearance from other pebbles, but enabled him to find anything. As the digging under supernatural direction never revealed anything, it confirmed the belief of the diggers in the devil, because he alone could have run off with the gold.

There should have been enough for good doctors to do, for salt meat, heavy pastry, and fiery rum made dyspepsia common, and cold houses produced rheumatism, and in the swampy regions the malaria-communicating mosquito flourished. The diet was not, however, altogether bad on the farms. Most of them had a "sarse" patch where vegetables were grown, and there was abundance of milk, butter, and cheese. The mainstay of the family, however, was the pork-barrel, but beef was also used a great deal. A good dinner consisted of boiled pork and potatoes, or salt beef, turnips, and stewed pumpkins.

The advice which the people gave one another shows what they considered to be their every-day evils and virtues. Scolding, back-biting women, and lazy, tipsy husbands were inveighed against, and the husband who did not help his wife received unmeasured censure. "A large woodpile is one sign of a good husband," they said. Profanity was a vile practice which should be stamped out. Above all things, the children of the family must be educated, the schools, the mentors insisted, being the safeguard of the country. Direct charity was the duty of all. Thus, a farmer is represented as being about to buy a lottery ticket, when a neighbor advises him not to throw his money away, and he changes his mind. He calls his son, "Here, Tom, take this five-dollar bill to the Widow Lonesome; tell her it is at her disposal; then hasten back to your school. I will to my team and my wood-lot."

XIII

THE sense of humor of a nation rises from the common people. It rests upon peculiarities and contrasts in characters and dispositions, producing strange remarks and situations which appear to be ludicrous to people of all classes. A touch of real humor makes all men kin, and a joke is a joke to the scholar as well as the clown. Foreigners usually found the Americans a solemn people, and merry they certainly were not; but they were developing a sense of humor so peculiarly their own that few foreigners understood it. Unfortunately, the record of it is meager, for the weight of English literary traditions hung so heavily upon the writers that, when they wished to be funny they tried to write like English humorists.

The fragmentary record is sufficient, however, to enable us to form a reasonably definite idea of what the people laughed at. Of course, many of the jokes were vulgar, as jokes at that period were everywhere. Many that were printed no publisher would now dare to put in the post-office. Respectable men roared over stories which the women were not permitted to hear, and they told stories before the women which made them laugh and blush at the same time. The head of the nation was one of these humorists. To the ladies of his acquaintance he made what they called "mischievous remarks," and in a social circle of men he produced uproarious mirth by jests which were often very broad. I have found some examples of his humor which could be quoted and others which I cannot quote. He was open to the charge of occasionally making a pun, but many of his contemporaries were worse offenders in this particular than he was. The wits of Philadelphia were having a debauch of puns, which even invaded the cultured circle of Dr. Wistar's parties.

Among the characters whom the people laughed at was the Dutchman of New York, with his large, square figure, great breadth of beam, and enormous coat and trousers made from an ancient pattern which no one but himself had ever used. He spoke English with an accent of his own, his nature was stolid and phlegmatic, and he adhered to the old way of doing things in a land where every one was regarded as ridiculous who did not grasp at novelties and inventions. Then there was the Pennsylvania Quaker, sanctimonious and solemn, of measured speech, "theeing" and "thouing" like a personified page from the Bible, who often gave pleasant astonishment by exhibiting worldly wisdom and effective repartee which were quite out of keeping with his joyless visage. The Irishman was a stock humorous character, amusing because of his brogue, his sentimental, unworldly nature, his reckless conduct, and his indifference to rules of logic, but he was not peculiarly an American possession. The two chief humorous figures who were our very own were the Yankee philosopher and trader and the negro.

The humorous Yankee was depicted as long-legged, sharp-visaged, blue-eyed, sandy-haired, with a long nose through which he talked, wearing garments always a little too small for him, which displayed his long bony hands and wrists and large feet and ankles. His manner was dry and serious, his powers of observation and penetration were extraordinary, and he expressed himself in original language. Often he was depicted as lazy and shiftless, being in this respect unlike his neighbors. He hung about in the villages and did odd jobs, told amazing stories and discussed theological subjects. This type was not as widely known as the Yankee trader, however, whose unscrupulous cleverness in over-reaching every one with whom he drove a bargain furnished a rich fund from which innumerable anecdotes were drawn. Already the story of the consignment of nutmegs made of walnut wood, which had been sent out from Connecticut, was national property.

Much of the sale of household and personal superfluities was by direct application of the vender, and to make a sale he must arouse a desire on the part of the purchaser to purchase his articles. He took a long journey to reach his customers, who lived far apart, and to compensate himself for the time consumed he placed the price of his goods at an immeasurable distance from the original cost. To be successful he must be sharp of wit, glib of speech, and active in his imagination, so he tried to create the good-nature and accommodating spirit which come to one who has been well deceived. By a knowledge of "soft sawder" and "human natur'" he compelled women, and men, too, to buy. He was both a diplomat and an orator. Thus, a clock-seller comes to a farm-house.

"Just to say good-by, Mrs. Flint," he says to the wife.

"What," says she, "have you sold all your clocks?"

"Yes, and very low, too, for money is scarce and I wish to close the consarn. No, I am wrong in saying all, for I have just one left. Neighbor Steel's wife asked to have the refusal of it; but I guess I won't sell it. I had but two of them—this one and the feller of it, that I sold Governor Lincoln. General Green, the Secretary of State of Maine, said he'd give me fifty dollars for this one, but I guess I'll take it back"; and so on, till the woman's sense of rivalry and curiosity is so aroused that she is determined to have the clock. After much persuasion he produces it and places it on the chimneypiece. The husband comes in and admires it, but he has a watch and does not think he needs a clock.

"I guess you're in the wrong furrow this time, Deacon," says the clock-seller. "It ain't for sale, and if it was I reckon neighbor Steel's wife would have it, for she gave me no peace about it." He looks at his watch. "Why, it ain't possible! As I'm alive, it is four o'clock, and if I haven't been two hours here! I tell you what, Mrs. Flint, I'll leave the clock in your care till I return."

So he winds it up and gives the key to the Deacon, telling Mrs. Flint to remind her husband to wind it every Saturday night. As he rides away he remarks to a companion:

"That I call human natur'. Now that clock is sold for forty dollars; it cost me just six dollars and fifty cents. Mrs. Flint will never let Mrs. Steel have the refusal, nor will the Deacon learn, till I call for the clock, that, having once indulged in the use of a superfluity, how difficult it is to give it up. We can do without any article of luxury we have never had, but when once obtained it is not in human natur' to surrender it voluntarily. We trust to 'soft sawder' to get them into the house, and to human natur' that they never come out of it."

The Yankee was put on the stage almost as soon as an American drama was written, and has done service in caricature on every stage in the land. He was not as well known in the South as in the North, but he appeared there among the country people occasionally, and always left a reputation behind him.

The negro was a Southern product, but he furnished humor for the whole country. Wherever he was he was laughed at. Those communities at the North which had only a few of them laughed at the few, and they had a monopoly of the humor of the South. They were the only really merry people in America. There were many reasons for it. They were by nature irresponsible, and in slavery they had no responsibility at all. For them it was to eat and be merry; their to-morrow was the care of others. Perhaps, too, the sadness of their hopeless bondage caused them to seek forgetfulness of their condition in the mirth of the moment. Like many humorists, they went quickly from laughter to tears. Until recently they had lived in an infant state of society, in the artless age when human nature shoots "wild and free"; when civilization has not cramped the exercise of the fancy and passion. Wonder and surprise were more easily excited in them than they were in a sophisticated people. They were still close to the time when they had spoken and acted in the "uncovered simplicity" of nature. They lived in a world of imagination and passion and were indifferent to truth and precision. They were rude poets as well as humorists. They personified domestic and wild animals and made them talk. The stories of Uncle Remus are all more than a century old. Themselves childlike in nature, they had a mental community with the white children and told them stories of talking rabbits, bears, and foxes, and of the strange doings of the creatures of the unseen world, which the children repeated to their parents, and thus the folk-lore was communicated by the little ones. They luxuriated in superstition, and had a hundred ghosts, ha'nts, charms, fetishes, and voodoos to the white man's one. Their emotions found expression in dancing and singing and in loud oratory. The more eloquent among them were preachers, and thundered forth discourses of amazing length which disclosed ludicrous notions of the personal interposition of Providence in human affairs. They pronounced English words in a way which was all their own, and they were gifted with an interminable flow of language. The negro's appearance was grotesque and he looked like a great, good-natured monkey. His sable skin, woolly hair, and enormous mouth brought laughter from all who beheld him. He imitated his white master with delightful exaggeration. If the master's manners were courtly the man's were majestic; if the former was dignified the latter was an embodiment of pomposity. When he heard long words he adopted them, adding some syllables to make them longer. If the tall collar was the vogue he wore one that covered his ears; if long coats were in fashion he wore tails that touched his heels. Like the humorous Yankee, he, too, was required by the people to be represented on the stage at an early period, and so popular was he that later he furnished material for a full theatrical show under the title of the negro minstrels. "Tambo" and "Bones," the two end men, making music by rattling bones and beating a tambourine, bandying jests and quirks, and the pompous interlocutor, usually addressed as "Governor" or "General," were fair exaggerations of negro characters that might be met with anywhere.

8

XIV

"RELIGION, OR THE DUTY WE OWE TO OUR CREATOR"

"AS the government of the United States is not in any sense founded on the Christian religion," were the words with which one of the articles in the treaty between the United States and Tripoli, signed in 1796, began. Washington was the President at the time, Timothy Pickering, of Massachusetts, the Secretary of State, and Joel Barlow, of Connecticut, the agent who negotiated the treaty. It was agreed to by the Senate without objection, so far as history records. During Washington's administration he issued two proclamations, being recommended to do so by Congress, calling upon the people to give thanks to God for their blessings and to pray for remission of their sins. In the first one, dated October 3, 1789, seven months after the new government had been in operation, he enumerated the "civil and religious liberty" which the people enjoyed as one cause for thanks, and advised them to supplicate "that great and glorious Being who is the beneficent author of all the good that was, that is, or that will be." In the second proclamation, January 1, 1795, drafted by Alexander Hamilton, he advised that thanks be given to "the Great Ruler of Nations." He purposely worded both proclamations so that they would be

acceptable to all who believed in a God. John Adams
was not so generous. His proclamation of March 23,
1798, appointing a day of public fasting, humiliation,
and prayer, recommended the people to implore the
mercy of God "through the Redeemer of the World,"
and he repeated the recognition of the Saviour in
another proclamation a year later. Jefferson issued no
proclamation of the character we are discussing, but
Madison was called upon by Congress to issue one
of thanks for the peace with England; and, although
he was urged by many people to make it a Christian
document, he followed Washington's example, and
worded it so that a non-Christian could accept it.
After his retirement from office he expressed the
opinion that Congress had erred in employing at public expense chaplains to open the sittings with prayer.
He said the chaplains must be members of some religious sect which was obnoxious to Catholics and
Quakers, of whom there were always a few in Congress.
The event proved that he misjudged, however, for
in 1832 Charles Constantine Pise, a Catholic priest,
was chosen to be chaplain of the Senate.

But there was really no connection between the
national government and religion, complete separation having been required by the fundamental law.
Because he believed them to be an encroachment
upon the spirit of that law, the President vetoed two
bills in 1811, one to incorporate an Episcopal Church
in Alexandria, then a part of the District of Columbia,
the other reserving a piece of public land in Mississippi
Territory for a Baptist church.

It must not be supposed, however, that the separation of church and state meant that the people and their leaders were irreligious. On the contrary, some, at least, of the leaders in the cause of religious freedom intended the separation to be an exaltation of religion into a thing above and beyond the reach of government. This was the President's position. The Virginia Bill of Rights, which may be said to have been the pioneer declaration on the subject, had said:

That religion or the duty we owe to our Creator, and the manner of discharging it, can be directed only by reason and conviction, not by force or violence, and therefore all men are equally entitled to the free exercise of religion according to the dictates of conscience.

This clause was phrased so as to avoid the use of the word "toleration," and was the result of an amendment offered by Madison, when a very young man fresh from Princeton College, intensely religious and suspected of an intention of going into the ministry. The argument used for the clause was the same that Mirabeau advanced twenty years later:

The most unlimited liberty of religion is in my eyes a right so sacred that to express it by the word "toleration" seems to me itself a sort of tyranny, since the authority which tolerates may also not tolerate.

Furthermore, the fathers of the Republic believed that religion and morality were welded together, and that national virtue could not exist without religious faith. They were in full accord with Washington's declaration in the Farewell Address:

Whatever may be conceded to the influence of refined education on minds of peculiar structure, reason and experience both forbid us to expect that national morality can prevail in exclusion of religious principles.

116

"RELIGION"

In 1815 the United States was the only country in the world which did not have an official religion. Religious toleration was general throughout Europe; individuals could hold such views as they preferred and attend any or no church, but they did so by permission and not by right.

When we examine this country in detail we find that not all the states were as liberal as the national government was. The conviction that virtue came from religion made many people think that the state must support the one to obtain the other. The Constitution of Massachusetts said:

As the happiness of a people and the good order and preservation of civil government essentially depend upon piety, religion, and morality, and as these cannot be generally diffused through a community but by the institution of the public worship of God and of public instruction in piety, religion, and morality—

therefore the legislature must require the people to make suitable provision for public worship and "the support of public Protestant teachers of piety, religion, and morality." New Hampshire said that morality and piety, "grounded on evangelical principles," were the best security to good government, and that to have them taught the legislature must see that provision was made for "public Protestant teachers." Massachusetts and New Hampshire had, in effect, a Church establishment. So had Connecticut; and it made a constitution in 1818 which proclaimed the right of freedom of worship, but allowed taxation for support of the churches. Vermont had an expression in favor of revealed religion. The Maryland Declaration of Rights allowed the legislature "to lay a general and equal tax for the support of the Christian religion"; New Jersey said that "all persons professing a belief in the faith of any Protestant sect" should be eligible to office; North Carolina that no person who should "deny the being of God or the truth of the Protestant religion or the divine authority either of the Old or New Testament" should be capable of holding any office or place of trust or profit in the civil department of the state. Rhode Island had religious freedom only for Christians. Tennessee said: "No person who denies the being of God, or a future state of rewards and punishment, shall hold any office in the civil department of this state." Pennsylvania put the atheists beyond the pale: "Nor can any man who acknowledges the being of a God be justly deprived or abridged of any civil right," etc. Complete freedom of conscience existed only in New York, Delaware, Virginia, Kentucky, Georgia, and Louisiana.

There were very few people who would have been affected injuriously by the discriminatory laws, even if they had been enforced, and they were not enforced. Belief in the divine origin of the Bible, in the miraculous creation of the world, in heaven and hell as places, in creationism, or that all living things, and especially man, were made substantially as they then existed, was well-nigh universal. Evolution, or the doctrine of derivation, was unknown. A few people still read the writings of the skeptics—of Voltaire and others of the French school, of Hume, of Kant; but the one most read was Tom Paine. The *Age of Reason* came to America by way of Paris, however, and was one of the products of the French Revolution, so its influence declined as the people became disillusionized with respect to that upheaval. The basis of Paine's attack on Christianity was its improbability, the similarity to pagan mythology, and the inconclusive proof of it; and this was the basis of attack by the other writers. Orthodoxy was as yet assailed only by philosophy, ridicule, and logic; it had received no serious wounds from scientific discoveries. That the earth was not the center of the universe was known; but geology had not yet revealed its slow formation. Darwin and his theories did not come till fifty years later.

Yet immediately after the Revolution there had been much infidelity in the country. Seven years of war had impoverished the churches and a great many of them had been destroyed. The Episcopal Church, the oldest and the strongest before the Revolution, was almost wiped out of existence by the war. Two-thirds of the clergymen were loyalists and had fled. It had been the state Church and fell to pieces when state support was withdrawn. The budding Methodist Church had depended for existence on John Wesley, an Englishman, who opposed the patriot cause, and many of the ministers had returned to British jurisdiction. The other churches might more easily adjust themselves to changed conditions, but before the readjustment came the wave of infidelity swept over the land. It came from France as a part of the affectation of French things and opinions which resulted from the alliance, and from the French Revolution, which Americans thought was an imitation of their own. But the French influence was artificial and soon passed; with it went the infidelity, and religion was enthroned again.

America was naturally its kingdom and the Americans were naturally its subjects. They came of religious stock. Back of many of them was the fact, in which they took great pride, that their fathers had settled in the land for religious reasons. While they were not, when compared with Latins, an emotional people, they were, nevertheless, strongly sentimental. Everybody who could read read poetry. It was a necessary mode of expression to them. They were dwellers in the country surrounded by phenomena of nature which they could not explain by natural causes. Scholars cultivating their intellects and killing their natural craving for religion were few and had little influence.

Religion came to its own through a series of revivals, close following upon one another and extending over the whole country. They began in Virginia in 1785, and lasted six or seven years in that state and the neighboring states. They appeared in New England in 1791 and became a characteristic feature of Congregational life. What was known as "The Great Revival" began in 1801 on the frontier in Kentucky, and swept northward, carrying thousands of people into the churches. The revival meetings were so large that no building could hold the people, so they gathered in the open. Often a meeting lasted several days and they camped out, so the meetings became "camp meetings." All the Protestant churches profited by the revivals, but the Methodists and Baptists profited the most, and then began their great career as popular churches. The Methodist traveling preachers reached the residents of remote districts. The vigorous style of preaching which they practised, and the fact that they were not usually better dressed or better educated than the average people in their audiences, made them popular with the masses, and the membership grew rapidly. From the time that the first Methodist preaching-house was erected there had been negroes in the Church, and in 1801 Zion Church, the first church exclusively for colored people, was erected in New York. By 1815 it was the most popular sect with them, dividing only with the Baptists.

That sect had already risen to a large membership. Starting in Rhode Island, it had gone through the Middle States and found a rich field in the South when the Episcopal Church was in a state of depression. It was the Church of the missionary and pioneer and went West with the earliest settlements. In 1812 it claimed a membership of nearly 18,000 in New York, of 35,000 in Virginia, of 13,000 in North Carolina, and about as many in South Carolina and Georgia, of 10,000 in Tennessee, and 17,000 in Kentucky. Probably it was the most populous sect in the whole country.

The Episcopal Church after a painful effort at resuscitation had at length established an American system of government, and in 1814 had a notable infusion of energy. New bishops were consecrated, many clergymen were ordained, old churches, long abandoned, were reopened, and the Church, as it stands to-day was put upon its feet. Outside of New England it was the Church of the intellectual and the well-born.

The Presbyterians had not suffered from English affiliations as the Episcopalians and Methodists had, but they derived fewer accessions from the Great Revival than the Baptists and Methodists did. They discouraged the hysterical, violent methods which characterized many revival meetings, and their clergymen were usually men of liberal education and not in complete sympathy with an ignorant crowd. Nevertheless, the Church had a normal growth and by 1815 numbered at least 30,000 members. Wherever the inhabitants were of Scotch-Irish origin there were Presbyterians.

The great Catholic denomination, now the largest of all, was then hardly as large as the Presbyterian. It had begun actively as an American institution in 1790 under the bishopric of John Carroll, and when he died in 1815 there were Catholic schools, convents, and colleges, a Catholic press, and at least one hundred priests.

The impulse to its progress came from a patriotic American, a member of a family noted for its service to the state. It was in religion as it was in every other institution—it progressed only when it joined the ranks that were marching on to the new nationality.

The preponderating Church in New England was the Congregational, and as it differed from the Presbyterian only in the matter of Church government, the two often acted together. Already Unitarianism had arisen in the Congregational Church in Boston and the battle between them was raging; but the separation had not yet been effected and the Unitarians outside of Boston were very few.

The Jews were a mere handful, probably not 5,000 in the whole country, grouped in several seaboard cities—Newport, New York, Charleston, Savannah, New Orleans, and Philadelphia.

Taking the religions geographically, the population of New England was overwhelmingly Congregational; in New York were many members of the Dutch Reformed Church and Episcopalians; in Pennsylvania and New Jersey, Lutherans, Quakers, Moravians, and Episcopalians; in the Middle States and the South, Baptists, Methodists, and Episcopalians; in the West, Methodists and Baptists. In Maryland were many Catholics, and they had a preponderance in Louisiana.

The prevalence of religion was general. It is true that the Indians were slow to yield to the Christian missionaries, having, in fact, a religion of their own, with a belief in a Supreme Being and a future state; but the negroes were all Christians.

They had been brought to America with the religion of their race, were worshipers of idols and fetishes, believers in charms and witchcraft; but under the white masters' orders they discarded their idols and knelt at the same altar with their masters. They never gave up their belief in charms and witches; but they became Christians almost as soon as they touched Christian shores.

All of the various sects in the country held it to be their mission to educate youth for admission to the ministry, and from this conviction came the colleges of the country.

XV

WEBSTER'S SPELLER

A NEW country, the population scattered over a great expanse, engaged in the work of conquering nature, working, under a popular government, steadily toward the glorification of the common man, is not the place where one should expect to find full cultivation of the higher intellectual qualities. The necessities are encouraging to action and antagonistic to study. Benjamin Franklin said it in the *Pennsylvania Gazette*, August 24, 1749, when he urged higher education upon the colony of Pennsylvania:

In the settling of new countries the first care of the planters must be to provide and secure the necessaries of life; this engrosses their attention and affords them little time to think of anything farther. . . . Agriculture and mechanic arts were of the most immediate importance; the culture of minds by the finer arts and sciences was necessarily postponed to times of more wealth and leisure.

The ideals of the people formed accordingly. They were in the fighting stage, and their greatest admiration was for fighting men. There was a man rising in the new Southwest who realized their ideals.

They had demanded that the war should produce a hero who should overtop all others, and they made one out of Andrew Jackson, a man who undoubtedly

had many heroic qualities. Popular at the close of
the war, his popularity grew steadily and became
overwhelming. The common people admired him
and chose him for their champion, and he was a man
to be admired. His intellect was strong, even though
it was narrow and uncultivated; he was of perfect
integrity, of glowing patriotism, and of chivalrous
nature. He was deep in prejudices, but he was absolutely free from class prejudice. Prince and pauper,
learned man and ignorant, were all equal in his eyes.
Philanthropy and courage shone out from his presence,
and wherever he went men turned to look at him and
felt that he was not an ordinary man. In fact, the
people's champion was a true knight, even though
he wielded a fence rail instead of a shining lance,
and the deadly twenty paces of a sylvan retreat took
the place of the crowded lists. His Rowena, who sat
trembling at home, waiting to know the chance result of a pistol-shot, was a faded woman of the frontier, who could quote no poetry beyond a few Methodist hymns; yet more romance had been crowded
into her life than any of Sir Walter's heroines ever
knew. Alas! the Waverley novels were coming out
at this very time and she never read a line of them.

Andrew Jackson was not a well-educated man and
his wife was hardly educated at all. He had been to
an "old field" school in North Carolina for a few
years—a rough institution where the rudiments were
taught by an ignorant teacher. He learned to express
himself well, but he spelled as he chose and his grammar was bad. Of science, the classics, literature, he
knew nothing. Here was the man who represented

the new order; here was the man who was the exponent of the masses of the people and whom they loved as they have loved no other President. Through him they took over the government which up to this time they had intrusted to gentlemen and scholars. With praiseworthy self-restraint they allowed the old order to pass without violent expulsion. In 1815 the profoundest scholar of government in America was the President. He had succeeded a man of whom it is hardly an exaggeration to say, as Ferdinand Lassalle once said of himself, that he was armed with all the culture of his century. Madison's successor was a graduate of William and Mary College, and Monroe's successor had studied in Paris and Holland before he graduated from Harvard. The choice of these men for the Presidency showed how forceful was the habit which had come from England, of conferring high public offices upon college-bred men. It was inevitable, however, that it should give way before the growing consciousness of power of a people whose surroundings were not of a kind to make the scholar their favorite type.

Nevertheless, there had been an earnest effort from the earliest settlement of the country to establish institutions of higher education. It had been fostered here, as it has been fostered from the earliest times in all lands, by religion, by government, and by private philanthropy; and the educational system went, as it has always done, from the top downward. There were colleges before there were academies, and academies before there were common schools, and the Church, the state and the rich man gave their attention to the first before they gave it to the last.

In 1638 John Harvard, a rich Congregational minister, left £800 to the newly established state college at Cambridge, and it was given his name. In 1691 Commissary James Blair asked Queen Mary for a charter for a college in Virginia where young men could be prepared for the ministry, and subscriptions were successfully solicited from rich and influential persons. The college was erected near the Episcopal church at Williamsburg and became the College of William and Mary. When the state of Virginia gave George Washington certain shares in the James River and Potomac River companies, he transferred part of them to the Washington Academy (now the Washington and Lee University) at Lexington, Virginia, and left the rest in trust for the benefit of a national university when it should be established. He never seems to have thought of giving the stock to encourage popular education. Thomas Jefferson, after much study of the schools of Europe, thought out the most scientific and far-reaching scheme of state education that had thus far been elaborated in America. The capstone of the structure was to be the university. He enlarged the Albemarle Academy into Central College in 1816, and it became the University of Virginia in 1819, but he had been dead for forty years before the state established a common-school system. It is true that there were many common schools in the country from the earliest times, but the main interest was in the higher institutions.

Harvard had recently become a Unitarian College;

Yale, founded in 1699, and Dartmouth, founded in 1769, were Congregational. Col. Ephraim Williams made a bequest for educational purposes in 1755, and with the aid of the state Williams College was established at Williamstown, Massachusetts, in 1793. It was not an ecclesiastical college, but it soon became a breeding-place for missionaries of the Congregational Church. King's College, afterward Columbia, in New York, and the University of Pennsylvania received royal charters in 1754, and were, of course, under the control of the Episcopal Church. In South Carolina the state established a college at Columbia which opened its doors in 1805. It was not sectarian, but the president was an Episcopal clergyman. The Presbyterians had the College of New Jersey at Princeton. It was powerful in the Middle States, was the parent of higher education in North Carolina, and the several Presbyterian colleges in Virginia owed their beginning to Princeton men. The Baptists had founded Brown University at Providence, Rhode Island, in 1764. The Catholics had several good academies, and the college at Georgetown had been opened in 1791. Naturally, the last sect to make an effort in the direction of higher education was the most popular with the common people, and it was not till 1829 that the Methodist Church founded Randolph-Macon College at Ashland in Virginia. It should be remarked, however, that while nearly all the colleges had their origin in the needs of the churches, they were not sectarian in their membership, and no student was barred from attending a college because he did not belong to the religious sect which controlled it. The form of organization of the colleges was copied from that of Cambridge University, England. The prescribed course was four years. The degree conferred was Bachelor of Arts. When the University of Virginia was opened it provided for an elective course of study, and already some choice was allowed at William and Mary; but in the other colleges all the scholars followed the same course. This included Latin, Greek, English literature, and rhetoric, mathematics, physics, chemistry, a little logic, psychology and metaphysics, political economy, a little history, and sometimes a smattering of German and French. In none of these studies was the course an advanced one, except in Latin and Greek. Boys entered college at fifteen or sixteen years of age, the average graduating age being twenty. There were no graduates' schools; but at the larger colleges it was common to find a few students who remained after graduation for a year's extra study of some special subject. After all, only a small proportion of the people goes to college, and it was a very small proportion in 1815. In that year 23 students graduated from Williams, 66 from Harvard, 69 from Yale, 40 from Princeton, 15 from the University of Pennsylvania, and 37 from the University of South Carolina.

Of professional schools there were few, and youths who wished to become clergymen, lawyers, or physicians studied under older members of these professions. There were a few divinity schools, however—one for the Dutch Reformed Church at New York, established in 1784, which was the oldest; St. Mary's

Academy at Baltimore for students for the Catholic priesthood, established in 1791; one for Presbyterians at Service, Pennsylvania (now at Chambersburg), established in 1794; the Andover Seminary at Andover, Massachusetts, established by the Congregationalists in 1778. The Princeton Theological Seminary began in 1812. There was no Episcopal seminary until one was established at New York in 1819, and none for the Baptists till that at Hamilton, New York, was opened in 1817. Any student might become grounded in theology, however, at the colleges, where it was part of the course, where the Bible was taught and the New Testament read in Greek.

The medical schools were multiplying. There had been one in Philadelphia since 1745, and in New York since 1750. The former became a part of the University of Pennsylvania in 1791; the latter the Medical Department of King's College in 1767 and the College of Physicians and Surgeons in 1813. Harvard (1782), Dartmouth (1781), the University of Maryland at Baltimore (1807), Yale (1813)—all had medical schools of good standing, that at Philadelphia being esteemed the best. Until 1813 it was the custom to confer the degree of Bachelor of Medicine first, and after a year more of study the Doctor's degree. Commonly, the course comprised two sessions of four or five months each. Notwithstanding the increase in the members of schools, not one practising physician in ten had ever taken a degree, nearly all of them having been educated in medicine in doctors' offices.

The young lawyers, too, came through the offices of older lawyers. There was only one law-school, that of Tapping Reeve and Judge James Gould at Litchfield, Conn. In had developed from an increase in the number of law students in Reeve's office. The course was fifteen months. In 1817 the University of Pennsylvania and Harvard established law-schools. There were no technical schools except the Military Academy at West Point, which had been established in 1802. It was the only institution where engineering was taught. There was no Naval Academy till 1845. The boy who wanted to become a naval officer sailed on a merchantman or as a midshipman on a man-of-war. He entered upon his career when he was a mere child, sometimes when he was nine years old.

To prepare for college many boys of the opulent class, especially in the South, received instruction from a family tutor—usually a young scholar who filled in a year or two after graduating from college by teaching before entering upon a profession. He was treated as a member of the family who employed him, and taught all the children who were old enough to leave the nursery. Frequently the parents taught their own children, however, and this was one of the causes of the strong family cohesion which was a characteristic of the time.

The greater number of boys and girls who received any education beyond the elementary obtained it at the grammar-schools or academies, where the studies for boys were generally regulated by the requirements of the colleges. There were some 265 of these institutions scattered through the country, and new ones were constantly springing up. A boy might enter when he was nine and remain four or five years. He underwent a classical course, usually with very little of science; but the academies differed greatly from one another in many respects, and reflected the individual views of the principals, who were nearly always the proprietors. Two illustrations will suffice to demonstrate this. Rev. Moses Waddell, a Presbyterian minister, had an academy at Willington, South Carolina, near the Georgia border, which was probably the most famous school in that part of the country. The recitation-hall was a log cabin, and situated near it were smaller log cabins where the boys lived. Every morning Dr. Waddell would come to the door of the recitation-building and blow a horn, when the boys would gather for prayers. When they were not reciting they studied their lessons in groups out of doors under the trees. If the weather was cold they built fires and sat around them. Waddell succeeded in exciting emulation among his scholars, and his graduates pronounced him an incomparable teacher. His course was classical, and the discipline appears to have been of the easiest. Of different character was the "American Military, Scientific, and Literary Academy" which Captain Alden Partridge started at Norwich, Vermont, in 1820, whence he moved to Middletown, Connecticut, and then back to Norwich, where in 1835 his school became the Norwich University. He had well-planned buildings, and those at Middletown served for Wesleyan University when it began in 1831. The boys wore uniforms, military discipline was enforced, the course was chiefly scientific and mathematical, and modern languages, especially French, were taught. He took his boys on

long excursions to historic points, and once they went
all the way to Washington by steamboat and on foot,
and met President John Quincy Adams. The hours
for meals, study, and recitation were those which
prevailed in most academies. Breakfast was at seven
o'clock in winter and a quarter before seven in summer; dinner was at one; supper at sunset. Study
and recitations began at eight in summer and nine
in winter, and lasted till one; were resumed at two
and ceased at four. From four to five there was
recreation; from five till sunset, study; and in the
evening, study and private lectures till ten o'clock,
when everybody must be in bed. The day began with
prayer, and on Sunday each cadet must remain in his
room, except when he was at divine service. The va-
cation was for six weeks, beginning with the first
Monday in December. The expense was about $275
per annum for each boy, which was more than the
cost at most academies. Some of the academies were
endowed and some had state assistance, but very
few were free. There were no high-schools till one
at Boston was started in 1821. There were no co-
educational academies. The Bradford Academy in
the Merrimac Valley, founded in 1803, was intended
for boys and girls, but after a short time it became a
girls' school. The higher classes studied Morse's
Geography, Murray's English Grammar, Pope's *Essay
on Man*, Blair's Rhetoric, and the Bible—a course
which it would be hard to improve upon. They were
taught embroidering and other accomplishments with
the needle. The movement for giving a girl the same
education as a boy was about to begin, however. In

1818 Rev. Joseph Emerson opened his Girls' Seminary at Byfield, Massachusetts, and taught such studies as boys learned. In 1821 Emma Willard started her girls' seminary at Troy, which was on the same plan as a boys' academy. A college course for girls was, as yet, not thought of. In the South girls were usually taught at home, by the mother or father or by the family tutor. Girls of poor parents might learn the rudiments at a village school taught by some poor woman, who received a pittance in return for imparting a pittance of knowledge, but even this apology for education was available to few. The prevalent idea was that it was not desirable to give girls much schooling.

But it was likewise a prevalent idea that education for boys was a luxury which the privileged classes alone could enjoy; but, as I have said before, this was a time of awakening, and one direction which it took was in the increase in facilities for popular education. Here, as with higher education, New England led the way. The best schools were there, the largest attendance, the keenest pursuit of knowledge. Primary schools were still sorry institutions everywhere, however.

In these schools there could be no grading, because all the children, young and old, within a given radius, must attend the same school, which comprised only one room and had only one teacher. It was kept in a frame or log building in which there might be as many as eighty scholars, all under one master. The smallest children sat on the front benches, immediately under the teacher's eye; the older pupils were at the back. The little ones might be as young as three years old, learning their A-B-C's, and there might be some youths who were nearly grown up. The discipline was very strict, the ferule, rattan, and cowhide being applied to refractory girls as well as boys without an age limit. In a few schools there was a whippping-post to which a bad pupil could be bound when he was being flogged, and there were instances of severe cruelty on the part of teachers. Notwithstanding the harshness of the system—perhaps because of it—mutinies took place occasionally, with rough-and-tumble fights between the teacher and scholars and consequent strife among neighbors, some of whom took the teacher's part, and others that of the scholars. One feature of the discipline and instruction has, unhappily, disappeared from American schools. The scholars were taught manners. When they came into the school-room in the morning the boys must bow to the teacher, and the girls make him a courtesy. They were required to make these signs of respect before and after reciting, and when they left the school-room. When they were dismissed in the evening they were told by the teacher to go home and "make their manners" to their parents. The school-house was never a good building, and often a very dilapidated one, being cared for generally by all and particularly by none. The school furniture comprised long benches, with rude writing-desks in front of them, and a high home-made desk for the teacher on a small raised platform. This desk was built of planks reaching to the floor, and behind it was a place of deposit for confiscated tops, balls, etc.

The school exercises were written in ink. Lead-pencils had been invented, but they were too expensive for school use, and slates had not yet been introduced. The scholars or the teacher made the ink by mixing ink-powder and water. Metal pen-points did not come into use till about 1830, and the teacher made the pens by pointing the ends of goose quills. Paper was expensive and was husbanded carefully. It was unruled, and lines were made with a ruler and a piece of metal lead. The district school was supported by tuition fees in the South, and attended only by children of the poorer class. In the West there were no classes and the district schools were used generally; as they were also in the East. The teacher was paid by taxes in the East, which were levied in the town or district. In some districts there were two terms—winter and summer—the latter kept by a woman when the men were all supposed to be engaged in farm-work, the former nearly always by a man. He received from six to twenty dollars per month as salary, and was boarded by different families in turn, in the vicinity of the school. The woman teacher received from four to ten dollars a month. Sometimes the teacher lived well and sometimes he starved. He was treated with respect as a personage just below the parson; but he was generally looked upon as a man who had an easy life, because he did not have to perform manual labor. It was in these schools that the great majority of the people received all their education. A child might enter when he was three years old; by seven he would be studying grammar; then he would learn to write and go into arithmetic. After he was ten years old his attendance at school was apt to become very irregular, for then he was old enough to do some work on the farm. The instruction was partly religious. The Bible was read in school every day, and the text-books had something of religion in them. The first book the child had was the primer. The New England Primer, published in 1813 at Concord, was entitled "The New England Primer, or an Easy and Pleasant Guide to the Art of Reading, to which is added the Catechism"—the catechism being a score or more of selections from the Westminster Assembly Shorter Catechism, which contained upward of one hundred and fifty questions. The catechism was committed to memory without any comprehension of its meaning, but so were most of the rules which the child learned. From the primer he progressed to the most universally used book that has ever been written by an American—Noah Webster's spelling-book. In 1815 it was already ten years old and had only started on a career, which lasted even to the school days of some middle-aged people who read these lines, by which time twenty-four million copies had been printed and sold. In 1818 Webster stated that more than five millions of copies had already been sold. It is hardly an exaggeration to say that one hundred years ago every child who went to school studied it. Starting in Connecticut and Massachusetts, it soon circulated through the rest of the country. All children learned to spell from it in the same way, to divide their words in the same way, and, in a great measure, to pronounce alike. It was called an easy standard of pronunciation. The schools, scattered so far apart, had this link to join them together. The book went out of use first in the home of its birth. It lingered for many years afterward in the South and West, and I dare say there are schools which use it even now. The arithmetic was taught in the earlier stages almost entirely orally and without books. The printed arithmetics were severely practical, being, they said, "adapted to the commerce of the United States." The new currency having been adopted in 1792, an important chapter was given to instruction how to divide, multiply, add, etc., in "Federal money." There was a section devoted to barter, which was the form of trade with many people in the country.

XVI

READING AND WRITING

NOAH WEBSTER called his speller "The First
Part of a Grammatical Institute of the English
Language," and it was part of a plan for American-
izing the English tongue. In the introduction he said:

This country must, at some future time, be as distinguished
by the superiority of her literary improvements as she is already
by the liberality of her civil and ecclesiastical constitutions. . . .
For America in her infancy to adopt the present maxims of the
Old World would be to stamp the wrinkle of decrepit old age upon
the bloom of youth, and to plant the seed of decay in a vigorous
constitution.

Up to Webster's time, says one of his eulogists,
"we had been living in a state of colonial dependence,
and were in the most complete literary vassalage to
the mother-country." We were as little children
"looking eagerly and reverently to the mother-country for our supplies." Webster and his followers
insisted that there was a connection between the literary and political life of the nation. A correspondent
wrote to him, November 23, 1790:

Did not many persons oppose the adoption of the Federal Constitution at first, who soon became convinced of its goodness?
If it had never been formed and presented to the public, anarchy
and ruin might have been the consequences; and so if a Dictionary

on a reformed plan of spelling should not be offered to the public, we shall jog on in the good old irregular, absurd way, and at last leave the world as servile in this respect as we found it. Is this the independent spirit of Americans? I should blush to own it —I deny it.

A writer in *The North American Review* for September, 1815, explained the difficulty in creating a national literature. It was, he said, the product of a national language; but America had a language which it had accepted from a nation totally unlike itself. The colonial state produced nothing, for the mother-country no more supposed that a colony could improve her literature than that it could improve her political or religious system.

So Noah Webster led a rebellion, and had a following of enthusiastic men who saw the vision of an independence as complete in letters as it was in government. It was to rest upon the broad basis of popular support, and was not to depend upon a favored class. In his grammar Webster insisted that it was correct to say "You was." "The compilers of grammars condemn the use of *was* with *you*," he said, "but in vain. The practice is universal, except among men who learn the language by books." Here was his purpose—to record the language as men used it. He worked toward his great end under disadvantage, because of the isolation of the communities of America. Writing to him in 1806, the historian, David Ramsay, lamented that there was so little literary intercourse between the states; but such as there was came largely from Webster's efforts. He traveled through the country, lecturing on language. Before the Constitution was adopted he petitioned the several state legislatures for copyright laws and obtained them from nearly all. This was the first official recognition of the existence of American authorship.

As everything living changes, so, Webster insisted, the English language must change from time to time, and he would have the changes in pronunciation recognized by changes in the spelling. So he offered *hainous* for *heinous*, *luster* for *lustre*, *humor* for *humour*, *doctrin* for *doctrine*, and a few other simplifications. For pronunciation he pleaded for that which was natural, and, if possible, for that which was used by the ordinary man. The English language must, in the course of time, be shaped by American usage, he thought. In his Compendious Dictionary he said:

In each of the countries, peopled by Englishmen, a distinct dialect of the language will gradually be formed; the principal of which will be that of the United States. In fifty years from this time the American-English will be spoken by more people than all the dialects of the language, and in one hundred and thirty years by more people than any other language on the globe, not excepting the Chinese.

There had been a few radicals who wanted to make a new language for the United States, and there was a more serious effort to stop calling the national language English. In 1778, when Congress prescribed the ceremonial to be observed in receiving the French minister, it said that his French address should be replied to "in the language of the United States."

On November 12, 1807, Webster wrote to Joel Barlow:

LIFE IN AMERICA ONE HUNDRED YEARS AGO

For more than twenty years, since I have looked into philology and considered the connection between language and knowledge, and the influence of a national language on national opinions, I have had it in view to detach this country as much as possible from its dependence on the parent country.

In his two-volume dictionary he said that many words commonly employed in England were foreign words here—those used in heraldry, in hawking, in speaking of feudal tenures, for instance; and that many American words had no uses in England— those used in our land-offices, "congress," "select-men," and the like; and that these differences must be recognized as natural and proper. Dr. Johnson said that "the chief glory of a nation arises from its authors," so Webster used American authors to illus- trate his definitions, and quotations from Washington, John Adams, Franklin, Madison, Ramsay, or Ham- ilton appeared in the same paragraphs with excerpts from Hooker, Milton, Shakespeare, or Dryden. Web- ster represented a sane and fearless radicalism. He did more than any other individual to give the American nation an independent property in the Eng- lish language. He was, without any rivals approach- ing him, the first American man of letters. In the same class with him at Yale, graduating in 1778, and, like him, born in Connecticut, was his friend Joel Barlow, who followed in his footsteps and attempted to do for poetry what Webster tried to do for the language and to give it the distinctive stamp of the new nationality.

The epic poem, "The Columbiad," was published in 1806 and went through four editions. The author

NOAH WEBSTER
From a painting by Jared Flagg

JOEL BARLOW
From a painting by R. Fulton

said he wrote it to foster the feeling of American
nationality, that his object was "altogether of a moral
and political nature," that he wished "to encourage
and strengthen in the rising generation a sense of the
importance of republican institutions as being the
great foundation of public and private happiness."
Again:

This is the moment in America to give such a direction to poetry,
painting, and the other fine arts, that true glory may be implanted
in the minds of men here, to take the place of the false and de-
structive ones that have degraded the species of other countries.

So Barlow sang of Christopher Columbus and the
discovery and settlement of America in a poem over
six hundred lines long, in a meter and in language
which were borrowed, exemplifying, in fact, the futility
of his own aspirations. There is hardly any one now
living who has read "The Columbiad" through, yet
the English is good, although the poetry is bad, and
the elaborate purpose of the author is industriously
sustained. When the poem appeared long poems
were a popular mode of expression, and the reviewers
generally spoke highly of "The Columbiad." Many
people bought the book, which showed that they
wanted a literature of their own. Doubtless many
people admired it. They were members of a young,
immature, and ambitious nation, and thought that
to be strong and noble which was in reality only fearless, crude, and bombastic. Nevertheless, I do not
believe that the book was ever read much. Barlow
was known as the author of "The Columbiad," but
"The Columbiad" was known only by the title on

the cover. In 1819 a commentator in the literary paper published in Alexandria, then in the District of Columbia, spoke of it thus:

That huge and incongruous mass of political monstrosities, "The Columbiad," is now scarcely considered worthy of criticism—and is by far a greater outrage upon the memory of Columbus than ever despotism inflicted on his person.

The periodicals all professed to have an ideal like Barlow's. Thus, *The Portfolio*, published in Philadelphia, which was one of the best, declared its object to be "the promotion of American literature, the cultivation of taste, the encouragement of the fine arts, the inculcation of sound morality, and the dissemination of general truth." The lesser literary papers claimed the same general purpose. Some of them were: *The Eye*, published by "Obediah Optic" at Philadelphia, begun in 1807; *The Journal of the Times*, at Baltimore, begun in 1818; the Boston *Weekly Magazine*, begun in 1816; and the *Columbian Telescope and Literary Compiler*, published at Alexandria, begun in 1819. All of them showed a creditable striving for literary expression. They were written in good English, they taught good morals, and they were patriotic. The *Columbian Telescope* was a fair example of its class, although it was not as good as some of the other papers. It was edited by "The Trio," being "Geoffry Whimsical," a humorous philosopher; "Solomon Studious," a tiresome pedant, who was eternally airing a cheap classical knowledge, a character who appears in nearly all the lighter literature of the day; and "Peter Quiz," a satirist of present-day habits and weaknesses. Nearly a third of the paper was devoted to "The Parnassian Bouquet," being verses, some borrowed and some original. The poets sang of love and friendship, admonished their readers to follow the path of virtue, told of humorous occurrences at convivial gatherings, and proclaimed the glory of Columbia. The heavy articles were reviews of serious books, and moral and semi-religious essays. Some of the papers had a great deal to say about art, and the Boston *Weekly Magazine* had a column devoted to the theater. All the papers had some humorous paragraphs. These papers were better than papers of the corresponding class are at the present day. The humor was richer, the articles, in both prose and verse, were more carefully written, more thoughtful, more informing, and the moral tone was higher. They were beneficial in their influence.

One of the lighter fortnightlies is read occasionally even at the present day. *Salmagundi, or the Whim Whams and Opinions of Launcelot Langstaff, Esq., and Others* was issued in New York for about a year. It was revived some years later, but not under the same authorship, and the charm had fled. William and Washington Irving and James Kirke Paulding were the authors of the issue of 1807. The theater, music, the fashions, follies, and amusements of New York society, were the topics treated with delightful humor and good taste. No names were given and the lampoons were harmless. It speaks well for the intelligence of the wealthier class of residents of New York that they were delighted with this paper. One like it could not now survive, because the tone is too high and the humor too innocent to suit the taste of the present day.

The monthly, bi-monthly, and quarterly magazines, such as the *Literary Magazine* and *North American Review* at Boston, *The Portfolio* and *Analectic* at Philadelphia, and the *Monthly Magazine* at New York, were better than the weeklies and fortnightlies. There were a great many religious reviews, and they also were literary periodicals. Almost every sect had one or more of them, and it is a fact which shows that they were not bigoted in tone that one must read some ways into one of them to find what sect published it. When Bishop John Carroll, the Catholic, died in 1815 the Protestant reviews generally eulogized him.

The South played no part in the literary development of the country. The reading class in that section was numerically small and very conservative in its habits. The planters read what English country gentlemen read—the classics, the English masters, and their own newspapers. They were slow to admit a new book. Very few libraries in the South contained the American books which were being read in the North and East. But the South had a civilization of its own and a part of it should be a literature, but it strove in vain to create it. It was not until 1828 that Charleston had the *Southern Review*, and not until 1834 that Richmond had the *Southern Literary Messenger*. Occasionally, the Southern presses issued a heavy book, and this was all, except the newspapers and political pamphlets, that the South contributed to literature.

READING AND WRITING

To name a few of the issues of the press will serve to indicate the direction of the public taste. In law there was Wheaton's *Digest of Maritime Law*, published at New York; in economics, John Bristed's *Resources of the British Empire*, also at New York; in history and biography, Belknap's *History of New Hampshire*, at Boston, and William Wirt's *Life of Patrick Henry*, at Philadelphia; in ethnology, Warden's translation of a French work on the intellectual and moral faculties and literature of negroes; in travel and adventure, John R. Jewitt's *Narrative of Adventures during a Captivity of Three Years among the Savages of Nootka Sound*, at Middletown, Connecticut, and Captain Porter's *Cruise of the Essex*, at Philadelphia; in humor and fiction, *John Decastro and His Brother's Bat, commonly called Old Crab*, at New York, and Hugh Henry Brackenridge's *Modern Chivalry, Containing the Adventures of a Captain and Teague O'Regan, his Servant*, at Richmond; in sensational fiction, Duyckinck's *The Sicilian Pirate*, at New York. Of poetry there were American editors of Burns, Campbell, and Thomson's "Seasons." There was a steady stream of religious books, ranging from a Charleston, South Carolina, publication, *A Dissertation on the Prophecies Relative to Antichrist and the Last Times*, by Ethan Smith, pastor of the Church in Hopkinton, New Hampshire, to John Foster's *Discourse on Church Musick*, published at Brighton, Massachusetts. The novels were few and were the most insignificant part of the publications. The public taste did not demand them, and for the time the production was slight. Charles Brockden Brown, the first American novelist, died in 1810, and there was no one to take his place for some years.

In 1809 Irving's *Knickerbocker's History of New York*, which was really a work of fiction, appeared. It was received with universal applause and established the reputation of the author. He was the first American to make a literary reputation in Europe, but he made it here when he applied his art to American life. A few years later the case of the greatest of American novelists illustrated again the insistence of the nation upon its own.

James Fenimore Cooper published at New York his novel *Precaution* in 1820. It was an example of slavish imitation and literary thraldom. The style was English, the scene was laid in England, the characters were English, and the English reviewers thought the book was by one of their own authors. It aroused no interest in this country and deserved none. The next year *The Spy* appeared. Here was a novel with an incident of the Revolution for the plot, the scene laid in a county in New York, the characters Americans. It leaped into success and became at once the most-read novel in the United States, and Cooper's career was fixed.

It must be remembered that the reading public of 1815 was limited, and that there were a great many people who could not read at all. People of this class now read, and a large mass of literature is provided for them; but in 1815 the servant girls, day laborers, and poor farmers who could read were so few that they had no literature of their own. They had to be content with the Bible and the newspaper. In fact, they read what more cultivated people read, but they read very little. Their imaginations were not excited by books and papers designed expressly for that purpose. There was no slum literature. The people of the slums were too ignorant to read it. There were no department newspapers, attempting to cover the whole range of human wants and make themselves indispensable to all classes of readers. Literature was held to be something higher than ordinary life; the printing-press was considered to be the vehicle for depicting mankind washed and in good clothes.

The newspapers varied greatly in merit, but they were all well written. They were not newspapers as we understand the term. There was no systematic co-operative news-gathering. The only reporting was of the proceedings of Congress and the state legislatures. The other news in a paper was picked up here and there from other papers and from letters sent to the editor, and there was nothing continuous about it from day to day. At seaports, however, the papers gave the entrances and clearances of vessels. One might read his newspaper for a month and not read of a crime. There was no fear of printing long articles. When the Hartford Convention issued its report January 4, 1815, the newspapers generally printed it in full, although it took up a page and a half of the paper and was an argumentative, closely reasoned state paper which no one but an intelligent man, well versed in the principles of government, could have read with understanding. Important speeches in Congress were often printed in full, occupying two, three, or more columns of a paper which had only four pages. It was the custom to print long communications over assumed names, such as "Cato," "Falkland," "Hampden," on political questions. They were polemical, nearly always able, and often profound. They were apt to reappear in pamphlet form. Under the law the statutes were promulgated through the chief newspapers, being printed *in extenso* on the first page. The papers were expensive. The Philadelphia *Mercantile Advertiser*, published daily except Sundays and holidays, cost eight dollars per annum; the Charleston *Courier*, also daily, the same price, but it issued a country paper three times a week for five dollars per annum; the Norfolk *Herald*, published twice a week, cost six dollars per annum; the Richmond *Enquirer*, published three times a week during the sessions of the legislature and twice a week during the rest of the year, cost five dollars per annum. The papers passed from hand to hand and were read by many who could not afford to buy them.

It is plain that people who read these newspapers must have had an extraordinary taste for affairs of government and that they must have had a knowledge of them. It is plain, too, that they must have had strong minds if they fed them on such strong mental food.

The newspapers conveyed to them, however, one form of literature which was calculated rather to stimulate their passions than to strengthen their minds; yet, as it was peculiarly American, it requires a word of notice. It was the custom of the newspapers to print cards or notices, signed by individuals who were responsible for their contents, denouncing other individuals who were named. Often a card was also printed as a broadside to be pasted up and distributed. On the trees near the court-houses, or in other conspicuous places where many people would be sure to see them, these notices could be found. They were interesting and ingenious compositions and their consequences were often deadly. They were worded carefully, so as to convey insult, denunciation, defiance, and contempt of the individual to whom they were addressed. They were the prelude to personal affrays, duels, or murders. They were common in the South and Southwest, but they appeared in all sections of the country. After the crisis which they produced had taken place, long circumstantial accounts of it and of the events leading up to it would be written by the witnesses, accessories, or principals. These accounts were minute in detail and were prepared with great painstaking, and from the original publication might spring a considerable body of printed statements. This form of literature was produced by the better educated men, but their example spread occasionally into the lower grades of society, as the following extract from the Norfolk *Herald* of June 24, 1815, will show. It comes from a man who had a grievance over a question of personal property:

NOTICE.

The designing hypocrite who comes under the appellation of *William Pendred* has wantonly seeked an opportunity of discrediting me in the public papers. . . . I am very sorry that I am reduced to the necessity of altercating with so ordinary a character as he is known to be. Though should I be the character who he alludes to respecting his brother's clothes, I assert him to be an infamous lyer, which would be sufficiently in my power to prove at any time when called upon.

And the following is from General P. J. Hays, of Tennessee, a man who stood high, a friend and devoted adherent of Andrew Jackson. It is undated and is found among General Jackson's papers:

To the Public:

Although I can never undertake to defend any man's conduct whether "*right or wrong*," I am not disposed to find fault with that filial sensibility which seeks to vindicate a father's fame. In accordance with it I have endeavoured to shew that Wm. P. Anderson's imputations against the character of my deceased father were unfounded, and that Anderson himself is so base as to deprive his assertions of all credit. These objects I believe I have accomplished. His son, R. K. Anderson, has, it appears, been instigated by a certain political Doctor in this place—who shines rather as a monkey than a catspaw—to meet the evidence I submitted of his father's dishonor by vague and vulgar abuse of myself—abuse as vile as his own character and which it is impossible for a gentleman either to utter or to notice. I cannot be drawn into a controversy with a person so disreputable as this Rufus K. Anderson, who is represented by his own father as given to thieving, and who in this case is notoriously the instrument of a calumniator, more contemptible, because more cowardly, than a highway robber—a calumniator who is proved to have lied away his own honor by the testimony of Messrs. Parrish, Foster, Fitzgerald, Black and Marshall.

XVII

GENERAL HAYS'S friend and patron, Andrew Jackson, was as familiar with posting literature and its consequences as any man in America. He had contributed both to the literature and to the consequences. In his propensity for quarreling and fighting he was an exaggerated example of a type of men who flourished in his day and in the part of the country where he lived. They were not bad men, but performed their public and private duties faithfully, were enterprising and industrious. They held human life cheap, however, and placed their notions of honor above everything else. They thought it no sin to hate and harbor the passion of revenge. At the same time they were loyal in friendship, devoted in kinship, and grateful for kindness. There was a great deal of the Indian's nature in them. De Tocqueville studied the red man and said that he was "mild and hospitable when at peace, though merciless in war beyond any known degree of human ferocity," and so it was with his white neighbors. They had to fight the Indians incessantly. Even in the more populous parts of the country they were removed by only a few years from constant Indian warfare. So, as they thought of Indians a great deal, they came to be like them, and were often ferocious and merciless in private warfare, when the opposing forces were two men who might possess all the domestic virtues. Physical bravery was the most essential attribute of a man, and he must be ready to endure suffering without complaint, like the Indian who sang a death song when burning at the stake. In at least two duels in which he was the second, General Jackson named as the distance between the combatants from six to nine feet, the weapons being pistols. In the duel in which he killed Charles Dickinson in 1795 he went to the field determined to kill. He said afterward that his purpose had been so strong that he would have been able to stand long enough to accomplish it even if he had been shot through the head. Instances of such predominance of will power were told of and believed. As a matter of fact, he did shoot Dickinson after he had himself been badly wounded. A few years later Armistead Thomson Mason, soon after he had retired as a Senator from Virginia, was killed in a duel in which six paces separated the principals, who fought with muskets. Instances of similar contempt for death could be multiplied. Many men kept guns or pistols exclusively for use in duels, and some of them with grim humor gave their weapons proper names. One of the most accomplished citizens of Georgia, a governor, soldier, poet, and artist, called his dueling rifle the "Hungry Tigress," and his neighbor had one which he called "Spiteful Sue." The ostensible cause of General Jackson's duel with Dickinson was a dispute over a wager on a horse-race; but there was a rumor that Dickinson and his friends wanted to get Jackson out of the way because of his increasing political importance, and there was another story that Jackson had heard that Dickinson had spoken lightly of Mrs. Jackson's reputation. Causes like these were the basis of many duels; but in their wake flowed a multitude of trivial reasons.

Young swaggerers and coarse bullies tried to get the name of being duelists. It added to their social importance, and they sought and gave insults without excuse. At a time when all men drank and nearly all drank too much occasionally, duels often came from the unpremeditated remarks of tipsy men. Not all the men who fought duels had fiery tempers or bullying dispositions, however. Some were benignant citizens, who reprobated the practice and only followed it because a refusal to do so would have subjected them to the unbearable charge of cowardice and have resulted in a loss of their influence in the community. Alexander Hamilton accepted Burr's challenge in 1804 because he knew that, if he refused, his career as a public man would be closed. In vain did the clergy protest against the duel as a violation of God's law; in vain did enlightened laymen denounce it as both foolish and wicked; no man dared to refuse a challenge if it was given for what was recognized as a valid reason, and few dared not to send one if their honor was assailed. Many duels were abortive, but these were not the rule. Rarely were the weapons swords or rapiers; nearly always the long-barreled pistol or the heavy musket was used, and most Americans were good shots.

The women were all opposed to dueling. When a

meeting was to take place the fact was hidden from them; but there were many women of gentle, Christian lives who stood aside and allowed their men to go to the field of honor as they allowed them to go into battle when their country was at war.

Dueling was a crime peculiar to the higher classes. It was remarked that "not one in ten thousand was entitled to leave the world in this manner." Nevertheless, many left it in this manner. There was hardly a family of the planter class in the South and Southwest that did not have one or more duels recorded in its annals. It was the custom of *The North American Review* to print in each issue a list of notable deaths by violence which had taken place during the preceding two months, and the list nearly always included some one who had fallen in a duel, oftenest in the South, often in the Middle States, and occasionally in the North and East. In New England, where there were few of the gentry, duels were of rare occurrence. The bad eminence of the South was due to the presence of a landed aristocracy which adhered to Old World customs, to a warm climate which produced an irritable physical condition, to idleness and the consequent gambling and drinking, to the intolerant and domineering temper which came to the owner of slaves. More duels took place in the South in a month than took place in the rest of the country in a year. It was not till many years after the time of which I am writing that dueling declined, disappearing first in the East and North, then in the Middle States, and last in the South, giving way before the softening influences of a general advance of civiliza-

tion and a modification of standards of honor produced
by the less frequent recurrence of wars.

Although dueling flourished in 1815, unlawful man-
slaughter by lynching had not yet come into practice.
When summary justice was visited it was by what
was termed "club law," an expression derived from
the voluntary organizations which existed in various
parts of the country for protection against criminals
where regular authority could not enforce the law.
These clubs proceeded in orderly manner and not as
mobs. Usually they warned their victims of impend-
ing punishment, the object being to make them move
away. Commonly they punished by whipping. Rarely
did they hang a man, and when they did they might
try him before an improvised court beforehand. They
illustrated the capacity of the people for self-govern-
ment rather than a spirit of lawlessness. There was
a great deal of irregular justice inflicted immediately
after the Revolution, when society was in a disordered
state; there was a great deal at a later period when
the idea of direct power of the people began to sink
in; but between 1792 and 1819, a transition period,
there was little. Lynching did not become an institution until after the Civil War, when a new species
of negro crime became prevalent.

There were a great many escapes from the law a
hundred years ago. Information that a crime had
been committed traveled no faster than the escaping
criminal, and the wild, uninhabited regions were an
asylum which was near at hand. There was no de-
tective system, and when a man was robbed, or when
his slave or apprentice ran away, he invoked the aid

of the public to apprehend the culprit and recover his property by an advertisement in the newspapers. The following from a Norfolk paper will serve as an example. It related to the escape of a negro woman who talked "very modest," but was "fond of dancing and smoking segars," and apparently to other property losses:

... I further make public that I have bought a blood-hound of the most furious kind; therefore I beg my friends will send no young children alone to my house, nor allow their servants to attempt the house by the yard way, without the greatest caution.

A great many criminals escaped punishment because the penalties prescribed for their offenses were too severe. The states had inherited the common law of England with its long list of capital offenses and barbarous punishments; and where the punishment went beyond all measure it was not enforced. Thus in New Hampshire the list of crimes for which the punishment was death included murder, arson, burglary, felonious assault, rape, and treason. Virginia had in her list selling a free man as a slave and stealing a slave. In Georgia, where a moderate code was adopted in 1811, counterfeiting was a capital crime, as it was in several other states. Yet counterfeiting was a common offense, the opportunities to commit it being numerous and the temptation too strong to be resisted. There were scores of different kinds of paper currency issued by local banks, crudely printed and easy to imitate, and, in consequence, much false money was in circulation. The severity of a penalty was often an indication that the crime was common and that an effort was being made to stop it by terrifying those who felt inclined to commit it. Under the law of North Carolina a convicted counterfeiter must stand in the pillory for three hours and have his right ear nailed to the pillory and cut off; must then receive thirty-nine lashes upon his bare back, and be branded with a red-hot iron on the right cheek with the letter *C* and on the left cheek with the letter *M*, besides forfeiting half his goods and chattels and suffering imprisonment. For the second offense—it is difficult to see how a man thus marked could accomplish it—the punishment was death. In Delaware, by an act passed February 7, 1817, a forger was fined and imprisoned, and then must "forever wear the letter *F* made of scarlet cloth sewed on the outside of his outer garment on the back between the shoulders, of at least six inches square." I have found no record of men with branded cheeks and only one ear wandering about the countryside in North Carolina, nor in Delaware of unfortunates wearing coats with a red *F* in the middle of the back. It must be that the punishment was inflicted very seldom.

Generally speaking, the criminal law was assuming a more merciful aspect, and was leaving out the old idea of vengeance and punishment for punishment's sake. The prevailing tendency was indicated by the code adopted by Maryland in 1809, which proclaimed as its object the reform of the criminal by a "mild and justly proportioned scale of punishment," and by the pronouncement of the General Assembly of Louisiana in 1820, "that it is of primary importance in every well-regulated state, that the code of criminal law should be founded on one principle— the prevention of crime."

To prevent the crime of piracy was one of the problems of the time, and a new variety had arisen, bred of the political commotions which now began to assume an acute stage in the Spanish-speaking countries lying off our Southern coast. It is true that the old days of great piracy on the Spanish Main had passed, but the West-Indian waters still held a great many sea robbers, some engaged in the slave trade, some bearing commissions as privateers, and some flying the black flag without pretense of lawful purpose. Some of the merchants of the surrounding ports profited by the robberies and encouraged them, and slave-dealers in the United States bought from them. The slave trade became unlawful in 1808, and in 1820 was declared to be piracy, but slavers did not respect statutes unless they were enforced. The trade was still lawful in Spanish dominions, and Havana especially was the resort of slave-vessels, whence many slaves were smuggled to the mainland. The federal government could only lessen the iniquity; it could not suppress it. The slave coast of Africa was so long that it was impossible to patrol it successfully, and convenient points on the Southern coast of the United States could be chosen for landing-places for the cargoes. Many thousands of slaves were smuggled in, scores of slave-vessels were captured, and the suppression of the slave trade presented a continuous problem for fifty-seven years. But the ordinary pirates of the West Indies did not confine themselves to taking slaves. All was fish that came to their kettle, and vessels with specie in their holds were their favorite food. The pirates were Spaniards, Portuguese, negroes, and a few English and Americans. One of the worst pirates that ever was hanged was already beginning his career. He was Charles Gibbs, born in Rhode Island, and executed in New Orleans in 1831, after he had confessed to the murder of nearly four hundred people. In 1822 Lieut. William Howard Allen, U. S. N., was killed off Matanzas, Cuba, while boarding a pirate vessel, and his death excited a great deal of indignation. The following year a fleet under Commodore David Porter was sent against the pirates, and inflicted such severe punishment that their power was broken. The new variety of piracy was more difficult to deal with, for it was sporadic in its recurrence and proceeded under cover of political purposes.

Immediately after our independence the rich domain of Spain, lying almost undefended by its owner upon our west and south, was a constant temptation to venturesome Americans who hoped to gain wealth and power by short routes. When Louisiana passed to our possession they turned their attention to the remaining Spanish territory lying on our southern and southwestern border and adjacent to our southern coast, and found, besides, a field for their activities by assisting the Spanish colonies in their revolt against the parent state. Everybody in the United States sympathized with the revolt, and the revolutionists received material as well as moral support; but many of those who went ostensibly to assist them

11   161

were looking only to their own aggrandizement and used the revolutions as a cloak for spoliations and smuggling operations. The first of these outlaws to establish an American base were three brothers, Jean, Pierre, and Dominique Lafitte. They had lived in Louisiana and were Frenchmen by birth, but Americans by preference. The leader, Jean Lafitte, had been a straight pirate, or, at any rate, was generally believed to have been one. They established themselves at Grand Terre, an island in Barrataria Bay, just west of the mouths of the Mississippi River, and their boats sailed as privateers under the flag of the new Republic of Carthagena. They gathered followers until the population of Grand Terre numbered about four hundred people. Residents of the neighboring country went there to buy plunder quite openly, and there was an active commerce between the Barratarians and Donaldsonville and New Orleans in Louisiana. Visitors who met Jean Lafitte reported that he was a mild-mannered man and a loss to good society, that he had a good cook and excellent wines— and some of the wines found their way to the tables of the connoisseurs of New Orleans. The Lafittes had ready money, and when they were indicted for smuggling four hundred and fifteen negroes into the United States and killing a revenue officer who sought to get evidence against them, the United States Attorney at New Orleans, John R. Grymes, resigned his office in order that he might become their lawyer, and Edward Livingston was the associate counsel. For a time they escaped punishment, but Commander Daniel Tod Patterson, of the navy, was sent against them and broke up their establishment. They re-organized and the British sought their co-operation in the campaign against New Orleans. Instead of giving it, however, they furnished valuable military information to General Jackson and asked permission to join his army. Some twenty or thirty of them, accordingly, worked the artillery in the battle of New Orleans, and on February 6, 1815, were pardoned by the President for their past offenses. A few may have become good citizens afterward, but others were soon heard of again at Amelia Island in the St. Mary's River, off the coast of Florida, and at Galveston Island, off the coast of Texas, where establishments like that in Barrataria Bay were made.

Galveston Island was taken possession of by Louis de Aury, a revolutionist of New Grenada, who was appointed Governor of Texas and Galveston in 1816 by the revolutionary government of Mexico. His ship was called *Mexico Libre* and sailed under the flags of Mexico and Venezuela. His followers were described as "the refuse of all nations and all colors collected from the mass of iniquity spread over the islands of the West Indies and Spanish America." Amelia Island was seized in 1817 by Gregor Mac-Gregor, "Brigadier General of the armies of New Grenada and Venezuela and General - in - Chief employed to liberate the Provinces of both the Floridas." He was a character somewhat more respectable than Aury, but his motives were the same—to gain power and wealth for himself. Neither the South-American nor the Scotchman cared a straw for South-American independence. MacGregor recruited his band of some one hundred and fifty men chiefly in the United States, from the loafers of Savannah and Charleston, but some of them were young men who had served in the war and joined him because they did not wish to return to the tame pursuits of peace. He was financed by an American mercantile firm, to whom he promised enormous tracts of land in Florida when his independent government should be established.

His treasurer, Irvin, and his civil governor, Hubbard, were Americans, and he bought his supplies in Georgia. After a time his money gave out and his enterprise was about to collapse, when Aury came over from Galveston Island and took command. The game then became too low for the Americans and they came home. Both MacGregor and Aury had issued many commissions to privateers, which fitted out in American ports and made Amelia Island their headquarters. Their chief business was intercepting slave-vessels bound for Havana and smuggling the slaves into the United States. They preyed upon Spanish shipping in particular, but took any other that promised profit. Amelia Island was claimed as American territory, and the President sent a land and naval force against it, and the outlaws were driven from both islands. These were the earliest of a long line of irregular expeditions, having their support in the United States, against established government in Spanish-speaking America. Robbery and smuggling, which were the only objects of Lafitte, and the chief objects of Aury, and in part the objects of MacGregor, gave way to a preponderance of political objects in the later filibusters.

PIRATES AND DEBTORS

The West-Indian waters were the Hounslow Heath of the sea, and there were many routes on the land also where the traveler was in danger from robbers. Where the temptation is there the crime will be found, and the travel of men with merchandise and money in small companies, or alone, through uninhabited regions, where there were no police, offered opportunities of enrichment which highwaymen did not neglect. There was no collusion with them on the part of men who did not themselves break the law, as there was with the pirates, and nobody profited by them except the keepers of the brothels and receivers of stolen goods. On the other hand, everybody used the highway, so there was general and cordial co-operation to apprehend highwaymen. Their depredations were infrequent in the most populous parts of the country; but there was no part where one could travel far without passing through regions that offered good places of escape to a robber. In the South were large tracts of canebrake and swamp where he could take refuge and feel secure. The borders near Spanish or Indian territory were favorite places for the outlaws. Escaping to Spanish jurisdiction, they were more apt to be welcomed than to be given up, and nobody cared to follow them far among Indians. They were taken usually when they came to the towns to spend their money and to pawn the watches they had stolen. The highway yielded a rich toll. One robber before he was hanged told how he had secured thirty thousand dollars from a single merchant who was on his way to the market to buy goods, and how he got ten thousand dollars from one robbery of the mail-stage. In the mail between North and South was much paper currency, and men buying and selling slaves were provided with large sums. The flow of money between the sections of the country was very large.

The supreme crime of the highwayman was to rob the mail, an offense against federal law punishable by death. In 1830 George M. Dallas, United States Attorney at Philadelphia, in prosecuting a mail robber put the situation truly.

"In no country on the globe, perhaps, is the mail exposed to greater danger than in this," he said. "The danger arises from the nature of our country, its vast extent, and the comparative sparseness of its population. We are on the threshold of a boundless and unexplored continent. Some of our mails travel through dark and dismal forests and deserts, over mighty rivers, through gloomy swamps, and on untenanted mountains, continually incurring all kinds of danger."

There was strong temptation to rob in the cities, too, for the watch was poor and the streets were dark after nightfall. Footpads were common and it was not safe to walk far at night. Nearly every citizen carried arms for his protection, however, and the criminal stood in greater fear of private punishment than he did of the city police.

When we consider the chronic crimes which have always afflicted civilized communities, we must remember that there was no large criminal class in the United States, there being, in fact, no good breeding-place for one. Nowhere was there a dense urban population; nowhere was there a large number of people sunk in poverty and vice and crime, contaminating one another. Individual cases of poverty and crime because of it were common enough, but poverty and crime were not propagated. The wayward youth with a deformed moral nature developed his criminal propensities, and weak natures succumbed to temptation. They were natural products and society was not responsible for them. On the other hand, while the danger of criminal contagion was absent the individual developed without the restraining influence and standardizing of conduct which come from the absorption of the individual by the group. It is probable that men allowed freer play to their passions than they do now and that crimes arising from the passions were more common. There were many illegitimate births. There were houses of immoral resort in the country districts, where they do not now exist. Many foundlings were picked up. Heavy punishments were provided for the mother who concealed the death, whether by natural causes or not, of her bastard. In New Hampshire she was set upon the gallows for an hour and then imprisoned. One of the most atrocious murders of the day was that of his illegitimate child by a farmer and his wife; another was that of his wife by a young man of good family connections who had become infatuated with an abandoned woman.

The causes of murder followed familiar lines— jealousy, cupidity, and mad passions moved men to kill, as they moved Cain when he killed Abel, and Eugene Aram when he killed the shoemaker in 1745, and Professor Webster when he killed Dr. Parkman in 1849. There was a dreadful murder in 1815 by a young man in Virginia, who robbed his victim in order to get money to enable him to pay a gambling debt.

As we have seen in a former chapter, foreigners generally criticised Americans for the eagerness with which they tried to make money, and declared that they were unscrupulous in the methods they employed. In plain words they thought them cheats. But Americans when they went abroad complained that they also were cheated. It would seem, in fact, that people have always complained of being cheated by unfamiliar methods. We had in America, however, certain phases of cheating which were our own. The desire to get rich quickly prompted men to take gamblers' chances, and there were, in consequence, many failures and bankruptcies which were essentially dishonest. There was a certain callousness toward bankruptcy which did not exist in England, for here it was hardly considered a disgrace. It was under control of state laws. The federal government had authority to regulate it, but there was no general bankruptcy law between 1803 and 1841. The state laws treated it variously and too leniently, and speculators took advantage of the opportunity they afforded to cheat their creditors.

On the other hand, embezzlement had not yet become a common crime—indeed, it was not yet a crime at all in many of the states. Punishment and redress could be accomplished by indirect means, but the direct crime was unknown to the common

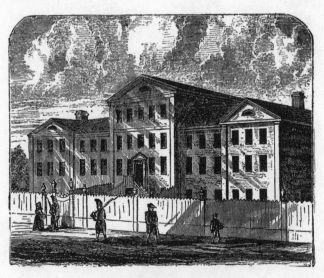

THE CITY PRISON, OR BRIDEWELL, WEST SIDE CITY HALL

THE DEBTORS' PRISON, SUBSEQUENTLY THE HALL OF RECORDS

law. Nor were there many embezzlements. Bankers and their clerks sometimes stole other people's money. The safeguards to prevent breaches of trust were not elaborate and the breaches of trust were rare. The great temptations in this direction arose at a later day with the coming of large corporations and central storehouses of money.

The offense of running into debt and failing to pay was punished by imprisonment. The insolvent debtor could, however, obtain relief from indefinite imprisonment by presenting his case in court. Nevertheless, there were prisons for debtors in the larger cities, and in the towns the jails generally contained a few of these unfortunates. There was much popular sympathy for them, and often it took the practical form of a subscription to pay a debtor's creditors and release him. Probably the debtor's prison at New York was the largest. It was situated on the park on the east side of the City Hall, nearly adjoining Chatham Street, and was a small stone building of three stories. It was open to visitors all day. The prisoners were obliged to furnish their own food and the Humane Society helped those who were unable to do so. In 1817 there were thirty-four men and one woman in the jail itself. But the limits of the jail extended to the surrounding country and embraced about one hundred and sixty acres. Within this area lived the great majority of the debtors, who furnished security against their escape, which was satisfactory to the jailer, and paid a small fee. There were between five and six hundred of these debtors. In spite of general disapproval of imprisonment for debt, it was allowed to stand as the law until New York led the way for abolishing it in 1831.

The great cause of debt, as it was of other crimes, was indulgence in strong drink.

XVIII

VICE

AS Bulwer Lytton said, when he was told that loaded dice had been found in the ruins of Pompeii: "Some of the virtues may be modern, but all the vices are ancient." [1] Nevertheless, some vices are practised more actively by one generation than they are by another and become in a sense the property of that generation. It cannot be claimed, however, that the vice of drunkenness was the peculiar property of the generation of 1815. Probably there was more of it than there had ever been before; but it may be doubted whether there was as much of it as there was a generation later. However this may be, it was a time-dishonored vice and impartial observers declared that it was the besetting sin of the Americans. Men were hard drinkers everywhere; they were supposed to be perpetually athirst; but the best that could be said for Americans was that they were no worse in this respect than the Irish, who were the worst in the world. It was estimated that they spent more money on strong drink than upon religion and education combined. The head of a well-

[1] I have borrowed this quotation from an official opinion written by James Brown Scott when he was Solicitor of the State Department.

to-do family spent hundreds of dollars a year upon his cellar, and a part of nearly every man's earnings went for strong drink. Soldiers, sailors, laborers, and working-men generally drank rum or whisky regularly every day. It was even served to the prisoners in the jails. There were many men who took a dram every morning before breakfast, who drank throughout the day, and took a "nightcap" just before going to bed. They were partially under the influence of alcohol all the time. There were others who began drinking in the afternoon and became intoxicated every day. The convivial spirits constituted a considerable proportion of the population. They took pride in their capacity for drinking and boasted of the amount of liquor they consumed. The Americans were not a wine-drinking people, except among the opulent class, who imported the wine. There was no wine of the country. The earlier stages of extensive agriculture were not favorable to grape culture and the minute care necessary to make wine. So distilling grain, fruit, or molasses was resorted to for drink. There was a large exchange of products with the West Indies, and heavy importations of molasses, which was made into rum, the liquor most universally used. No restriction was put upon distilling and the product was not taxed until after the Constitution went into effect, when the imposition of a federal tax raised a rebellion in Pennsylvania, because it was a novelty and was thought to be an infringement upon a right which the farmers had always enjoyed. So, with ardent spirits accessible to all, many became addicted to their use. There was a general complacency toward drinking. A drunkard was held in contempt, but a man who got drunk did not incur disgrace. *The Literary Messenger and American Register* of Boston in the March number, 1807, had some humorous paragraphs on "The Miseries of Social Life," and gave this as one:

On entering the room to join an evening party composed of remarkably grave, strict, and precise persons, suddenly finding out that you are drunk; and what is still worse, that the company has shared with you in the discovery, though you thought you were, and fully intended to be, rigidly sober.

Even at funerals spirits were served, and at town meetings the most sober men drank at the taverns. Nobody dreamed of absolutely stopping the evil; to mitigate it was the utmost hope of the reformers. Earnest efforts were made in this direction. Benjamin Franklin had shown the folly of drinking, and Dr. Benjamin Rush treated the question from a medical standpoint in 1784. These and the teachings of other wise men had an effect. The churches battled with the evil, but the outlook was not encouraging.

The first temperance society was organized near Saratoga in 1808. It was called the "Temperate Society," and the members agreed not to drink rum, gin, whisky, or wine, under a penalty of twenty-five cents for each offense, except at public dinners. No member should become intoxicated, under a penalty of fifty cents. One of the members who had a farm and was in the lumber business related how it had been his custom to buy a hogshead of rum for his laborers each year, but, since he had embraced the temperance doctrine, he had diminished the amount materially. He found it necessary, however, to provide liquor for some of his laborers, who would not work for him unless he did so. A temperance society appeared in Massachusetts in 1813. There was one at Morristown in 1825, each member of which pledged himself not to drink more than a pint of apple-jack a day, a quart having been the allowance up to that time. The Methodist Church directed its efforts to preventing its ministers from distilling and selling liquor. It was not till 1836 that the efforts for reform became a crusade for total abstinence. Then it was that strong drink was banished from use in the family and at social entertainments, from the workshop and the harvest field, and that there appeared, as a consequence, innumerable tippling houses or saloons, the offspring, as the recorder of the movement has stated, "of the American temperance reformation." Afterward serious attention was given to the question of invoking the law to enforce temperance or total abstinence. James Appleton made a report on the subject to the Maine legislature in 1837, and Neal Dow passed his law in 1851. In 1840 the "Washingtonian movement" began in Baltimore. Three reformed drunkards got other drunkards to reform and sign a pledge not to drink. They got others; the practice spread, and the whole country was ablaze with oratory from men who related their experiences when they were slaves to their appetites. We are told that there was at one time 600,000 of these reformed drunkards. Most of them returned to their bondage after the novelty of virtue had worn off. There was no such thing as an inebriate-asylum in the world till that at Binghamton, New York, was opened, the corner-stone being laid in 1858.

But the work of the country was not done by the drunkards in 1815 any more than it has been since. Probably there were fewer drunkards in public life than there were at a later period, because the public officials came in the main from a more refined class.

Going along with the drunkenness, the two being the chief vices of the time, was the vice of gambling, which had the sanction of the law everywhere to the extent of the lottery, which had been a favorite mode of raising money from colonial days and was regularly invoked by the Continental Congress to prop up the tottering finances of the country. Afterward it was used by the states for all sorts of purposes—to build churches, schools, hospitals, and roads. It was such an easy and certain mode of raising money that it continued to be resorted to even after its demoralizing influences were generally admitted. It was reasoned that it did public good even if it worked private harm. It was the poor people especially who supported it, instead of saving their surplus. It was antagonistic to habits of saving. In 1833 a society was organized in Pennsylvania to advocate its suppression. Public opinion indorsed the movement. Soon official lotteries ceased; then all were forbidden by law.

That form of gambling which was practised by more people than any other, except the lottery, was betting on horse-races, and everywhere in the country to a greater or less degree horse-racing was indulged in. It was not lawful in New England, nor in New

York between the years 1802 and 1821, and was put under the ban in Pennsylvania in 1820; but nothing could prevent horse-lovers from testing the speed of their horses, or stop emulation among them, and where there were no tracks there were races along the road or scratch races before the taverns.

In New England running-races never became popular, and the interest in horse-breeding was not so strong as it was in the other parts of the country, but it was there, especially, that the trotting-horse was developed. In 1810 a Boston horse astonished the country by trotting a mile in less than three minutes at Philadelphia. The line of trotters did not begin till 1824, however, when Trouble went a mile in 2:43. The races were usually under saddle, but in 1810 a light two-wheeled sulky was experimented with and soon afterward races were trotted under conditions similar to those which now prevail, but the distances were usually two or three miles.

There was no interest which so much pervaded all classes and all sections as the interest in horses. Every one had to notice them, whether he had a natural liking for them or not. They carried him wherever he went; he was absolutely dependent upon them for a hundred necessary purposes. It was deemed a quality of manliness to ride and control a horse well. The idea of a gallant and admirable man was a man on horseback. No one described the attributes of a noted individual without speaking of his abilities as a horseman. Even President Madison, although a man of sedentary tastes and without any fondness for sports, had a fine stallion on his farm

176

in Virginia, and owned an interest in a race - horse
with Dr. Thornton.

While the home of the race-horse was Virginia, the
whole South and Southwest, and to a less extent
the Middle States, were breeding horses from English
and Virginia stock. As it happened, the greatest
horse in the country, Messenger, was owned in New
York. He died in 1808 at Townsend Cock's stable
on Long Island. The greatest race of the generation
was that between American Eclipse, a New York
horse, against Sir Henry, a Southern horse. It took
place in 1823 on the Long Island course, and it was
estimated that one hundred thousand people saw
Eclipse win. Everybody knew the names of the great
horses; everybody took an interest in the great races;
and thousands of people bet on them who did not
bet on other events. The country storekeeper, who
acted in some sort as the banker for his patrons,
would sometimes advance the stakes on a race to a
customer, receiving his payment in produce delivered
from time to time. When Messenger died every human being in the United States knew it who was old
enough to know anything. It was regarded as a
national calamity. He was given a military funeral
and volleys of musketry were fired over his grave.

The oldest track in the country was the Washington
course near Charleston, where races took place every
year in the latter part of February. Beginning on
Wednesday, they lasted for the rest of the week, and
on Friday night the great jockey-club ball took place.
The races were free, a stand was provided for the
common people, and there were special accommo-

dations for ladies. The schools were closed so that the pupils might go. The whole population gathered at the course, and many visitors came from other states. At a race meeting there were not many races in a day, and not many horses entered a race. In fact, there were few horses which were capable of the severe test that a race put upon them. The distances were two, three, or four miles in heats. The principal event was usually a four-mile race, and it often happened that the best horses would run twelve miles before one of them had won. The great qualities they exhibited can be appreciated when the time they took to cover the course is considered, for they ran the third heat almost as fast as they did the first. Taking the time from a race in 1811 at Charleston, the first heat was run in eight minutes and fourteen seconds, the second in eight minutes and two seconds, and the third in eight minutes and thirteen seconds—which was not considered notably fast going. There was no regular circuit racing. The meets, except at Charleston, were not at stated periods, but took place as the result of the challenge of one horse-owner by another. Thus, the *Richmond Enquirer* for March 25, 1815, announced that a match race would take place at New Market (Petersburg) on April 27th, between James J. Harrison's horse by Sir Archy against Abner Robinson's Optimus for a purse of five thousand dollars, in heats of two miles, best two in three. On the following day, for a purse of two hundred and fifty dollars, there would be a race under the same conditions open to any nag. The advertisement was inserted by a tavern-keeper who offered to reserve accommodations for gentlemen with their servants and horses, who intended to come to the races. The sectional rivalry showed itself in the races. The localities from which the horses came were laid stress upon and called forth demonstrations of local pride. In 1806 there was a great race at Washington, D. C., in which horses from Maryland, Virginia, Pennsylvania, and New Jersey took part. It was looked upon as a contest for supremacy between four states.

Let no one who has seen a professional horse-race of the present day suppose that it gives him an adequate idea of the course a hundred years ago. The colts which sprint a few hundred yards and cannot maintain a racing speed for a full mile are poor imitations of the horses which used to circle the track four times, take a rest of half an hour, do it again and then again. The old racing demonstrated all the fine qualities of the horse, and the modern racing is his degradation. The sport which was under the control of horsemen who gambled has fallen into the hands of gamblers who race. They know nothing about horses, and few of them can ride. To them the race-track is only a great roulette-wheel and the horses only expensive balls. The elements of the crowd have changed. A few rich idlers, a large number of professional gamblers who systematically follow the races from place to place, men from the streets who like to gamble when they can, all transported to the meeting in trolley-cars and automobiles — by any other means than horses—have taken the place of the indiscriminate gatherings of earlier days, when lawyers, doctors, even a few clergymen, farmers, rich and poor, public officials, clerks, apprentices, small shopkeepers, horse-traders, and blacklegs came together, impelled by a common interest. We have lived to see editorials written on the "Passing of the Horse." Many years ago he ceased to have any usefulness for purposes of travel. A machine-driven car is now supplanting him for city and suburban purposes also. He is even being pushed off the country roads. He is rapidly becoming only the drudge of the farm. It is true that he lingers as a toy of rich men, but they will soon discard him, because he has no basis of usefulness to them. The children have been born who must live their lives without an interest which has been the concern of mankind since before the days of Job, and has influenced the minds and characters of many millions of men. The deep-reaching changes which modern inventions are making have a remarkable illustration, the full significance of which we cannot fathom, in the elimination of the interest in horses.

Many of those who were the victims of the passion for horse-racing also found a means of combining gambling and sport by following the ancient amusement of cock-fighting. Here, as in horse-racing, Virginia was the pioneer, but the pit which was most steadily in use was that at New Orleans, which, having been a Spanish town, had retained the taste for a sport in which Spaniards have ever taken peculiar delight. In Maryland, however, there was much cock-fighting, and to a less degree it prevailed throughout the country. The most important mains were those fought by the cocks of one locality against those of another. The law did not notice the sport particularly, and it was not considered an evil, except in New England, where all games were deemed to be sinful.

Nor had the law as yet need to notice the fighting of men in a ring before spectators for stakes. Such fights occurred, but there were no elaborate preparations or advertisement, and the general public took no notice of them. A good fighter became known to other ruffians, but there was no recognized champion American pugilist. A negro from Georgetown, D. C., named Molineaux, appeared in England in 1810 and claimed the title. His boasts were believed and he fought with some success; but very few people had heard of him in America. The first ring fight under rules was fought in 1816 between Jacob Hyer and Tom Beasley; but it would never have been remembered if it had not been that Jacob Hyer had a son named Tom who became the first champion prize-fighter of the American ring some twenty-five years later, and his fame was so great that his father's exploits were recalled.

But the gambling spirit which found an outlet in betting at sports more or less coarse and cruel also sought simpler and more direct means of satisfaction. Accordingly, there was much card - playing, dice-throwing, billiard-playing, and table-gaming, and establishments were provided where men who demanded facilities for ruining themselves could be supplied with everything that was necessary for the purpose. Unhappily, the universal custom of marrying early caused suffering and hardship to innocent wives and children of the wretches who gambled away their substance and died in their youth among the unclean. The evils of gambling had become acute, and there was an outcry against it. In this year old Parson Weems, still calling himself the former rector of Mt. Vernon Parish (which he had never been, for there never was such a parish), issued a pamphlet in Baltimore in which he depicted in lurid, but not exaggerated, colors the horrors which resulted from gambling. There were many other writings to the same effect. Hardly any one dared to defend gambling. In all the states except Louisiana gambling-houses were forbidden by law. Nevertheless, they flourished to a greater or less extent throughout the country. At the summer resorts, especially the springs of Virginia, there was gambling during the season. Games were found wherever there were race meetings. The round or banking games were the same as those which now prevail, but the names of some of them have probably been changed. There was roulette, "the wheel of fortune," "black and red," "equality," "E. O.," and "A. B. C.," but the favorite game was faro. A certain "Major" Robert Bailey flourished at this time, and after he had run his race and ruined himself a number of times and dragged others down with him he wrote an interesting account of his career. He kept a faro-bank at the Sweet Springs and the Berkeley Springs in Virginia, where he had a large and profitable patronage. At the Berkeley Springs he had a boarding-house or hotel, over which he and his handsome mistress presided, where the cuisine was excellent and the drinks were mixed by an expert whom he had brought from Philadelphia. His guests included foreign diplomats, people of fashion, and profligates young and old. He went to Philadelphia, where, in a room in the Mansion House Hotel, he fleeced his visitors at faro. When he was in Washington he lived at O'Neill's and must have enjoyed an acquaintance with the future Mrs. Eaton. He consorted with men of fashion, as the list of his creditors when he went into bankruptcy shows.

In Richmond there was Mr. Strass (or perhaps Strauss), who had a gambling-resort which was well patronized. He provided a good dinner for his guests, who paid for it indirectly. Some of the inveterate gamblers of the town dined with him every day. A novice entering his rooms was surprised at some of the people he met there, for among them were citizens of high standing and seemingly respectable lives —solid family men, church members—evening wolves who walked the streets by daylight clad in the garb of innocent sheep.

There was a vice of the day which we do not call a vice. To break the piety of the Sabbath by following amusement or doing work was considered to be a wicked and a vicious act. The observance of the day was the care of the law. It was supported by the argument that Sunday as a day of rest was a necessary civil institution, but the law was made for religious purposes and had its basis in the Fourth Commandment. An ominous revolt against the extreme features had arisen and received encourage-

ment from the federal government. The post-offices
in the larger towns, to accommodate their patrons,
fell into the way of opening their doors for a time on
Sunday to receive and deliver mail. In 1810 Congress passed a law requiring postmasters to deliver
mail every day in the week. There must have been
a wide-spread demand for this innovation; but in the
nature of things it was not as loud and clamorous as
the voice of the opposition, which expressed a conviction that one of the most sacred and essential of
divine institutions was being assailed. The cry went
up that the morals of the country were being ruined.
Petitions poured in upon Congress to repeal the law.
They came by the hundreds from New England and
by scores from the rest of the country. The denominations forgot their differences and spoke in concert
against the impious innovation. The petitions were
alike in tenor. "That the Sabbath," said one from
Fannettsburg, Pennsylvania, in 1815, "according to
their [the petitioners'] belief is an ordinance of God,
instituted from the beginning of the world, and always
regarded by believers in revelation as a blessing,"
etc. The conscientious observance of the day, said
another from the West, "constitutes one of the best
foundations of the virtue and happiness of any people."
One argument against the law was that it conflicted
with state laws which forbade such labor as the delivery of the mail required. The battle raged for
years; the archives of both Houses of Congress are
loaded with the petitions, and several good reports
were made upholding the American doctrine of freedom in religious observances. The enemies of the

law feared, with reason, that it would prove to be an opening wedge in breaking up the perfect quiet and inaction on Sunday which they wished to maintain.

Still, the quiet and inaction prevailed to a notable degree everywhere in the country; but in New England it assumed an extreme of solemnity which made Sunday the most disagreeable day of the week. De Tocqueville gives us a description of a New England city on Sunday, which might be applied in a less degree to all the cities in the country except the foreign city of New Orleans. He said that all social movements began to be suspended on Saturday evening. The streets were in solitude and silence. Chains hung across them in the neighborhood of the churches. The shutters of the houses were half closed. Now and then a solitary individual glided silently along the deserted streets and lanes. The city seemed to be dead. On Monday morning, at early dawn, the rolling of carriages was heard, the noise of hammers, the hum of a busy population. The city was alive. In Massachusetts the law of 1792, confirmed in 1816, forbade not only all working, but all games and recreation, and decreed that no one should travel, no ship leave the harbor, no one lounge at the tavern, and that any person in health who without sufficient reason should omit to worship God in public for a space of three months should be fined. No hackney carriage could drive into Boston or leave the town on Sunday, unless the driver had a certificate of permission from a justice of the peace. There was some laxity in enforcing the law, and in 1814 complaints were made to the legislature, which passed resolutions advising all ministers to read the laws on the subject of Sabbath observance to their congregations and to preach to them on the subject of obeying them. A society was formed "for the suppression of vice in general and particularly of profanity, intemperance, and the profanation of the Lord's day." It met at Burlington, Middlesex County, in 1814, and took into consideration especially the increasing violation of law by traveling on Sunday. Steps must be taken to punish the violators, so that the people might continue to enjoy the Sabbath "in the same uninterrupted quiet and solemn stillness as the fathers of New England enjoyed it." The law must be invoked. "Vice may be bold and clamorous," said the association, "when opposed only with timidity, but will at once shrink from the grasp of loyal authority sanctioned by public opinion," and as religious observances on the Sabbath were "more effective in restraining vice and enforcing moral duties than civil laws," it was the duty of the state to guard over them. What was the custom in Massachusetts was the custom in all New England. Perhaps the Sabbath was even more severely observed in Connecticut than it was in Massachusetts. The day in New York was a little freer, but in Pennsylvania it was solemn enough to suit the strictest. In the South the customs were less severe, but everywhere the day was set aside for religious observance, rest, and abstinence from amusements.

Somewhat akin to the vice of Sabbath-breaking was the vice of swearing and blaspheming which was an offense against the divine command exclusively. All the states had laws on the subject, but they did not enforce them. The habit of swearing was well-nigh universal and went unrestrained; but blasphemy would have been punished if there had been occasion for it. The law of Maryland, passed in 1793 and adopted by Congress as the law of the District of Columbia, may be cited as an example of the extreme horror of blasphemy which the community felt. It was in force in 1815, but nobody was tried under it. It provided that any one who should blaspheme or curse God, or deny our Saviour Jesus Christ to be the Son of God, or should deny the Holy Trinity, the Father, Son, and Holy Ghost, or the Godhead of any of the three persons, or the unity of the Godhead, should for the first offense "be bored through the tongue and fined twenty pounds," and for the second offense be branded on the forehead with the letter *B* and fined forty pounds, and for the third offense suffer death.

XIX

THE WICKED

WHEN a person was arrested in 1815 for violating the law he was confined in the county
jail, the state's prison, or the penitentiary. He fared
badly in any one of them. Even if he entered prison
with a gentle heart and virtuous desires he came out
a hard criminal and an enemy of society. Some of
the prisons were dirty, and some were clean; some were
lighted and ventilated, and others were not; some had
humane masters, and the keepers of others were brutes;
but in all of them the criminals were confined indis-
criminately, young and old, the most abandoned with
the most hopeful, youths fourteen years old with
patriarchs of crime, the suspected with the convicted,
misdemeanants with felons, debtors with murderers.
Classification had not yet been undertaken. There
were six, twenty, even thirty prisoners in a cell. In
some prisons they worked; in most they did not, but
idled away their days, told vicious stories and con-
cocted further crimes. Liquor was served with ra-
tions in some prisons; it was purchasable in all. The
prisons were, in fact, seminaries of crime.

But the penitentiary system had been established.
Imprisonment had been substituted for more acute
suffering as punishment after conviction. It was

188

based upon the expectation that it would not only deter from the commission of crime, but would reform the criminal and turn him into a useful citizen. The penitentiary at Philadelphia was the first one established, and Pennsylvania was the mother of a reform which stands as one of the milestones to mark the progress of civilization. William Penn had substituted imprisonment and labor for the death-penalty in the early days of the colony, but the English government had disapproved the change and ordered a return to the sanguinary punishments of the common law. After independence the state revived its plan. It suited the Christian spirit of the Quakers. Edward Livingston in his work on criminal jurisprudence said of them:

> In every society for promoting education, for instructing or supporting the poor, for relieving the distresses of prisoners, for suppressing vice and immorality, they are active and zealous members; and they indemnify themselves for the loss of the honours and pleasures of the world by the highest of all honours, the purest of all pleasures—that of doing good.

So in Pennsylvania capital punishment could be inflicted only upon those who were found guilty of murder and treason, and the branding-iron and stripes had disappeared from the criminal law. In 1790 the penitentiary was built and the cellular system introduced. Each prisoner was confined alone; he could not contaminate or be contaminated; if he did not reform he did not corrupt. But it was confidently believed that he would reform, and for the three years the system had prevailed the results had been promising. Unfortunately, the penitentiary became crowded and solitary confinement was abandoned. The prison then became no better than any other. Upon the revival of the original plan humanitarians pinned their hopes.

The other states had followed Pennsylvania in putting up penitentiaries and accepting the humane principle they stood for, but none of them had as yet a system of solitary confinement. A penitentiary at New York was built in 1796, at Richmond in 1800, at Charlestown, Massachusetts, in 1804, at Windsor, Vermont, in 1808, at Baltimore in 1811, at Cincinnati in 1816. Connecticut had modernized the old prison at the Simsbury copper-mines. By 1821 fourteen of the states had penitentiaries. But the public was asking, where were the reformed criminals? In truth, there were none, and it was plain that the new system had failed to produce any. In consequence, a serious sentiment began to manifest itself in favor of returning to the old way—of increasing the list of capital crimes, of inflicting personal cruelty in public, of making the criminal law a pitiless and terrifying master to the wrong-doer instead of a firm but merciful parent. Against this reaction the gentler spirits of the time contended resolutely. They insisted that cruel punishments did not deter from crime as effectively as milder punishments did; that they aroused feelings of rebellion against the law and of hatred and revenge in the criminal himself and in those who from similar education and association sympathized with him; that the experience of a thousand years had shown that crimes had been most common when the laws against them had been

EDWARD LIVINGSTON, AUTHOR OF THE CRIMINAL CODE FOR
LOUISIANA

From a painting which hangs in Whig Hall Princeton University

most severe. Besides, the infliction of cruel punishment brutalized society. It could not see its agents act a cruel part under its orders without itself being degraded. To these arguments the merciful doctrines of the New Testament were always added, and always with effect upon a population which was composed almost entirely of zealous Christians. Various organizations were formed to relieve the miseries of ill-treated prisoners; but a part of their propaganda was always advocacy of the penitentiary system. The individual writers and workers had the same objects. The Society for Alleviating the Miseries of Public Prisons in Philadelphia, the Massachusetts Society for Prison Discipline, the Society for the Prevention of Pauperism in New York, and Caleb Lowndes, a Quaker writer, Mathew Carey and Edward Livingston, with many others, worked with the same purpose. The great hope which they never lost sight of and never lost faith in was that a way would be found of reclaiming the criminal. In the face of poor facilities for experimentation, and even of failure of experiments when the facilities were good, they never ceased to believe in the innate nobleness of man, and to prosecute the search for the method by which the germ of virtue which lay in the nature of every man might be developed, and the criminal transformed into a man of rectitude and self-respect. They were not, generally speaking, under delusions with respect to the duty of society to itself as well as to its enemies. Their great hope at this time was in solitary confinement, and they wished to give it a fair trial, although they knew that it was a terrible punishment. In 1816 the state of New York, following the Pennsylvania system of 1790, built the prison at Auburn. The prisoners were not allowed to see or speak to a human being, nor to hear the human voice. The experiment was abandoned because many of the prisoners went mad under torture by comparison with which the rack and thumbscrew were mild correctives. From the abandonment came, at a later day, the system of working the prisoners in company but in silence, and separating them at night. In 1818 the legislature of Pennsylvania decreed that the conventional sentence of imprisonment at hard labor should be changed to solitary confinement — "such an entire seclusion," said the law, "of convicts from society and from one another, as that during the period of their confinement, no one shall hear, or see, or be heard by, any human being except the jailor, the inspector, or such other persons as, for highly urgent reasons, may be permitted to enter the walls of the prison." It was some time, however, before the state had the means of trying this method. A serious detriment to all the experiments that were being made was the use that politicians made of the offices in the penitentiaries. The scientific humanitarians complained bitterly that the prisons were in charge of untrained and incompetent keepers, the friends of politicians, and that they were changed as often as the political complexion of the appointing power changed. This was the rule to which there were a few honorable exceptions. There was complaint, also, of the use of the pardoning power by the governors of the states. Tender-

hearted citizens signed petitions for pardon in unworthy cases; the governors erred upon the side of
mercy; the criminals hoped for pardon instead of
striving to reform; the many who were disappointed
were embittered by the spectacle of unjust discrim-
ination.

Of the reformers the one whose writings showed
the deepest research and the most philosophical consideration of the subject was Edward Livingston, and
his work on the Criminal Code for Louisiana placed
him among the first social scientists of the world,
being received with as great appreciation in Europe
as it was in the United States. It is impossible to
read his chapter on the "Code of Reform and Prison
Discipline" without recognizing the statesman-like
manner in which he applies his erudition, humani-
tarianism, and philosophy. He had great hopes in
the revival and proper application of the Pennsylvania system, but he would add to it preliminary
houses of detention, where the suspected and the
unconvicted should be confined, and houses of refuge
and industry, where prisoners who had shown signs
of regeneration might find employment and subsist-
ence after leaving prison and before acceptance by
society.

Even if the solution of the problem of reforming
criminals was still in the dark in 1815 public opinion
had left behind the barbaric idea of retaliatory punishments for crime, and humanity had scored a
triumph.

XX

THE same reformers who gave their attention to the proper mode of dealing with criminals also took concern for poverty and the best methods of dealing with it. Originally, the only institutions which cared for the poor were the churches. They had their poor-boxes in America as they had them in older countries, and the clergy distributed the alms. They did not abandon the practice, but as population increased and became more diverse in its elements the churches could not reach all the poor and had not resources sufficient for their relief.

Everybody in the United States believed with Mathew Carey that this was "a country far more prosperous than any other portion of the habitable world." Nevertheless, it had its derelicts, unfortunates and physically incapacitated, who were not able to make a living for themselves and must be supported by others. Most of them—in fact, nearly all who were not immigrants—were supported by the charity of individuals. I have said in a previous chapter that the members of the community were closer to one another than they have become in the specialized life of the present day, and knew one another better. So the misfortunes and distresses of some were known to the others and were relieved by direct ministration. This form of charity was considered to be a virtue, and it was encouraged. No question arose about its pauperizing effect. In fact, it had an advantage in this respect over institutional charity, for the person who helped his unfortunate neighbor had personal knowledge whether or not the case was a worthy one. In consequence of the personal aspects of beneficence those who received it gave loyalty and gratitude in return. These qualities also were held to be virtues. It would have been hard, on the one hand, to find an individual who held direct charity to be an economic error, or, on the other, one who believed that a part of the possessions of the successful or fortunate belonged of right to him.

This was the age of the predominance of the family. It was still the microcosm of the state, and accepted responsibilities toward poor and disabled members. The well-to-do families had many dependent members, women chiefly, but old and worthless men also. The law could be invoked to compel families to care for their own. In Pennsylvania, for example, one who could not support himself must be supported by his father or grandfather, or by his mother or grandmother, or by his children or grandchildren. Edward Livingston proposed that the obligation be extended to the collateral ancestors and descendants also.

For the helpless, friendless poor, without ties or kindred, the communities, cities, towns, or counties generally made legal provision. If there were only a few of them they were boarded with private families; if they were numerous enough almshouses were built for them. The Friends of Pennsylvania had established an almhouse as early as 1713. There was a city almshouse in Philadelphia in 1730. By 1815 all the cities had them. They served to accommodate a great variety of unfortunates—orphans, foundlings, the sick and insane, besides ordinary paupers. In the almshouse at New York in 1809 there were five hundred and thirty-eight adults, two hundred and twenty-six children, and one hundred and sixty-six sick in the hospital. In the Boston almshouse in 1823, out of some three hundred inmates seventy-eight were sick, seventy-seven were children, and nine were maniacs. Lying-in rooms were included in most of the almshouses. Attached to them were houses of employment where paupers who were able to work were required to render some return for their support. In the seaports and fast-growing cities the poverty was greatest, especially among foreigners who worked at digging or on the streets. When the winter came their work stopped and they must be fed and housed lest they die. Of the inmates in the New York almshouse not one in five was an American.

One of the earliest efforts to remedy the evils of indiscriminate association in the poorhouses came in the founding of orphan asylums. The Orphan Asylum Society of the City of New York was organized in 1806, being the first in the United States. It developed from the Society for the Relief of Poor Widows with Small Children, a woman's association founded in 1797, the members of which went about the city rendering succor to poor women and children. It was the first woman's charitable organization in New

York. They found many orphans, and were impressed with the injustice of associating them with grown paupers, so they induced other philanthropists to join in providing a separate asylum for them. In 1807 they were supporting twenty orphans, and thereafter the number increased rapidly. In 1811 the legislature granted the asylum five hundred dollars, and this was the beginning of state recognition of its duty to assist in the work of educating orphan children to be good citizens. The Roman Catholic Church opened an orphanage in New York in 1817. In 1815 one was started in Washington, with Mrs. Madison at the head of the board of managers and a number of ladies associated with her. Orphan asylums soon multiplied and became a regular part of the policy of dealing with the unfortunate classes. They were always started by private benevolence, but many of them received assistance from the public taxes afterward.

Associations for charitable purposes were not many nor important. There was one in New York called the Association for the Relief of Respectable, Aged, Indigent Females, formed in 1813, probably the earliest effort to establish a home for poor old ladies. There was a Female Charitable Society at Providence, Rhode Island, organized in 1802, and the Washington Benevolent Society of Massachusetts, organized on Washington's birthday, 1812, with the chief citizens of Boston as members. These organizations had a limited field. The day of combination and co-operation had not come.

The problem of dealing with the insane was being

discussed, but had not as yet been solved. The Pennsylvania Hospital, which was the oldest in the United States, having been opened in 1752, had been projected partly with a view to giving treatment to the insane, and half the building was given over to them; but it was not entirely a free institution, and in 1815 only admitted some twenty-five lunatics.

The treatment of the insane was practically the same throughout the country. If they were violent they were sent to jail; if they were harmless they went to the almshouse or were boarded with private families. When hospitals were erected they were received there, but they had no hospitals of their own. The well-to-do families sent insane members to the hospitals or kept them at home or employed private keepers for them. Many thousands of insane people, who ought to have been in asylums where their comfort and health could be cared for by trained attendants, roamed at large, often to their own injury and always to the injury of normal persons, who became familiarized with the sight of their affliction and indifferent to it. Some brutal individuals made sport of it, and it was a common sight to see a crazy wretch followed by a tormenting crowd of boys and men. The provision for the insane in Pennsylvania was not so good as it was in New York, but was equal with that of other states. The Friends opened an asylum at Frankford in 1817 which accommodated fifty patients. The Pennsylvania hospital held in all about two hundred. There was no provision by the state government till 1848. There was no asylum in Washington till 1841. There was none in Massachusetts till 1839. It was not until 1839 that the insane were moved from Bellevue in New York to a hospital of their own, this being the beginning of the Bloomingdale Asylum. In 1826, of one hundred and eighty-four patients in the hospital eighty-two were insane. The treatment they received was barbaric. Heroic methods prevailed in the treatment of most diseases, and the violence of insanity was dealt with by violent methods. It is not necessary to open this record of horror. It was the benevolent Dr. Benjamin Rush who invented a "tranquilizing chair," in which a frenzied insane patient could be strapped so cleverly that he could not even move his head, this torture being administered with the idea that it quieted him.

There was not a school for the deaf and dumb in the country, and there were only twenty-five in the world. In 1817 Thomas Hopkins Gallaudet opened his school for deaf mutes in Hartford, and in the same year one was started in New York, but there were no others for many years. There was no institution for the blind until a generation later, that at New York, established in 1831, being the first one. But in 1820 several young physicians opened the New York Eye Infirmary in two rooms at No. 45 Chatham Street and rescued hundreds of people from blindness. Until then affections of the eye were commonly supposed to be incurable.

From the almshouse and treatment of sick paupers developed the public hospital. When the new almshouse was opened in New York at Bellevue in 1816 it included two hospital pavilions, whence came Bellevue Hospital. The patients were numerous enough, but they did not receive much care, for in 1817 there were more than two hundred of them attended by one visiting physician, who came twice a week, and one house physician, who also compounded all the medicines administered. The Pennsylvania Hospital existed apart from the almshouse, but most of the patients paid for treatment. The Philadelphia Hospital was a part of the almshouse and was opened about 1812.

People who could avoid it never went to the hospitals. They looked upon them with dread which was not ill-founded, for most of them were overcrowded and unsanitary, and those who entered were more apt to die than to recover. They were intended as charitable institutions limited to the sick poor who were without homes. The earliest hospitals in Pennsylvania had been for sick strangers exclusively.

XXI

DOCTORS

GEORGE WASHINGTON died on December 14, 1799, when he was sixty-seven years old. Until his fatal illness he was in full manly vigor. The new century came in with solemn thoughts of the great services he had rendered his country. In truth, no man had ever done more for a country than he had done for America; but his work had been finished for nearly three years before his death, and there was no promise of further public usefulness for him. Events had taken a new turn and were leading into paths which were strange and uncongenial to him. His last remarks before he took to his bed with the ailment from which he died were in criticism of James Madison, spoken "with some degree of asperity," as Tobias Lear relates, and Madison was soon to be President and his party in the ascendant. History has no regrets to record at the removal from the stage of an actor who has played his part. Nevertheless, it is highly probable that General Washington would have lived for some years longer if his doctor had treated in the proper manner the disease of which he died. He was attacked by inflammation of the upper part of the wind-pipe, or what the doctors now call acute edematous laryngitis, a very dangerous malady under any circumstances, but Dr. Craik, his physician, did not examine his larynx, for there was no instrument then invented to enable him to do so. He was given an emetic, purged, bled, and blistered, and the seat of his disability was not directly treated at all. No patient suffering as he suffered would now receive the treatment he received. Yet Dr. Craik was a skilful physician, and his two consultants were also good doctors, and their diagnosis of the case was doubtless correct. No other doctor would have done any better than they did.

The causes of few diseases were known, and the treatment of all was wrong. The great specific of the day was mercury, which Dr. Benjamin Rush called the "Samson of the materia medica," but opium was freely administered, and Peruvian bark. The most efficacious part of the treatment, however, as nearly everybody thought, was blood-letting. There was a small number of doctors who protested against it, but they were overwhelmed by the great majority of doctors and laymen who were loud in its praises. They thought that it lessened the morbid and excessive action in the blood-vessels and removed fever, that it lessened pain, induced sleep, prevented hemorrhages, and was a safeguard against relapses. The doctors prescribed it for all sorts of fevers, for pulmonary consumption, diabetes, asthma, idiocy, hysteria, madness, catarrh, gout—for everything, in short, except a few hopelessly debilitating ailments where it would certainly kill. The bleeding was not generally performed by a physician, but by a barber who was a specialist in this branch of surgery. He cut open a vein in the arm, the neck, or the foot. Occasionally an artery would be lanced; but that was a very dangerous way of taking blood and was resorted to rarely. Leeches and the cup were used sometimes, and toward the end of the practice were the usual way of drawing blood. Bleeding was freely practised in treating disease until about 1850. Even now, in some of the older towns, an old barber may be found whose sign proclaims him to be also a "cupper and leecher."

Before a patient was bled he was given an emetic and a purge and mercury to produce excitement and inflammation of the glands of the mouth and throat and abstract excitement and inflammation from the more vital parts. This was especially desirable if there was morbid congestion and excitement of the brain. Besides this, the patient was usually blistered. After complete depletion had been accomplished there would be nothing for the disease to work on, and the patient should recover. If any one looks with horror upon the course of treatment he can reflect that the profession in 1815 looked with horror upon the course which had been followed by the doctors of the generation before them. And, whatever may be said of the medical profession in America, it must be admitted that it represented the most advanced knowledge of the day. Benjamin Rush died in 1813, when he was the most influential physician in the country. His contemporary and successor as the head of the profession was Philip Syng Physick, also of Philadelphia. Both were graduates of the medical school at the University of Edinburgh; so were David Hosack,

who led the profession in New York; Ephraim Mc-
Dowell, of Kentucky; John Collins Warren, of Boston, and many others. The Scotch school was in the
ascendant, and the Scotch school was thought to be
the best in the world. Medicine was practised here by
the pupils of Dr. William Cullen, a great light in the
history of medical science. He was the first physician to generalize the phenomena of disease; but he
was devoted to theory, and said it did not matter
whether practice or theory came first; so his followers
were disposed to subordinate practice to theory. Dr.
Rush in the lectures he delivered to the medical students at the University of Pennsylvania quoted from
Cullen a great deal and said that in medicine there
were ten false facts to one false theory; but Rush
introduced into the science the teachings of John
Brown, also a student at Edinburgh, who had com-
bated Cullen's generalizations. The layman need not
enter into a consideration of either school, as both
are dead. A greater than Cullen, John Hunter, of
London, of whom it has been said that he "laid the
foundation of all those improvements in surgery,
physiology, and comparative anatomy which have
been made since his time," was the preceptor of Dr.
Physick and of several other American doctors. In
fact, Physick practised with him for a time and declined his offer of partnership in order to return to
Philadelphia.

The American physician was essentially a prac-
titioner, however. He had so much to do that he
could not undertake research. He was ruled largely
by authority, and he contributed little to medical

science, although his practical habits enabled him to add something to the advance of surgery. In 1790 Rush offered some new principles in medicine, suggested by his observation of the peculiar phenomena of diseases in the United States, and from this grew what he and his followers called "an American system of medicine." They traced all diseases to morbid excitement produced by irritants acting upon debility. All prescriptions were applied to forming and fluctuation states of disease.

The country was in the main a healthful place of abode. There was a great deal of fever, which it was believed came from the exhalations of marshes, from decayed vegetable matter, from old rotting timber, stagnant water, bad sewerage, and lack of drainage. The fevers were classed as remittant, malignant or yellow fever, and chronic or nervous fever. They also called the last-named typhus, and did not separate typhoid fever from it till 1829. The doctors treated all fevers on the theory that they could be broken up. It was not till 1822 that Dr. Jacob Bigelow, of New York, suggested that many diseases were self-limited and that their duration could not be limited by art. The changes in climate and exposure produced a great deal of catarrh, and all catarrhs were lumped together. There was much rheumatism. It was considered to be an external disease due to cold and damp. There was a form of malignant sore throat which became epidemic occasionally and killed many children. It was really diphtheria, but was treated as croup. Much suffering and disease was occasioned by decayed teeth, and the only dentists were a few in the large cities. The free consumption of ardent spirits with salt meat and bad cooking produced a great deal of dyspepsia. There was always an increase in sickness among the men of a community after a public dinner had been held. Dr. Rush thought that diseases of the mind were increasing, and attributed them in part to the intemperate political feeling and the excitement of the pursuit of wealth by speculation. No nerve diseases were classified as such. Pulmonary consumption carried off its thousands every year. It was regarded as incurable and was treated with the usual heroic remedies; but the fact that life in the open checked it was understood. It was remarked that Indians did not have it. There was a great deal of gout. It was held to be quite distinct from rheumatism, because, as Dr. Hosack explained, it came from internal causes, and rheumatism never did. By laymen generally it was considered to be proof that he who had it lived well and that his ancestors had lived well, that he had an excusable fondness for good wines and rich cooking and was of virile, manly habit. It was supposed to separate him definitely from the laboring part of mankind. The doctors said it followed gluttony, drunkenness, and debauchery more than any other causes, but the other causes were so amiable—as, for example, long exercise of the understanding in study—that a man who was sick with the gout never concealed it. If he was sick with some other ailment it might require inquiry to discover what it was, but if he had the gout the disease was proclaimed. There was no dispute about the remedies—bleeding, purging, an emetic, salivation, blistering. The faculty sought for a quick remedy, for, as Dr. Rush said, "Who has not read of the most interesting affairs of nations being neglected or protracted by the principal agents in them being suddenly confined to their beds or chairs for weeks or months by a fit of the gout?"

What made the death-rate high at various times in certain parts of the country were the epidemics of disease. Several which had scourged Europe had not yet visited our shores. The bubonic plague and cholera were not yet known. An epidemic of influenza swept over the country from South to North in 1789, and again in 1807, from Northeast to the South and the West, and there were a great many deaths from it—how many was not recorded. In New England between 1806 and 1817 what was known as "spotted fever" prevailed in many parts. It was treated as typhus, but was probably typhoid. Smallpox existed more or less all the time. It was accepted as a matter of course; but, the population being scattered, it had no such material to work upon as the dense populations of Europe afforded, and the mortality from it was not nearly so great. Inoculation of the smallpox virus was practised to a small extent long before Jenner's discovery. The first virus of cowpox was sent by Jenner to Dr. Benjamin Waterhouse, of Boston, in 1800, and by 1802 vaccination was common in that city. Dr. Hosack at the same time introduced it in New York, and the doctors of Philadelphia adopted it. Dr. Waterhouse sent the virus to Thomas Jefferson, and he had some three hundred people in

Washington vaccinated. Many reputable physicians, however, refused to believe that giving a person cowpox would render him immune from smallpox. Further, a prejudice arose against inoculation, which still lingers, from the fact that occasionally it communicated other diseases. It made its way, however, and by 1815 the terrors of smallpox had diminished to a great extent.

Far worse than the smallpox or than any other disease, more dreaded, more fatal to the communities which it visited, more discussed and studied, was the yellow fever. It was essentially a city disease; there was little or none of it in the country; and, while it made its way occasionally to towns in the interior, it belonged chiefly to the seaports or river ports near the sea. It appeared as far north as Portland, Maine, and at Portsmouth, Boston, Providence, New Haven, and New London; but it was more terrifying than dangerous at those places, the deaths from it being relatively few. Every year or two Baltimore, Norfolk, Wilmington (North Carolina), Charleston, and Savannah had it. New Orleans had it worst. There was some of it every summer, and some summers hundreds of deaths from it—800 in 1817 and 2,190 in 1819. The two cities which it visited with most fatal effect were the two largest, Philadelphia and New York. In Philadelphia in 1793 it killed more than 4,000 people in a population of 55,000; in 1798, when two-thirds of the population had fled, it killed 3,500. In subsequent years there was a small number of deaths, and it gradually disappeared. In New York in 1795 732 people out of a population of 40,000 died of it;

in 1798, 2,086; in 1803, 606; and in 1805, 262. It has been practically unknown in that port since 1822. The description of the epidemic of 1793 in Philadelphia will apply with modifications to the epidemics in other cities—even to the last one in New Orleans in 1878. Most of those who could do so fled into the country, but after the disease had begun its ravages they found few communities that would receive them, and many had to stay at home in consequence. They were afraid to walk the streets, and shut themselves up in their houses, with the shutters closed. Smoking was supposed to prevent infection, and women and children could be seen puffing cigars. Others chewed garlic or put it in their shoes to keep off the fever, being recommended to do so by the doctors. Gunpowder, tobacco, niter, were burned in all the houses, and they were sprinkled with vinegar. Those who ventured abroad held handkerchiefs impregnated with vinegar or camphor to their noses, or carried pieces of tarred rope in their pockets, or had smelling-bottles filled with what was known as "thieves' vinegar," a concoction which it was said had been used at Marseilles during the plague by certain thieves who successfully robbed the dead. Many people bled themselves, being afraid of infection from the barbers because they had bled infected persons. Three of the four newspapers of the city stopped publication, and the public offices were closed. The dead were buried without ceremony or attendants at the funerals. A person with signs of mourning on his person was avoided. The well deserted the sick; the living deserted the dead; the hearses in the streets were the only sounds of travel.

Dr. Rush and Dr. Physick, who began his American career in time to fight the epidemic of 1793 and to have the disease himself, became the leading authorities on yellow fever, and were convinced that they knew its origin and how to treat it. They bled copiously and gave enormous doses of calomel, rhubarb, and jalap, with a low diet and cooling drinks and applications of cold water to the body. They saved a great many of their patients; but Dr. Edward H. Clark says of Rush, that his "pathology was erroneous and his therapeutics atrocious." Rush's printed observations of the disease were important in future investigations, however. In 1800 "Peter Porcupine" (William Cobbett) published a newspaper called *The Rush Light*, which ran for seven numbers and was devoted to abuse of Rush's methods and personal villification of him, and in consequence Rush sued him for libel, and he was fined five thousand dollars. But Dr. William Currie, a more responsible antagonist, was bold enough to protest against the accepted methods of treatment, declaring that they weakened the patient too much. He also insisted that the disease was not communicable from infected bedding and similar sources and that it invariably came as an importation from the South. He had a following, but the great preponderance of intelligent public opinion was with Rush's school. Of the origin of fever they thought as Dr. Pinkard said: "To look for it in ships and vessels, or to strain the eye across the ocean, in order to fix its birthplace on the opposite coast of the Atlantic, or to trace its descent from the slaves of the Indian seas, was to overlook the reality in search of a phantom. It needs no foreign parent; the prolific earth is its mother; its father the bright god who governs the day."

Nevertheless, there were quarantine regulations in all the ports, but they did not keep yellow fever out, as the trade was large with the West Indies, and especially with Havana, where the fever always existed. The gradual disappearance of the disease was due to stricter quarantine enforcement; but the people of a hundred years ago knew about as much of its cause as we did until the army surgeons made the wonderful discovery of the communicating mosquito a few years ago.

The doctors in America did their best to extend their influence and knowledge. There were medical journals of good repute in Philadelphia, New York City, Rochester, Baltimore, and Boston. There were state medical societies in all the states, which fixed the standard of medical education. As we saw in a previous chapter, there were medical schools at Yale, Harvard, Dartmouth, Columbia, Brown, the University of Pennsylvania, and the University of Maryland. One was opened at Transylvania University, at Lexington, Kentucky, in 1818; at Bowdoin College, at Brunswick, Maine, in 1821; at the College of Physicians and Surgeons, in Fairfield, New York, in 1816; at Cincinnati in 1821; at Castleton, Vermont, in 1820. Between 1810 and 1819, 1,375 physicians were graduated. In 1815 the medical apprentices at the almshouse and the students in the hospital and the university in Philadelphia were given permission to attend the surgical operations in the Pennsylvania Hospital, and this was the beginning of the clinic.

A doctor was a surgeon and even a dentist as well as a physician, but in the country the blacksmith sometimes relieved his neighbors of toothache by rough extraction. A few dentists were practising, however, in New York and Philadelphia, the first ones having come from France. The art of making artificial teeth was understood; and John Greenwood, one of the earliest dentists in New York, made a fine set out of ivory for General Washington in 1790 and again in 1795. It was not until 1839 that a dental school was established, the Baltimore dental college being the first.

There was a strict limitation to the powers of surgery, not only because of the ignorance of the causes of disease, but also because there was no anesthesia, that discovery not being made till 1846. A patient who was operated upon lay conscious and writhed in pain as the knife cut into him. His cries rent the air, and he had to be held forcibly upon the operating-table by strong attendants. Under these conditions operations must be performed very rapidly and could not be very complicated. The record of American achievement in surgery is creditable and showed originality and daring. In 1809 Dr. Ephraim Mc-Dowell, of Danville, Kentucky, performed an operation upon a woman which has since become common and has saved many lives; but at the time the profession refused to accept it, and he derived no credit from his discovery. Dr. Richard S. Kissam, of New York, performed the operation of lithotomy, or cutting for stone in the bladder, with great success. In 1818 Valentine Mott, of New York, tied the innominate artery, a feat never before accomplished. Wright Post, also of New York, performed a successful operation for aneurism of the femoral artery in 1813. In that year John Ingalls, of Boston, made an amputation at the shoulder-joint. Dr. Walter Brashear had made one at the hip-joint at Bardstown, Kentucky, in 1806. The most celebrated of all the surgeons, the father of American surgery, was Dr. Physick. Until his death in 1837 no sick or injured man thought he had had the full benefit of medical science or surgical art unless he had been a patient of Dr. Physick's.

Dr. Hosack and his colleague in New York, Dr. Samuel Bard, were the pioneers in the science of midwifery. In 1807 Bard published the first American book on the subject, and the same year Hosack was made professor of midwifery and surgery in the College of Physicians and Surgeons. That branch of the profession still hung upon the borders of respectability. Until Dr. William Shippen had lectured upon it at the University of Pennsylvania in 1780 no student learned it. It was not a compulsory course for the doctor's degree at that school till 1843. It was still largely in the hands of old women, and a considerable proportion of women died in childbirth.

The profession was harassed by radicals, revolutionists, charlatans, and quacks, but it fought them off and was in complete possession of the field. It had never heard of Hahnemann, although he was laying down his peculiar dogmas at this time and proclaiming the efficacy of very small doses of medicine. The regular school believed in furious doses and thought there was curative quality in the nauseous taste of its medicines. The first appearance of Hahnemannism in the United States was when Dr. Gram began practising in New York in 1825. Strangely enough, there was some discussion among the doctors of Mesmer's theories of curing disease by animal magnetism. He was known partly because Dr. Franklin had served on the committee which investigated his claims in Paris and Lafayette had once been his pupil. Of course, his methods were regarded as nonsensical, but there was a general understanding that a doctor to be successful should make his patients believe in the curative powers of his treatment. Many people followed the charlatans. In a former chapter we saw that thousands resorted to a faith-curer in Vermont. They advertised as the same class does now. In a Savannah or a New York paper you read the same proclamation of the wonderful cures effected by Dr. ——'s snakeroot, which cost only twenty-five cents a bottle.

XXII

COOKS

DO the people make the country, or does the country make the people? We are fond of speaking of man as the conqueror of nature, but does not nature govern him quite effectively? If the climate of a country is such as conduces to health and energy in the man, and the soil yields abundantly for his food, he will thrive. His surroundings will adapt him to them. Some of the emigrants to America have come from crowded countries where each family has farmed an area of a few acres, and at first they have been appalled at the prospect of farming a hundred acres or more; but, unless they have passed the learning age, they have accommodated themselves to the larger area. It is impossible that their natures should not expand with their industry and that they should not become hundred-acre men in their ideas, so to speak. After all our boasting, then, it would seem that the American continent, being a magnificent domain, gave a magnificent destiny to the people whom it nourished. The greatest credit that they can properly claim is that they left behind them the outworn customs with which centuries of usage had burdened them in Europe, and that they preserved the liberty with which the New World clothed them when it received them.

"The destiny of nations depends upon the manner in which they nourish themselves," and the Americans of one hundred years ago had a right to look forward to the future with confidence, for there were no people in the world so abundantly supplied with food as they were.

When Captain John Smith came to Virginia he found the Indians cultivating corn, and from this beginning it became the most universally used food of the white settlers. The Indians pounded it in a stone mortar and made it into meal. Adding a little water, they formed it into a cone which they cooked in the hot embers of a fire. The white man put a similar cake upon a hoe and put the hoe on the fire, whence came the hoe-cake and corn bread. Indian corn was believed to be the most wholesome single article of food in the world, and the one most capable of feeding the whole man. There were few people in the United States one hundred years ago who did not eat it every day of their lives.

In due season all the domestic food animals of Europe were imported and thrived in every part of the country; and beef, mutton, pork, and the barnyard fowls became plentiful. Besides these, there was a great variety of game—turkeys, geese, ducks, pheasants, pigeons, and smaller birds, all so plentiful in their appointed seasons and places that the people were free to feed upon them. Venison, too, was available in all parts of the country and was eaten almost as much as beef. What is now food which only the rich man can enjoy was then accessible to all classes of the population. The waters abounded in fish—

cod, carp, mackerel, salmon, shad, bass, and a hundred other kinds. Shell-fish were found along the coast and in the adjacent rivers and bays. Only the interior regions were without oysters. Terrapin were plentiful in the rivers and bays from Pennsylvania to Florida, and sea-turtles on the Southern coast. All the common garden vegetables were grown—Irish and sweet potatoes, peas, beans, cabbage, cauliflower, carrots, parsnips, celery, artichokes, and a number of others. The tomato was almost the only garden food they missed. They called it the love-apple, and, as it was a variety of the nightshade, they thought it to be poisonous and only used it to make sauces. By 1830, however, it was eaten generally. Small fruits were plentiful—cherries, pears, peaches, and apricots. The finer varieties of apples were cultivated in some orchards, but apples were eaten raw to a very limited extent. They were mixed with meat or boiled with cider to make apple-sauce, but they were raised chiefly for cider, and for this the small, knotty apples were supposed to be the best. Such berries as strawberries were so plentiful in the wild state that they were cultivated very little. The forests yielded a multitude of nuts, and the peanut was known, but had not yet become a product of systematic cultivation.

This was not the land of the gourmand. Fine cooking was a detail of life, and the Americans were indifferent to details. As in speaking they were careless of their grammar and only sought to make their meaning clear, so in eating they did not demand elegance in the cooking if the food itself was good.

They were preoccupied with things which seemed to them more important than eating, and were unwilling to spend much time or thought upon the table. They ate quickly and only to live. The comfortable fat man with smooth flesh upon his bones, with round face and stomach—the product of leisurely appreciation of the pleasures of the table—was a rare product. The typical American was a lean man.

The cooking of the poor American was generally bad. His wife fried nearly everything, because it was the easiest and quickest way of cooking it. She made bread and pastry which were indigestible enough to ruin the character of the people. There was a limit to the harm she could inflict upon corn meal and salt pork, however, and these were the chief articles of diet. Undoubtedly, the bad cooking was one of the causes that produced the cadaverous, shambling men and sour-faced, flat-breasted women who were met with at every turn of the road in the South and often enough in other parts of the country. It was one of the causes, too, of the habit of drinking rum or whisky. The liquor was used to satisfy an appetite which had been irritated by ill-cooked food.

The professional cooks of the country were negroes, and the national cookery came from them. They were taught the art by their white mistresses, but they had a natural aptitude for it and made it their own. They liked the heat of the kitchen, and preferred the desultory labor of cooking to any other form of work. They were proud of the praise they received from their masters and mistresses when they performed it well. It gave them a position of importance in the house and flattered their self-esteem. Their own pleasures were sensual, and they were very fond of eating, so they cooked with appreciation. While their cooking varied in the different sections of the country, in its general characteristics it was the same, and it was marked with the tropical origin of the cooks. The trained palate could tell if the food was cooked by a negro in New York as well as in Savannah. Probably the best cooking was in New Orleans, where the negroes had been taught by the French or creole settlers; but traces of creole cooking penetrated to the North. The race of good negro cooks lasted until the rise of the second generation of negroes after the Civil War. It has now almost disappeared, because the free-born negroes take no pride in domestic service and refuse to learn the art which their mothers in bondage practised with so much success.

But it must not be supposed that the people who were rich enough to own or hire negro cooks were the only ones who lived well. On the farms in the well-settled portions of the country the prosperous and thrifty housewives were too intelligent to live uncomfortably, and epicures who had catholic tastes testified that their gastronomical experiences were agreeable when they enjoyed the hospitality of American farm-houses. The most interesting tribute came from the greatest authority, Anthelme Brillat Savarin, a French statesman who fled from France at the time of the revolution and spent several years of his exile in the United States. He gave lessons in French at Hartford and played the violin in the orchestra of the Park Theater in New York. He returned to France in 1796 and became a judge of the court of cassation. He died in 1826, and his classic work, the *Physiologie du Gout*, was published after his death. It contains many pleasing allusions to the good eating he enjoyed when he lived in the United States. He described the abundant dinner he had at a farm-house in Connecticut—the superb piece of corned beef, the stewed goose, the magnificent leg of mutton, vegetables in plenty, and at each end of the table an enormous jug of excellent cider; and after dinner the daughters of the house prepared excellent tea.

In a primeval forest near Hartford Brillat Savarin shot a large wild turkey, and the feast which followed the next day he set down as a noteworthy event in a life of gastronomical adventures. He declared that the turkey was "one of the most beautiful presents that the New World had made to the Old," and he called attention to the fact that while it had been domesticated in all the countries of Europe, in America alone was it found in a state of nature. It was, he said, the favorite food of all classes, and they were united by this preference. When the farmers wished to make a feast they chose for the principal dish a turkey; so did the artisans and the workmen; so did the politicians and financiers. Dr. Johnson, writing his dictionary in 1755, defined a turkey as "a large domestick fowl supposed to come from Turkey," but the American origin of the fowl was generally known at a later day. It was plentiful enough in 1815 to be accessible to all but the poorest people.

Equally accessible to everybody and equally prized by all classes of the population were the oysters, which existed in the greatest profusion in the bays and rivers along the whole coast, but were thought to reach their perfection in Chesapeake Bay. Oyster-houses were common in the cities, where they were eaten raw on the shell. At Le Count's United States Refectory, at the corner of Fifth and Chestnut Streets, in Philadelphia, was a famous oyster-bar, presided over for many years by John Gardener, who opened so many oysters that he became an authority on their habits and printed the result of his observations in an amusing and instructive pamphlet.

But the people were fond of other and less wholesome food than turkeys and oysters. There is an account of Mrs. Madison at breakfast at Monticello buttering her muffin carelessly and being told how she ought to do it by one of the young children at the table. Thus from childhood to old age the Southerners were eaters of hot bread; but the evil existed in all parts of the country. Buckwheat-cakes and flapjacks were eaten immoderately in the East, and hot rolls, muffins, and biscuits were on every breakfast-table in the South. There was a cheerful interchange of products between the sections, and buckwheat-cakes were in the South and hot rolls in the North. Foreigners generally commented unfavorably upon the habit of eating hot bread, and declared it was the cause of much of the ill health of the people. American physicians also advised against it; but admonition was in vain, and it has continued without appreciable diminution to the present day.

The custom of eating salted meat, especially pork, was not confined to America, but was more prevalent here than it was elsewhere. Nearly everybody in the country districts and many in the city regarded salt pork as the staff of life. The hogs were killed late in the autumn and their meat eaten every day in the year. Even to this day in certain sections of the country the word "meat" is commonly understood to mean pork. Probably the constant use of salted meat was another reason for the thirst of the people. Pork in the shape of hams was eaten by everybody, and a well-furnished dinner-table was considered to be incomplete without it.

The custom of serving dinner in courses was not practised as we now practise it. Ordinarily, the whole dinner was on the table at the same time, but for a special feast there might be two courses of the same character and each a dinner in itself. The attractiveness of the table depended upon the symmetrical arrangement of the dishes and upon their garnishment. There would be nine or ten large dishes upon the table, besides a number of smaller ones. The tablecloth would hardly be visible. An opulent man giving a dinner-party would serve something like the following: for the first course, "cod's head," being the head and shoulders of a fresh codfish, a dish much esteemed at the time; pea - soup, venison, chickens roasted, boiled ham, beef collops, which corresponded with beefsteak; potatoes, celery, parsnips, jelly, pies, and marrow pudding. For the second course, turkey poults (young turkeys), scolloped oysters, roasted rabbits, wild ducks, lamb, smelts, haricot (usually written "harrico," being a mutton ragoût), several vegetables, cherry tarts, and stewed pippins. Then there would be brought in some ice-cream by itself. It was considered to be a great luxury, and it was eaten on rare occasions. The decanters of wine were distributed about the table. The servants placed the dishes on the table and changed the plates and knives and forks from time to time. The largest dishes of meat were carved by the host and hostess, and the person nearest a dish was expected to help his neighbors to it. Thus they all fed one another, and everybody was busy. The wine-drinking began early in the feast, and the people drank one another's health individually and collectively. After the second course the cloth was removed, the wine was replaced, fresh glasses were put on, and probably a fresh vintage, with nuts and fruit. The hostess then withdrew with the other ladies, if there were any; but the dinner-party was a pleasure generally reserved for men. Around the bare mahogany they drank lightly or heavily, as the case might be. At these dinners discussions of importance often took place as the madeira or claret circulated, agreements for political action were reached, the fate of ambitious aspirants for public office was determined, financial projects were arranged. How many acts done in the cold light of day were the result of suggestion or encouragement coming from men who were warmed with wine and good feeding sitting at the dinner-table is beyond power of calculation. One illustration can be given, but similar instances could be multiplied. It was at a dinner-party given by Thomas Jefferson to Alexander

Hamilton in 1789 that an agreement was made by which the Capital of the United States was located upon the banks of the Potomac and the general government assumed the debts of the states. It may be that those communities where dinner-giving was common exerted greater influence upon national affairs than communities where the men seldom ate and drank together enjoyed.

After the wine-drinking at a dinner-party the surviving guests went to the drawing-room and drank tea with their hostess. Coffee did not figure on these occasions, and it was not as generally drunk as it was at a later period. In fact, the consumption in the next thirty years increased by more than twelvefold. The tea-drinking or the uninterrupted wine-drinking might run into supper, in which case the party would not break up till eleven o'clock at night. The dinner having begun at three o'clock, which was a late hour even in the cities, there would have been about eight hours of continuous eating and drinking. At some tables an innovation in the courses was being adopted by serving the fish and soup as a first course by themselves, but nobody had yet thought of a dinner of eight or ten courses. Silver forks were used at the dinner-party, but for every-day purposes steel three-pronged forks were universal. As they did not hold some kinds of food very well, it was not considered inelegant to convey food from the plate to the mouth with the knife.

Naturally, it was only a small proportion of the people who went to private dinner-parties, but the public had opportunities of accomplishing something of the same result by attending the public dinners which were given in the towns and villages and attended by people from the surrounding country. The reason, or the excuse, for holding them was to celebrate notable anniversaries or events or to do honor to public men. A great many were given on the 4th of July and the 22d of February, and there were a number in honor of the Treaty of Ghent. Often they were political gatherings designed to influence public opinion. A local committee managed the feast and sold the tickets to any one who cared to pay for them. They cost about a dollar each, or perhaps more, some dinners being more expensive than others. The shopkeepers, proprietors, people of all classes except the laborers, attended them. It was easy enough to load the long tables with substantial food and with liquor, punch, and wine. If a band of music was obtainable it played before and during the dinner. Usually it could not play afterward. The local militia escorted the lion of the occasion in procession through the streets to the dinner. If there was a cannon available it thundered salutes to persons and sentiments. The committee drew up a long list of toasts, to which were added by various guests what were called "volunteers." Most of the toasts were printed in the newspaper after the dinner, and they were supposed to show the trend of public sentiment. They aimed to be epigrammatical expressions of that sentiment. A few will serve to illustrate their general character. At the dinner given early in 1815 to Commodore McDonough at Trap, New Castle County, Delaware, near the place of his birth, one toast was: "The

American character, as much caressed since, as it was despised before our late struggle—Honor to the brave men, both on the sea and land, who, at imminent risk of their lives, brought their country into notice and established its national character."

At one given June 15, 1815, at Fairfield, Vermont, to General Wooster: "The Constitution of the United States—the basis of our independence, the cement of our Union—may it be kept sacred and inviolable as the tables of stone in the Ark of the Covenant."

At a dinner given to General William Henry Harrison at Petersburg, Virginia, in March, 1817: "The people—brave, patriotic, virtuous; free, sovereign, and independent. Four guns."

"The American navy—the ocean and the lakes, the grand theaters of its glory. Two guns."

"The Spanish patriots—contending for liberty. Whilst we sigh for their misfortunes we glory in their triumph. Two guns."

There might be twenty toasts or more at a dinner, and a man who drank them all must have got very tipsy, but many of the diners did so independently of the toasts. In a former chapter we saw that the members of the first temperance society excepted public dinners from their agreement not to drink; and in another place, that the doctors said there was always an increase in the amount of sickness in a town after a public dinner. They were demoralizing assemblages. What with the music, the speechmaking, the hurrahing, the cannon-firing, and the drinking, there was excitement enough to tear the nerves of the participants asunder. The only thing that can be said in their favor is that they brought men of different classes together on a plane of common interest and enabled them to know one another at their worst. The whisky-bottle is a rough promoter of democracy.

XXIII

DISCONTENT

"WHEREVER we travel through Christendom —in Europe, America, or elsewhere—we find great numbers of men, of all descriptions, very much dissatisfied with their condition, or, in other words, with the state of society with which they are connected." This true statement was in the introduction to a pamphlet published in London in 1789, entitled "A Plan for a Free Community upon the Coast of Africa . . . with an Invitation, under certain Conditions, to all Persons desirous of partaking the Benefits thereof." It was signed by two men from Sweden, one from Prussia, and one American; but their names are unimportant, for they are now unknown to fame. That dissatisfaction was prevalent in Europe was true, but the dissatisfied element in America was small. There was really nothing to cause dissatisfaction. There was no social injustice. One class was not exploited by another class—in fact, there was no such word as exploitation. There was no privileged class. If a man had the elements of success in him he succeeded. There were individuals who complained because they were unfortunate, and there were others who looked for perfection in human affairs and attributed its absence to a false constitution of society. These were only individuals; they constituted no group of the population.

The foundation of the national prosperity was the land, and good land was abundant. Under the law the national lands were sold for two dollars per acre. One-twentieth of the purchase price must be deposited to pay costs of survey and registration, which amounted to $11.00; one-fourth of the total price must be paid in forty days; one-half in two years; three-fourths in three years, and the whole in four years. The immediate capital necessary to obtain 640 acres was not more than $331. An able-bodied man of good reputation could borrow it. Later the price was reduced to $1.25 per acre, and various laws were passed by which a settler could, under certain conditions, obtain land for nothing. Besides these national lands were the great tracts held by several of the states and by individuals, parcels of which could be bought on terms so easy that they were accessible to everybody. There was a great deal of speculation in land, but the speculators themselves, demoralizing as their influence was, were active in obtaining settlers for the new land by selling it to them. The farming was done, as it had been done for hundreds of years—with the plow, the horse, and by hand. There were no important inventions in agriculture till 1831, when McCormick made his reaper and Manning his mowing-machine. To be a farmer on an equality with other farmers required little capital.

The rich men of the country had not yet become a power to excite general alarm. They, too, were only individuals. The largest fortunes were made in shipping. The adventurer sent American products abroad in his own ships and exchanged them for foreign products which he brought home and sold at an enormous profit. It was a simple and direct form of commerce, which did not carry with it the idea that the individual was enriching himself by the labor of others. One of these shippers was Israel Thorndike, of Boston, who died in 1832, leaving a fortune of more than two million dollars. He was described as the richest man in New England. William Bingham, who died in 1804, had been perhaps the richest man in America. He owned two million acres of land in Maine, and the largest house in Philadelphia, but the basis of his fortune was laid in the West Indian trade. The shippers sent their vessels into every sea—to Turkey, China, and East India as well as Europe and the West Indies. Stephen Girard, in Philadelphia, had amassed a great fortune. He died in 1831, leaving nine million dollars. He was a banker, but his wealth began in shipping. John Jacob Astor, in New York, was an exception to the rule that the great fortunes came from shipping. He became rich as a fur-trader and was already buying large tracts of land in the city and contiguous to it. His was the only great fortune of the day which has survived to the present time. Individual fortunes were rising in New York, but a man who had one hundred thousand dollars was among the few who were called very rich. There were not five millionaires in the city. Exclusive of the United States bank, there were eleven banks in New York and ten in Philadelphia. Six of the New York banks and four of those in Philadelphia had a capital of over one million dollars. There were some rich bankers, but their wealth was uncertain, for this was the period of state bank-making. Between 1812 and 1817 there were three times as many of them as there had been in previous years, and an enormous increase in the volume of circulating bank-notes. All the banks except those in New England suspended specie payments in 1814 and bank-notes fell in value. The result was in 1819 the first great financial panic in the country, many business failures and much distress. An effect of the speculation and the bank failures was to create a popular prejudice against banks in general, which bore fruit some years later when General Jackson was President and fought the Bank of the United States.

Along the Hudson River and in the central part of New York were a few large landholders, whose ancestors had obtained their lands by Dutch grants, and who had let them out on a sort of feudal tenure. After the Revolution they retained the ownership and obtained some state lands as well, and had tenant farmers. The injustice of paying rent to proprietors who had no part in developing the land caused serious discontent among the tenants, which finally culminated in 1841 in an attempted revolution which became known as the anti-rent war. The condition was local and is an interesting illustration of the fact that where injustice prevailed discontent took form. It was an exception to the rule that the land was cultivated by those who owned it. The great tracts of wild lands held for speculative purposes were not farmed at all, until they were sold to cultivators. As a matter of fact, they were not needed.

After the land the wealth of the country was chiefly in two items, shipping and slaves, each being computed as worth two hundred and twenty-five million dollars.

The planters of the South were rich men—that is to say, they had the attributes of wealth in the form of servants, horses, large houses, abundance of food, and fine clothes. They traveled occasionally and sent their children to the best schools. They were capitalized at a large sum, because their slaves were very valuable, being worth from one hundred and fifty to fifteen hundred dollars each. So a man who had fifty slaves and a thousand acres of land would be worth some forty thousand dollars, a respectable fortune. But he had no stocks or bonds or money out at interest. On the contrary, he was apt to be paying interest, for he was often in debt. He lived by the labor of others. He exploited a lower class of men whom he kept in bondage. He was privileged. The system of society in which he lived was built upon palpable social injustice. The observations which have been made here about the absence of a basis for a discontented class in the United States do not apply to the South. There the voice of discontent was suppressed, but there the discontent was deep and serious. We should look to find from these conditions projects for reform, and we do not look in vain.

There were many plans for freeing the slaves. To use the proceeds of the sale of public land to buy them from their owners; to emancipate all who should be born after a certain date; to allow them to buy their own freedom by their labor—these and many other projects were put forward with the best intentions. The chief argument against them was that they made no provision for removing the blacks after they were free, and the conviction was general that a large population of free negroes could not safely exist in the same country with a white population. From this conviction came the plans for sending the freedmen back to the continent from which they had been stolen. These projects were the noble fruit from an evil soil. Their object was to encourage emancipation which should come from philanthropic motives, by showing slaveholders a happy and prosperous state composed of black citizens in Africa. The free blacks, too, whose position in the United States was always uncertain and often deplorable, would be free in fact, and would have opportunity to develop all that was good in them— an opportunity which they could not have as long as they lived in the United States. Finally, there were the Africans themselves, sunk in savagery, ignorance, and superstition. The American blacks, free, Christianized, and with some education, would be as missionaries among them, and would lead them out of their mental and moral darkness into the light of Christianity and knowledge.

The first efforts at colonizing American negroes in Africa were made in England, where certain English philanthropists, under the lead of Granville Sharp, planned to send the negroes who had escaped to English jurisdiction during the Revolution to Sierra Leone. They had been sent to England, where they were a public charge and a demoralized and useless part of the population. A strip of territory on the West Coast of Africa was bought for them, and arrangements were made to send them there. Many of them refused to go; many ran away, and the ships for Sierra Leone finally sailed with less than seven hundred colonists, only about a third of the number for whom the colony had been planned. From various causes, the basis of which was the incapacity of the colonists and the perfidy of the agents who were in charge of the enterprise, the scheme failed. Some of the colonists were killed by the natives, many died of disease, and only a remnant was left to drag out a miserable existence in a miserable land.

Nevertheless, certain American emancipationists thought the experiment might be tried with better prospects of success under other conditions; and John Jay, who was always an emancipationist, and the Rev. Samuel Hopkins, of Rhode Island, who had proposed colonization of free negroes in Africa as early as 1773, wrote to Sharp on the subject. He replied discouragingly, but William Thornton, who also wrote to him, would not accept discouragement. Thornton had recently chosen the United States for his home and wished to free the large number of slaves he had on his plantation in the Island of Tortola, one of the Virgin Isles in the West Indies. He was reared a Quaker, although he left that persuasion when he married a Philadelphian who was an Episcopalian.

Of soaring ambition and daring thought, young and enthusiastic, he burned with a desire to do some act which would elevate humanity and make his name immortal. He thought the English colony had failed for reasons which he could remedy. For one thing, the colonists were helpless because they had been freed too suddenly. He would have them obtain their freedom by their own exertions and become gradually accustomed to relying upon themselves. Moreover, the freedmen's new home must be an independency. They must erect a new nation. He interested his friend Brissot de Warville in Paris in the plan, and Brissot brought in other Frenchmen. Thornton intended to go with the colonists himself, and, doubtless, had visions of being the head of the new nation and carrying out some of the many plans for a great state which grew in his fertile brain. His work extended from 1786 to 1791, during which time he traveled in Rhode Island and Massachusetts, and also made addresses on the subject of colonization in Pennsylvania. About two thousand freed negroes in New England expressed a willingness to go to Sierra Leone. Thornton hoped that the legislature of Massachusetts would send them, but when he approached some of the members he found they were unwilling to transport the negroes so far. They proposed, instead, to send them to the most southern part of the public lands of the United States, between the white settlements and the Indian country. To this Thornton would not agree. Thus situated, he said, they would be exposed to massacre by the Indians; and, moreover, if a black territory were established in the United States the inhabitants would never be given political rights. So the scheme fell through, and his restless mind turned to another subject—the building of a great city upon the banks of the Potomac for the capital of the American nation. He proposed at a later day the purchase of negro slaves by the government and their employment upon public works pending their emancipation, and that the island of Porto Rico should be bought from Spain and made a home for them. The public mind was ready for none of these things, and the idea of negro colonization slumbered for twenty-five years, when it was awakened under greater promise of success than it had ever had before.

On December 21, 1816, the American Colonization Society was formed at a meeting in Washington over which Henry Clay presided. The first president was Bushrod Washington, a judge of the Supreme Court, the nephew of General Washington, and the owner of Mt. Vernon. Most of the members were slaveholders who lived in the hope of finding a practicable way of accomplishing emancipation. Money was raised by popular subscription and bequests. The government gave its patronage to the plan and appropriated one hundred thousand dollars to send the freedmen to the country which the society selected for them. The scheme at first took on the appearance of a popular movement. The eagerness with which enlightened Southerners embraced it shows how earnestly they wished to rid themselves of the incubus of slavery. Opposition to the society developed in a few parts of the South, however, where it was looked upon as hurtful to the pecuniary interests of the planters and slave-dealers. It depended for its income too much upon voluntary donations. Church collections and the proceeds of ladies' fairs were a part of its resources, and a very uncertain part. It required a large and assured income to carry out the tremendous purpose it was designed to accomplish, and it did not have it. From the beginning the society fell too much into the hands of clergymen. They had the missionary project of converting the Africans too much in their minds. Practical men cared nothing for the souls of the Africans; they were concerned with the hideous evil which existed at home, and they doubted the efficiency of a society which clergymen were managing. The freed blacks themselves showed no eagerness to go to Africa, and they could not be compelled to go. After all, the society was a very small organization to grapple with a very large problem. If everything went well with it the results would still be hardly noticeable in a population of more than a million blacks. It staggers the imagination to suppose that the leaders of the society should have expected to establish a prosperous community in such a place as that which they chose for settlement. One of the agents whom they sent to report on it died of the fever. The climate was hopelessly enervating to those whom it did not kill outright. Nevertheless, a few thousand misguided American negroes went from time to time to the new land, and finally established the republic of Liberia, an independent nation, under the protection of the United States, probably the least important country in the world, the feeble child of a devoted and wholly futile effort to free the country from the worst evil that has ever afflicted it. Hardly any slaves were emancipated in order that they might emigrate. Nevertheless, the Colonization Society was talked about long after it ceased to deserve notice. It exists even now and administers a small income which yet belongs to it, and now and then sends a few American negroes to join their unhappy brothers in Africa.

XXIV

EXCRESCENCES

THE efforts for the betterment of the American blacks were a legitimate outcome of American conditions, but there were certain communities in the country established for the betterment of their own members which had no such basis. These communities were not indigenous; all were imported.

The Shakers are the oldest, and there are still about one thousand of them left in fifteen societies in New York, Massachusetts, New Hampshire, Maine, Connecticut, Ohio, and Kentucky. The membership is diminishing, and their total disappearance is only a matter of time. It is remarkable that they have held together for so long. In 1815 the sect had reached its greatest prosperity and numbered some five thousand people. The founder was an ignorant English working-woman, Ann Lee, who came to New York from Manchester in 1774 with two women and six men who believed her to be the "Mother in Christ" and called her "Mother Ann." She worked as a washerwoman for two years, when she and her little band formed a community at Watervliet near Albany. In England she had been persecuted for her religious pretensions, and in this country she was imprisoned on the charge of being a British spy in 1776, but was

pardoned by Governor Clinton the following year
and thereafter suffered no molestation from the law.
At different times, however, there was some popular
animosity toward her followers, and they were harassed by mobs on several occasions. The recruits who
joined her sect were the products of the frequent
religious revivals. At a revival which took place at
Mt. Lebanon, Columbia County, New York, in 1780,
a number of the participants joined Mother Ann's persuasion and founded a community at that place, which
became the parent of the other societies. In 1781 she
made a missionary journey through New England and
several communities were started. Her death in 1784
had no effect on the progress of Shakerism, and following the great revival in Kentucky in 1805 villages
were established in that state, Indiana, and Ohio.
One pledge which the brethren and sisters took said,
among other things:

"We do by these presents covenant and agree to re-
nounce and disannul every band, tie, and relation of the
flesh and to hold ourselves free and separate from all that
pertains to the corrupt generation of fallen men," etc.

The Shakers believe that Christ appeared on earth
for the second time in the person of Ann Lee, and
that they are enabled by their faith to "take up a
full and daily cross against the world, the flesh, and
all evil" and "to follow Christ in the regeneration
by which they believe God according to His everlast-
ing promise will gather together in one all things in
Christ which are in heaven and upon earth." They
are loyal to their country and declare that their
belief is perfectly consistent with civil rights. They

believe in liberty of conscience and "that all souls whom God has created are free and have a right to believe according to their own conviction and to act according to their own faith." They are non-combatants, however, and regard military service as sinful. They believe in celibacy for themselves, but have no objection to marriage among people who are not of their elect. They require their members to confess their sins to an elder. They believe they must live separated from the world and holding their property in common. They are spiritualists, and Mother Ann and other departed shades often appear at their meetings. Mother Ann herself claimed the power of divine healing of the sick, and, according to the testimony, effected several miraculous cures. At their meetings there is singing, dancing, marching, and whirling, besides exhortation and prayer. A great many of them have reached a stage where their lives have become sinless. Originally professing the Quaker creed, they were known as "Shaking Quakers," but they soon became a distinct sect and accepted the designation of Shakers. Their civil and religious government are in the same persons, deacons and deaconnesses, and elders and eldresses, who appoint their own successors. The women and the men are upon a perfect equality. They are careful to keep the sexes apart, however. Everything is ordered with rigid regularity. The meals are eaten in silence, the men and women at separate tables, and no amusements are permitted. As everybody works and the strictest economy prevails, they have attained material prosperity. The fact that they are absolutely honest in their dealings and thorough in their work is an additional reason for this. The regularity of their lives has produced some notable cases of longevity among them. These figures were given by one of them for the communities of Hancock, Massachusetts, and Mt. Lebanon, but the last figure seems incredible: Fifty-three of the members lived to be more than ninety years old, of whom thirteen died when they were more than ninety-five, four when they were over one hundred, and one after he had lived for one hundred and twenty years. I have seen a great many of their hymns, prayers, and narratives of experiences. They show the perfect self-confidence and strength of conviction of ignorant minds. They do not show weakness of intellects, but narrowness. Those who came after Mother Ann were better educated than she was; in fact, she could neither read nor write; but there have never been any cultivated people among the Shakers. While the Shakers were English in their origin, their membership was drawn mainly from Americans, but there was always a fair proportion of foreigners.

The Harmony Society, which is the next oldest community in the United States, was foreign in its origin and always remained so in all essentials. The members did not vote, although they were naturalized as American citizens, and their recruits came from Germany. They used the German language. George Rapp, the founder and guiding spirit of the community, was of a far higher grade of intelligence than Mother Ann. He was better educated, less pretentious, and his creed and conduct were less unreasonable. He claimed no divine origin or power, and he did not believe in spiritualism. He fled from Württemberg, where he was born, because he and his followers were persecuted for practising their religion. With three hundred families, constituting seven hundred and fifty men, women, and children, he built the town of Harmony in Butler County, Pennsylvania, in 1805, but the soil and climate did not suit them, and in 1814 they moved to the valley of the Wabash in Indiana, where they built a second Harmony. In 1825 they moved again, to Beaver County, Pennsylvania, where they built the town of Economy, and where the remnant of the sect, now not a dozen members, still resides. The community was industrious and honest, its industries were diversified, and it became very rich. George Rapp died in 1847, when he was ninety years old, and the Harmonists drifted on without the master guiding hand. Originally they were not celibates; but in 1807 they decided that marriage distracted people from higher duties and was not consonant with their belief in the original dual nature of Adam, and there were no more marriages among them. The cardinal point in their creed was that the second coming of Christ was near at hand, when the millennium would come and the earth would be like the Garden of Eden before the fall of Adam. The great object of life, therefore, was to be ready for the reappearance of Christ, and Rapp expected to present his followers as worthy of divine favor. The communistic mode of life they thought was a command of Christ.

In 1818 another band of persecuted Germans came to America from Württemberg. They settled in Tuscaroras County, Ohio, where they founded a village which they called Zoar, after the little city in which Lot found refuge when Sodom and Gomorrah were destroyed. At first they were not communists, but, finding it difficult to hold the members of their sect together because of their uneven fortunes, they adopted communism as a convenience. They were celibates till 1828 or 1830, when they permitted marriage, but they never encouraged it. Like the followers of Rapp, they came to escape religious persecution, and they proselyted only in Germany. They prospered fairly well, but they did not have as great cohesive force as the Harmonists or Shakers, because their creed was much milder. They did not have as able a leader as Rapp. They called themselves Separatists, and merely disapproved of the forms and ceremonies of the established church of Germany. True Christian life, they said, requires no set forms and ceremonies. They were opposed to military service. They retained the rules which they made in Germany, which were applicable there and had no application here. They had a simple government, the officers being elected by majority vote, the women having a vote equally with the men. Their religious meetings were held only on Sundays and all the people did not attend them. They were of the German peasant class, and they did not progress beyond it. There were never more than five hundred members of the community. It decreased and passed out of existence in 1898.

EXCRESCENCES

When George Rapp and his followers left their land and buildings in Indiana they sold them for one hundred thousand dollars to Robert Owen, of Lanark, who thus acquired, ready made as it were, the plant for a more important social experiment than Rapp's; but Owen's experiment was inspired by an entirely different purpose from Rapp's and belongs to a different period. It marks, in fact, the beginning of socialism in the United States. It was the outcome of the factory system. It was an effort to overcome the injustice of employing large bodies of men to create wealth and of not permitting them to receive a fair proportion of the wealth which they created. It was not directed to their spiritual welfare; on the contrary, it tended to concentrate their attention upon their material well being. It has its place in the economic history of the United States under conditions which did not exist at the time of which I am writing, when there were no large American factories.

In 1813 Owen wrote his essay on "A New View of Society," and it found its way to America where a few idealists welcomed it. In a former chapter I spoke of the New York Society for the Prevention of Pauperism. It was a practical charitable organization which dealt with poverty under existing conditions; but another society was formed about 1820 entitled "The New York Society for Promoting Communities," the organizers being four ministers, one attorney, five physicians and surgeons, a printer, three teachers, a merchant, a builder, and one whose occupation was not stated. It had as its object to "convince the pious of all denominations that their duty is to constitute and establish in every religious congregation a system of social, equal, and inclusive rights, interests, liberties, and privileges to all real and personal property" which would cause "self-love to expire in social love" and introduce the gospel of peace on earth and good will to men; and "when the inclusive system became general the present government of exclusive rights and properties would be supplanted by the government of Jehovah and his annointed, the Prince of Peace." It said: "The heartrending statements which were made known during the discussions of negro slavery do not exhibit more afflicting scenes than those which, in various parts of the world, daily arise from the injustice of society toward itself." So this society intended to abolish poverty, crime, and injustice. I cannot find that it got any adherents or founded any communities. It printed extracts from Owen's "New View of Society," all unconscious that Owen was an infidel and would soon proclaim the fact.

The three communities, the Shakers, the Harmonites, and the Separatists, were the only ones in the United States one hundred years ago, and they were mere excrescences on our national life, superficial appendages without organic significance. They excited little attention at the time and made no impression on the normal progress of the nation. A few people under strong religious excitement found among the Shakers conditions which enabled them to continue their exaltation; but in Harmony and Zoar there was nothing to attract them. There were

EXCRESCENCES

reasons why Mother Ann and Rapp and the Separatists should have come to America; they were persecuted in Europe; but there was no reason beyond their own preference for their living in separate communities in this country.

XXV

THE GOVERNMENT

EXCEPT for the few groups of communists who lived by themselves all the people in the United States in 1815 took a personal interest in the political affairs of the country. They were busy making a living, but they were not so engrossed by their industry that it excluded the government from their thoughts. They were still considering the nature of that government. They knew that it was not a democracy, and the utmost lengths to which those who wished it to be a government of the people, and argued that it was, cared to go was to call it a democratic republic. Everybody believed in representative government. The governors of eight of the eighteen states were elected by the legislatures, and not by the people directly. It was considered to be enough that the people should directly elect their Representatives in Congress and their local officers. The legislatures had chosen the delegates to the Continental Congress and the delegates to the convention which framed the Constitution. The Constitution itself was not ratified by a vote of the people, but by conventions of delegates whom the people had selected to decide for them whether or not it should be accepted. The people still believed that the electoral college chose the President. No voice was raised to demand a direct election by popular vote of Senators. No one proposed that the people should vote directly on proposed legislation.

Nevertheless, this was understood to be a government of public opinion, and it was generally agreed that no important measure should become law until it had been publicly discussed and a sentiment for it had been manifested. It was not generally believed that a count of heads was the best way to ascertain what the public sentiment was. Universal manhood suffrage was being experimented with, but was not yet accepted as a safe basis of government. In twelve of the states voting was conditioned upon ownership of real property or payment of taxes.

The electors felt the responsibility of their power and had a good understanding of public affairs. They read pamphlets and articles, and listened to speeches on pending political questions which were thorough and even erudite discussions. The nature of the information which those who understood the voters put before them shows that their intelligence was held in respect. This is not to say, however, that the demagogue was not busy with them. If a country is governed by an individual there will be people near him who will try to influence him to their advantage by flattering him and playing upon his weaknesses. If the people govern there will always be designing men who will try to use them by arousing their passions and making them false promises. It would seem that courtiers who deceive the monarch and demagogues who deceive the masses are the worst forms of an evil which afflicts all governments. In 1815 the United States was governed by the middle class, who were not easily worked upon by tricks and lies. There was no powerful moneyed class, and there were no great groups of ignorant voters such as now cluster in the large cities. Unless the surviving evidence—the books, the published debates in Congress and the state legislatures, the pamphlets, newspaper articles, and private letters—is wholly misleading, demagogic appeals to the governing power were not a conspicuous feature of political life one hundred years ago.

Public opinion was forming steadily in the direction of the belief that the United States was a nation, but it had not yet formed in that belief. It was common to speak of "the Nation," because there was no other word to describe the country as a whole, but it was not considered to be a nation for domestic purposes. Against a foreign country the states stood as one power; but at home the country was thought to be an aggregation of political entities, each of which had most of the attributes of sovereignty and might assume them all. They had voluntarily given certain sovereignty to the federal government, and were free to recall it. National laws were drawing the bands tighter, and each year the union became more and more difficult to break, but the right to break it existed, as most of them believed.

In 1794 Oliver Ellsworth, of Connecticut, and Rufus King, of New York, had an interesting private conversation with John Taylor of Caroline, of Virginia, all three being Senators at the time. King and Ellsworth proposed that there be an amicable dissolution of the Union, because the sections could not agree on any government measure; but Taylor would not consent, and thought the differences could be accommodated. He reported the conversation to Madison, who was then the leader of the House, and Madison was disposed to think that King and Ellsworth had been trying to frighten Taylor; but this point is not important to our inquiry. They would not have made a treasonable and unpatriotic suggestion for strategical purposes. They did not consider their suggestion to be either treasonable or unpatriotic; nor did Taylor and Madison so consider it. So far as their attitude toward the Union was concerned there was no real difference between the opposing parties at this time. The party which was in power wished to continue the union; the party which was in the opposition threatened it. In the first Congress both parties would have dissolved it under a little pressure. Business came to a standstill, and there seemed to be no object in Congress meeting, because the South could not get the North to agree to locate the capital in the South, and the North could not get the South to agree that the general government must assume the war debts of the several states. Having weathered this storm, the Federalists began to think of disunion a few years later, as we have just seen. The exciting cause of their dissatisfaction was that the opposition Senators opposed the confirmation of John Jay as Minister to England, and favored a sequestration of British debts, because Great Britain had not paid for the slaves she had carried off during the Revolution.

There was no vital issue at stake between the parties, and no serious injury to the rights of either could have come from the success of the other. When the Federalists passed the Alien and Sedition laws it was the turn of the Republicans to talk of disunion, and plans were discussed, especially in Virginia and North Carolina. In 1811, when Louisiana was about to be admitted as a state, a Federalist, Josiah Quincy, of Massachusetts, threatened disunion in the course of the debate in the House of Representatives. The ground of complaint was that the new territory was so large that it would dwarf the old states. That the nation would gain prestige was of no consequence alongside of the fact that Massachusetts would lose it. Again the Federalists threatened disunion, and seriously considered it because of the hardship inflicted by the commercial restrictions imposed before and during the War of 1812. The hardship was real, and the opposition to the measures was excusable. To pursue the subject further: in 1832 the Republicans of South Carolina threatened disunion, because they thought the tariff weighed heavily upon them. The disturbance was local, and the union sentiment had attained such force that the country accepted Andrew Jackson's argument in his proclamation addressed to the nullifiers that an overt act of disunion was treason. Thus the march had gone forward—from tolerance of the union, to general consent to it, to intolerance of opposition to it, to denial of the right to withdraw from it. In 1815 public opinion had reached the third stage and regarded disunion sentiments with intolerance. Because of their attitude toward the

Union the members of the Hartford Convention and their friends became marked men and lost their national influence. From now on devotion to the Union and the Constitution deepened into affection and became synonymous with patriotism.

One reason for this forward movement was that a regular and simple way had been found to prevent the Constitution from being violated, and that this way was now generally understood. It was clear that until there was a way by which the government could protect itself from violations such violations were likely to be met by withdrawal.

Suppose that a majority in Congress, being of the same party with the President, chooses to pass unconstitutional and oppressive measures; what is to prevent it? In truth, there is nothing to prevent it; and if the President signs them they become law. But is there no way of arresting the operation of such laws? Any one would answer promptly, "Yes, the Supreme Court will declare them void." In 1798, however, few people would have made that answer, and in that year Congress passed despotic measures dangerous to liberty and believed by a great part of the people to be palpably unconstitutional; and the President signed them, and they became laws. They decreed that the President could send out of the United States any alien whom he might consider to be dangerous to the public peace and safety. There was no appeal. He could have sent away all the aliens whom he did not like under the pretense that their presence was harmful to public tranquillity. The object of the law was not to prevent paupers, criminals, diseased persons, and members of an obnoxious race from settling in the United States, but to provide the President with the means of suppressing the voice of antagonism to the measures of his political party, some of that antagonism having come from aliens who had recently settled in the United States. At the same session of Congress another law was passed requiring an alien to live in the United States for at least fourteen years before he could be naturalized as a citizen. The object of this law was to keep aliens within the power of the law, permitting their expulsion as long as possible. Then a law was passed inflicting fine and imprisonment upon any one who should utter in speech or in print scandalous or insulting language against the government or its officers. Free speech and a free press could be silenced by this law.

Where was relief from the operation of these laws to be sought? The Supreme Court did not then command, nor did it deserve, general confidence. The Chief Justice was Oliver Ellsworth, who had, while still Chief Justice, been sent on a mission to France, when the office was essentially a political one. The judges were Samuel Chase, an avowed violent Federalist partisan; Iredell, Cushing, and Paterson, all known to be strong Federalists. It is beyond doubt that the court, if the laws had been brought before it, would have upheld them. Thus far, in fact, it had never declared an act of Congress which did not affect the judiciary to be unconstitutional. It was a semi-political body, and politicians, as the historian of the court states, "bivouacked in the chief-justiceship on

their march from one political position to another."
If the court had upheld the laws one party would
have murmured against the decision. If, on the
other hand, it had declared them void the other party
would not have accepted the decision. In fact, public opinion would not have supported the court. It
is fortunate that the authority was not then subjected
to a strain which might have destroyed its future usefulness. So, eliminating the court, the opponents of
the laws, by resolutions adopted by the legislatures
of Virginia and Kentucky, proposed a complicated and
impracticable method of meeting violations of the
Constitution. As the states, they said, had ratified
the Constitution, it was their creation, and they had
power over it. Consequently, when an obnoxious,
oppressive, and unconstitutional law was passed the
states could arrest its operations within their respec-
tive borders. To this proposition all the New England states, New York, and Delaware replied in dis-
sent; but the rest of the country probably agreed to
it. In 1814 New England put forward the same doctrine, and no state replied to it. There was general
apathy toward the theory, because a power had been
developed in which all had confidence, which would
guard the fundamental law from violation. In 1803
John Marshall, the Chief Justice, handed down the
decision of the Supreme Court in which it asserted
for the first time that it was the right and duty of
the court to pass upon the constitutionality of acts
of Congress, and if they were unconstitutional to
declare them void. It is true that the framers of
the Constitution had always believed that the court

had this power, but they had no idea how its exercise would operate. Here, as in all government affairs, the personal element entered as an important factor. The court of John Marshall and his associates, among whom were now several jurists who had no political record, could do with safety what Oliver Ellsworth and his partisan associates would have done with peril.

By 1815 the functions of the several branches of the government were understood, but the second chamber of Congress, the Senate, was looked upon as of less importance than it became in the public view at a later day. For this fact it had itself to thank. Had the first sessions been open to the public, as the sessions of the House were, it would have had public influence equal or superior to that of the House. It was supposed that it would occupy high position in the new government, and at first the ablest characters sought admission to it. The first Senate was a strong body in its personnel. Oliver Ellsworth, George Read, Charles Carroll, William Paterson, Robert Morris, Rufus King, Richard Henry Lee, and James Monroe were among the members. But it held its sessions in secret, so that it might not be influenced by public censure or favor. In consequence, it could not exert public influence itself. It exercised its power untrammeled, but it deprived itself of power. Wise action taken in secret and eloquent speeches which nobody heard were wasted. The public, being ignorant of what it was doing, became indifferent to it or perhaps suspicious of it. Thus the impression at the beginning of the operation of the government was not favorable to the Senate; and, being a neglected or even unpopular body, there was no eagerness to serve in it, and the membership fell off in quality. John Vining took George Read's place; John Henry, Charles Carroll's; William Bingham that of Robert Morris; and so on. On February 20, 1794, the Senate opened its doors to the public, but it took some years to overcome the popular indifference which had come in the beginning. In 1815 it held very few members who were of the first rank of public men. Henry Clay had been in the Senate from 1806 to 1807, and again for a year from February 5, 1810, to March 3, 1811, when he resigned to go into the House, because from the House he could lead the country. For the next ten years the obscurity of the Senate continued; but in 1823 Thomas H. Benton, Martin Van Buren, and Robert Y. Hayne were there. In 1827 Daniel Webster entered; in 1831 Henry Clay returned; and they were joined in 1832 by Calhoun. The pre-eminence of the Senate was settled.

As I have said, everybody took an interest in public affairs; but as the "era of good feeling" began there were no radical differences of opinion on political subjects and no issues before the people which they regarded as involving vital principles. As a consequence, politics descended to a lower level than it had occupied before. The heroic age had passed, and we were entering upon the day of small things. We were about to illustrate the truth that when a country is happy its history is dull. The large things had been disposed of, and, issues failing, the interest now centered in the officers. The chron-

icler of the time must concern himself with a
"dull, dismal labyrinth" of politicians' activities,
which they covered over with a cloak of cant,
but which had as their only object the gaining of
offices.

XXVI

THE PRESIDENT

IN the early days of the operation of the government of the United States there was a latent fear that the President would sooner or later develop into a king. He had so many functions such as the old king had exercised; he had so much authority over others; his general primacy was so well defined that it required little imagination to picture him using his power so as to extend it and continue it. Confidence that the office was a safe one and would not absorb the other functions of the government came as a consequence of the unselfish patriotism of the incumbents. In fact, the Constitution left some important features of the new government almost at the mercy of the individuals who should first be intrusted with the responsibility of putting them in operation. An ambitious man being President might have continued in office for more than two terms; there was nothing in the law to prevent his re-election as long as he lived; he was commander-in-chief of the army and the navy; it might have required a revolution to dislodge him. But the first President commanded universal confidence. It was known that he preferred farming to governing and that he would go back to his crops as soon as he could. The power of the Presidency actually diminished under John Adams. He left the ordinary duties of the office to his subordinates. He was surrounded by faction, and the strength of the opposition party was growing steadily. Thomas Jefferson, who succeeded him, was the personification of opposition to large governmental powers. Unless he turned traitor to every political principle which he had ever uttered he could be depended upon not to stretch the functions of the Presidency. He used them actively and passed them on in good working order to his successor. Nothing had yet occurred to alarm the people. James Madison's record in public life was a guaranty that he would preserve the balance of power in the government. It was he who had proposed in the convention which framed the Constitution that there should be a President and had defined his duties. His ambition was to see that the government, whose frame had come from his hands, should prove a success. So, by 1815 there was a feeling of confidence in the institution of the Presidency, for nothing had yet occurred to arouse apprehension that a President would try to deprive the people of their liberties.

To everybody the President was the most important man in the country. There were a few ignorant people who could not have named the Secretary of State; there were many more who could not have named the Chief Justice; but no one could have been found who did not know that the President was James Madison. Thus far the Presidents had been men of broad and accepted reputation, to whom the office had come as the climax of long public service.

There had only been four of them; the republic was very young; and the fourth was less familiarly known to the great body of the people than any of his predecessors had been. Yet he had had a longer public career than any of them.

In 1768, when he was seventeen years old, James Madison entered the sophomore class at Princeton College, and he and several of his classmates founded the American Whig Society for the purpose of debating questions of government. In 1836, when he was eighty-five years old, he wrote his last message, "Advice to My Country," in which he admonished posterity to cherish and perpetuate the union of the states. During the whole of this long period, for sixty-eight years, he was continuously concerned with problems affecting the government of America. He began his public service in 1774, and terminated it when he left the Presidency in 1817. During a period of forty-three years he had been almost continuously in public office. There was no man in the United States to whom the title of statesman could so appropriately be applied.

Some of the description of a great statesman which Buckle gives in his analysis of the talents of Burke applies to Madison. He employed his learning with sobriety, and his political principles were practical. Although his mind was stored with ample material for generalization, as a legislator he did not generalize. He regarded statesmanship as an empirical science. He was well aware that in political practice the statesman must deal with human nature, human weaknesses, and human passions, and that his function is to direct or follow, not to force, public inclination. He was fully alive to the distinction between the broad generalizations of philosophy and the principles of politics. He never doubted for a moment that the people were his masters. So much of Buckle's picture of the statesman's mind he realized; but not all of Burke's political code, as Buckle expounds it, fitted him. He would have agreed that political principles were but the product of human reason; but he would have denied that it was a statesman's duty "to shape his own conduct, not according to his own principles, but according to the wishes of the people for whom he legislates and whom he is bound to obey." He would have insisted that a statesman should shape his conduct according to his principles and leave the people to remove him from his office if his conduct ran counter to their wishes. He would have insisted upon the validity of general principles in politics, and he would have denied that it was not an object of government to preserve particular institutions, if those institutions were, in his view, essential to the preservation of principles. In fact, no American statesman would have proclaimed that he must obey the public demand, even if it required from him action which he believed to be wrong in principle. The public itself would have withdrawn its confidence from an agent who obeyed it and at the same time declared that he believed the action it required of him was wrong. It would have regarded his course as immoral. It required that its agent should have a conscience, or, at any rate, should make it believe that he had. It recognized no distinction between political morality and private morality. What was wrong in private life was wrong in public life. The political principles of Madison were the political principles of those whom he represented. If he and they had not so believed they would have parted company.

The President was a man of versatile scholarship and interests. He knew French and Italian; he had studied Hebrew; he kept up his knowledge of the classical languages. He had a taste for art, as his house at Montpelier demonstrated. It was designed for him by Thornton, and is a model of good taste in architecture. The interior was decorated with many works of art, some of which were of real excellence—Cardelli's busts of Jefferson and Adams, for example, and the marble medallion of himself by Ceracchi. The grounds about the house were laid out artistically, and repay the study of the landscape-gardener at the present day. He delighted in the beauties of nature, with which he had been surrounded from infancy. He was a scientific farmer and wrote learned addresses on agriculture. He was learned in theology, having at one time studied with the thought of becoming a clergyman, and had read the French and English philosophers and skeptics. He was a naturalist, read Buffon, and added to Buffon's information. He knew something of ethnology, especially with reference to the origin of the Indians. He studied law; but this science, political economy, and social science all belonged to his erudition in political science, in which it is not an exaggeration to say that he had exhausted the record of human experience and reasoning.

Happily for his usefulness, Madison understood the people of Virginia thoroughly, and was in complete sympathy with them, so he had a constituency upon which he could rely. He was always a little in advance of them, and on occasion skilfully led them forward. He did so when, using an agent to act for him, he obtained from the legislature the invitation to the states for a general convention to consider interstate trade regulations, when the legislature was jealous of increasing federal power. From this invitation came the Annapolis convention, from which came the Philadelphia convention which framed the Constitution.

Madison was accused of violating his convictions when he broke with Alexander Hamilton and joined Jefferson's party when the opposing parties formed, but there was no reason why he should not have been convinced that Hamilton's system of government was dangerous and unwise. All Virginia and most of America were so convinced. But if he believed that the charges made against Hamilton, in the effort to break his power, were true, his brains were working with unaccustomed feebleness. When men engage in political warfare they commonly lose their heads and something of their morals and deal foul blows as well as fair—

In wretched interchange of wrong for wrong
'Midst a contentious world, striving where none are strong.

This period of political warfare was the weak point in Madison's career. The utmost that can be said (and it is not much) is that he was not as vindictive nor as vituperative as most of his contemporaries were.

To the generation of statesmen who were rising in 1815 Madison was already one of the figures in the pantheon. The chief of these new statesmen was Henry Clay. In his early life he had followed Madison, and he enjoyed the friendship and confidence of the President. In 1829, when Clay was at the height of his popularity, in the course of a private conversation he gave it as his opinion that Madison was our greatest statesman and the first of American political writers. This opinion of his writings had reference to his numbers of *The Federalist*, his pamphlets, speeches, articles, and state papers. The most notable of his writings, the journal of the debates in the convention which framed the Constitution and the explanatory introduction, had not yet appeared.

I am not prepared to say that Clay's opinion was too strong. The writings of Madison cover a great range of subjects, which they treat with philosophic wisdom. At the present day there is hardly a decision of the Supreme Court dealing with constitutional construction which does not quote them as authority. They contain a wealth of authentic narrative history besides, and judicious discussions of those problems of government which are perennial.

The Constitution of the United States was the crowning work of the revolutionary period of our history. It preserved for posterity the liberty which the Revolution won. Madison was the chief agent in calling together the convention which framed it. He drew up the plan of government upon which the convention based its work. He was confessedly the leading member of the convention. He was the chief agent in accomplishing the ratification of the Constitution. He was the leader of the House of Representatives, and consequently of Congress, when it adopted the measures which put the Constitution in operation. In constructive statesmanship no other American had a record the equal of his.

His course while he was President did not add to his reputation. For the first time he was in an office where success required large administrative talents, and he had never had administrative experience. He found himself at the head of a nation in arms, and here his deficiencies were conspicuous. He hated war. All his life he had been searching for governmental policies which would render war unnecessary. Without enthusiasm for fighting he could not inspire the nation with enthusiasm for the war. He watched the law and kept his own powers within cramped bounds. What the occasion demanded was a lusty warrior who would take all needed authority and settle the question of legality afterward. The war having terminated, the government had suffered no harm— there was that much to be said in favor of Madison's caution.

The position which he occupied with the people was peculiar. They held him in respect, but he was hardly more than a name to them. He was the friend and coadjutor of Jefferson, and would carry on Jefferson's system of government. He had been a member of the Continental Congress, and was the father of the Constitution. They felt grateful to him and had confidence in him, and that was all. How could it be otherwise with a man who was only five feet six and a quarter inches tall, with a small, wizened body and a weak voice?

His countenance was solemn and not handsome. So far as the public knew him he was always an old, sad-eyed man. There was never any of the dash and fire of youth in him. He made no open-air speeches, except among his immediate constituency in Virginia. He never courted public attention. All of his published speeches and state papers were able compositions, solid, closely reasoned, profound, and stately, but with no illumination from catching phrases, no inspiring appeals, nothing to warm the public heart.

He had his enemies, but he himself hated no one, and those who disliked him were not many nor were they bitter. At one time they said he was in secret league with Napoleon, but they could hardly have believed so nonsensical a charge. They said he sold himself to the Clay Republicans, exchanging his war message to Congress for a renomination for the Presidency, and this shocking accusation many people believed and some historians have repeated. It was never proved, and recently discovered documents have disproved it. His character was assailed less than that of any of his contemporaries of similar public experience, and was, in fact, unassailable. The dislike for him entertained by those who had suffered from the commercial restrictions of his and Jefferson's administration was mitigated after the peace, when most of them became prosperous again, and he went into retirement pursued by no anathemas.

It was his misfortune to be made fun of. Washington Irving, going to Washington in search of an office in 1809, wrote in a familiar letter:

Mrs. Madison is a fine, portly, buxom dame, who had a smile and a pleasant word for everybody. Her sisters, Mrs. Cutts and Mrs. Washington, are like two merry wives of Windsor, but as to Jemmy Madison—ah! poor Jemmy! he is but a withered little apple-John.

When war was declared Richard Rush, then the Comptroller of the Treasury, wrote to his father that the President had visited the War and Navy Departments, "stimulating everything in a manner worthy of a little commander-in-chief, with his little round hat and huge cockade." It is a pity for his fame that he should have been obliged to be "a little commander-in-chief."

After the capture of Washington some verses were published in New York in the style of John Gilpin, entitled "The Bladensburg Races." The President is made to say to his wife:

Quoth Madison unto his spouse,
  "Though frighted we have been
These two last tedious weeks, yet we
  No enemy have seen."

To which, after another verse, his wife replies:

"To-morrow," then quoth she, "We'll fly
  As fast as we can pour
Northward, unto Montgomery,
  All in our coach and four.

"My sister Cutts, and Cutts, and I,
  And Cutts's children three,
Will fill the coach; so you must ride
  On horseback after we—"

MRS. JAMES MADISON
From an original painting by Gilbert Stuart

JAMES MADISON

This last verse was an allusion to Mrs. Madison's sister and family, who frequented the White House during the Madison administration.

The flight progresses from Bladensburg

> Then might all people well discern
>   The gallant *little man*,
> His sword did thump behind his back,
>   So merrily he ran.

In private life, especially in Washington, Madison played rather a secondary part. Strangers who went to the receptions at the White House gave long descriptions of Mrs. Madison, and had only a perfunctory sentence about the President. He was a very modest man and did not shine in a large assemblage. He liked to see his wife the center of the circle, and was content himself to stand quietly on the edge. He never talked for show. Serious visitors who sought for information on political history found him an inexhaustible mine of information, frank, communicative, and amiable; but casual visitors who hoped to hear only words of wisdom from him, and to carry away with them some remarks which fitted his character as the father of the Constitution, were apt to be disappointed. In fact, they might dine at his table and hear nothing but banter from him during the whole dinner. After dinner, if the men who sat around the table drinking their wine were his friends, the ladies from the adjoining room might hear loud roars of laughter from the President's guests, who were enjoying the President's broad and irresistible jokes. The sorrowful hazel eyes were often lightened by a mischievous twinkle, and the solemn mouth covered remarkably good teeth, which made the whole countenance look gay when he smiled.

To what extent was the President typical of his time? He belonged to the days which were passing and not to those which were coming. When he left the Presidency he retired definitely from public life, as his predecessors in that office had done, and the partisan personal bickering which soon became the most conspicuous feature of politics did not interest him. When the Missouri bill came up, and ten years later the nullification movement, he raised his voice and spoke his views; but in spite of every effort no one could get from him an opinion on the merits of the various politicians who were seeking public favor. His mind was occupied with the past, with the events of the Revolution, but particularly with the making of the Constitution, its meaning and the intention of its makers, and on these points his pronouncements were accepted as oracular.

But, as I pointed out in a previous chapter, his administration, as it progressed, set steadily away from the old order, and before it closed became fairly representative of the new. When it closed William H. Crawford was the Secretary of the Treasury; the position of Secretary of War was vacant for the time, Crawford having been transferred from that office. The Attorney-General was Richard Rush, and the Secretary of the Navy was Benjamin W. Crowninshield. Crowninshield represented the new republicanism of New England and the departure of that section from the Tory federalism which had hitherto any other officers over whom he had influence as agents to further his political fortunes. He was the first public man to erect an effective political machine. He became a powerful factor in the politics of the country. He called himself a Jeffersonian Democrat, but he was not identified with any public measures involving broad principles. His management of the finances of the country was not notable. His main interest was in the manipulation of political groups with a view to securing the offices, and, having secured them, to so administer them as to retain them. Politics was with him and his followers simply a contest for office. The forces behind men like Rush and Crowninshield were insignificant compared with the force behind Crawford.

dominated it. Rush was a Pennsylvania Republican, a member of an old and influential family in Philadelphia, where old families still had influence.

The genius of the new order in politics was the Secretary of the Treasury. William H. Crawford was educated for the law, but became a member of the legislature of Georgia when he was twenty-one years of age. He came to the Senate and served for a time as president *pro tempore*. Madison sent him as Minister to France in 1813, and he entered the Cabinet in 1815, first as Secretary of War, from which office he went to the Treasury Department in 1816. He served till John Quincy Adams became President in 1825. He was a candidate for the Presidency in 1824, and came near being elected by the House of Representatives. He was a man of some parts as a lawyer, and closed his long career as a federal judge. He was a large man of bluff, democratic personality. He had a large circle of personal friends who were really devoted to him and thought him a great man. As Secretary of the Treasury he had many subordinates, and his activities among minor public officers extended beyond his department. In 1820 he succeeded in having an act passed prescribing four years as the term of office of United States attorneys, collectors of customs, and a number of other minor officials. Thus, automatically and without the trouble of dismissal, a large number of offices were constantly falling vacant, there was a constant stream of applicants, there was incessant flow and life among the rank and file of politicians. He systematically employed the officers of the Treasury Department and

XXVII

PATRIOTISM

WHEN Benjamin Franklin was shown one of the medallions of the Society of the Cincinnati in 1784, and was told that the design had been criticized because it more resembled a turkey than an eagle, he said he wished it had been a turkey.

"For, in truth, the turkey is in comparison a much more respectable bird, and withal a true original native of America. Eagles have been found in all countries; but the turkey is peculiar to ours. . . . He is, besides (though a little vain and silly, it is true, but none the worse emblem for that), a bird of courage, and would not hesitate to attack a grenadier of the British guards who should presume to invade his farm-yard with a red coat on."

The patriarch had the same idea that possessed all his fellow-countrymen—everything must be our own, even to the symbols of heraldry. But he was a little unjust toward the eagle, for the Continental Congress, in adopting that bird as the central feature of the American arms, had required it to be "the American Eagle displayed proper," meaning the bald eagle, which is found only on this continent.

The spirit of Americanism was manifested everywhere. The President should not become a king,

18

such as other countries had, but a chief executive with circumscribed powers, a chief such as no other country had. The government must be our own in all respect. Its various features might resemble the features of other governments, but they were not identical. The same spirit went into lesser things; nothing was acceptable unless it bore the American stamp. Dictionaries, the very language, novels, poetry, plays, even art, education, prison discipline, medicine, the churches, must be American if they were to find favor and success on this continent. Happily, we were isolated and could develop unvexed by any rival civilization. The sea was our eastern boundary; on most of our north and all of our west was an uninhabited empire; and on the south were an inferior people who made no impression upon the people of the United States, except, by the contrast of their feebleness, to make their English-speaking neighbors more certain of their strength. There were no rivals near us and no foreigners within our borders. The immigrant came to stay. His dominating desire was to merge himself in American life. He obtained American citizenship as soon as the law allowed him to do so. He imbibed American institutions and forgot the institutions he had left behind him. He learned our language and often failed to teach his children his own mother's tongue. There was always present a fear that the immigrant would interfere with the normal development of American life, but in reality he became more American than the natives themselves and embraced the American idea with a convert's zeal.

PATRIOTISM

American nationality developed without the over-shadowing element of personal loyalty and devotion, which is one of the romantic features of the history of European states. The blending of affection and duty and the personification of patriotism have given much of the poetic coloring to the history of the countries from which Americans came, and that we have lived our national life without it is one of the reasons why people who read only for their pleasure think our history is dull.

Far back in the history of the world the patriotism was always personal, being, in fact, only an enlarge-ment of the devotion and subjection of the child to the parent. The head of the house, the patriarch, the leader of the tribe or clan, was the protecting father of his people. The kings were always kings over the people, and not over the land. The fact survives in the titles of some of the monarchs who now reign. The king of Belgium is King of the Belgians, of Den-mark is King of Denmark and the Wendes and the Goths, of Sweden is King of Sweden and of the Goths and the Vandals. In the course of time society ad-vanced from the nomadic and pastoral stage and be-came agricultural. It gained its sustenance by culti-vating the soil, and became fixed in its place of abode. From this condition a new idea of nationality arose—that it was appurtenant to the place of birth and resi-dence and was not derived from personal subjection and fealty alone. From the patriarchal state had arisen the doctrine of citizenship by descent, by kinship, by blood—the *jus sanguinis* of the Roman or civil law; from the agricultural state came the doctrine that citizenship was based upon the land—the *jus soli* of the English or common law. The newer doctrine did not supplant the sentiment of loyalty to a personal sovereign; but it introduced a new element into it. When nationality became territorial and not wholly personal the country took over the loyalty and devotion which before had been monopolized by the patriarch or monarch. Then the man personified the land where he dwelt and whence he derived his sustenance. It became the fatherland, and he expressed his devotion to it by giving it the feminine pronoun *she* or *her* when he spoke of it, as he did when he spoke of his mother or his wife. Centuries after the reason for it had departed the old feeling of personal loyalty lingered, held in men's minds by the survival of an organization of society which had been based upon it. It lingers yet, a survival of medieval times without logical excuse in the modern state.

When America was settled the earliest pioneers came with the sentiment of personal loyalty still in their minds, but here it had nothing to feed upon. There were no visible requirements by the monarch of his subjects, no constant personal duties for them to perform. He was thousands of miles away. There was no royal court, no royal family, no royal army; there were no castles, no pageants; there was nothing to remind the people of the splendor or power of their king. A sentiment cannot live indefinitely upon nothing but recollection. The king was only a name in America, and the sense of personal loyalty to him steadily decreased.

But the European brought with him also his feeling

of attachment to the soil, and that he transferred immediately to the new soil which nurtured him. Thus, while the memory of devotion to the old king grew weak, the attachment to the new country grew strong. Nevertheless, when the Revolution came there were many Americans with whom the sense of loyalty and duty was still so strong that they would not embrace the patriot cause. For the most part, however, the loyalists were people who had recently come to America, or who had recently been back to England, or had relatives there, or were officers of the king, or were connected with the official class. The great body of the people threw off their personal allegiance without a pang of regret. The crown had long since ceased to occupy a place in their hearts.

The attachment to the soil was necessarily an attachment to that part of it which the American knew, and that was his state rather than the continent. I have shown before that the American of 1815 did not travel; that, in fact, he could not; that he did not write many letters, as it took so long to get an answer and the expense of carriage was considerable; that he married a girl of his vicinity because he knew none other; that his schooling, if he got any, he received in his neighborhood; that he derived little information from the newspapers; in short, that his interests and affections were circumscribed by a very small area. Before 1789 the government did nothing to enlarge his sphere. The Revolution had enlarged it, and for eight years he had seen the glimpse of a broad continental nationality, but he lost sight of it afterward. A union loosely linked together by a government which existed only by sufferance and had no authority or power of its own; a government over which no person presided as chief, which was managed by agents who had no power to act without orders, in some sort a flimsy nation composed of thirteen independent parts any one of which could destroy it at any time by affirmative action or even by no action at all; a government so constituted that it could not have any recognized leaders—such a government was more calculated to stifle continental patriotism than to arouse it. When all aspiration for a continental patriotism seemed about to die, by a feat of statesmanship it was given a reviving stimulant by the new government. This new government operated directly upon the individual and caused him to feel his duty to it; and after a time it awakened his loyalty, too. It had a visible chief to preside over it, and national leaders to direct it and stimulate interest in it. There was the personal element, the absence of which had been one of the weaknesses of the old government. Soon patriotism meant devotion to the United States as well as to one state. By the time of the close of the War of 1812 patriotism was generally understood as being continental as well as sectional. As time went on inventions and discoveries made travel easy and quick, and the communication of intelligence became almost instantaneous, the sections of the country were brought close together, and the continental patriotism increased with great rapidity. After the artificial barrier of slavery which stood in its way had been removed it became a fact of universal acceptance. The people liked to believe that this condition was fostered by the national government, and soon after 1815 those who wished to please them, and who truly represented them, fell into the way of putting the adjective "glorious" in front of the word "Constitution" whenever they spoke of it.

BIBLIOGRAPHY

THE chief manuscript sources of this book are:

The Madison, Jefferson, Andrew Jackson, Thornton, Dolly Madison, Margaret Bayard Smith papers; the House of Representatives collection; the Benjamin Rush lectures; note-books of Dr. Edmund Physick; autograph letters of physicians (Toner collection); Shaker papers; billing-heads of stage lines—all in the Library of Congress. Mr. O. G. Sonneck's work on *Early Opera in America*, now in press, which he was good enough to allow me to see.

The newspapers are:

New Haven Connecticut Journal, Richmond Semi-Weekly Enquirer, Washington Daily National Intelligencer, New York Evening Post, Boston Gazette, Charleston Courier, New York Spectator, Poulson's American Advertiser, Philadelphia Mercantile Advertiser, Norfolk Herald, Niles Weekly Register —all for 1815 or approximate dates.

The other periodicals are:

Boston Weekly Magazine, 1816; *Evening Fireside*, Philadelphia, 1806; *Columbian Telescope*, Alexandria, 1819; *Norfolk Repository*, 1807; *The Hive*, Washington, 1811; *North American Review*, 1815; *Literary Magazine*, Philadelphia, 1807; *Monthly Anthology*, Boston, 1811; *The Polyanthos*, Philadelphia, 1814; *Academic Recreations*, New York, 1815; *The American Review*, Philadelphia, 1812; *The Eye*, Philadelphia, 1808; *Journal of the Times*, Baltimore, 1818; *The Portfolio*, Philadelphia, 1815; *Boston Weekly Messenger*, 1815; *Atheneum*, Boston, 1817; *Analectic Magazine*, Philadelphia, 1815; *American Baptist Magazine*, Boston, 1817;

BIBLIOGRAPHY

The Churchman's Magazine, Elizabeth-Town, N. J., 1814; *The Christian's Magazine*, New York, 1811; *Quarterly Theological Magazine*, Burlington, N. J., 1813; *The Panoplist*, Boston, 1815; *The Guardian*, New Haven, 1819; *The Latter Day Luminary*, Philadelphia, 1818; *The Adviser, or Vermont Evangelical Magazine*, Middlebury, 1815; *The Methodist Magazine*, New York, 1811; *The Christian Disciple*, Boston, 1815; *The Almoner*, Lexington, Ky., 1814; *The Christian Spectator*, New Haven, 1819; *The Alleghany Magazine*, Meadville, Pa., 1816; *The Christian Journal*, New York, 1817; *The Christian Herald*, New York, 1816; *The General Repository*, Cambridge, Mass., 1813.

Of general works:

Autobiography of N. T. Hubbard, New York, 1875; *The Description of the City of New York*, by James Hardie, New York, 1827; *Blunt's Stranger's Guide to the City of New York*, by E. M. Blunt, New York, 1817; *Reminiscences of an Old New Yorker*, by William Alexander Duer, New York, 1867; *Reminiscences of an Octogenarian*, by Charles H. Haswell, New York, 1896; *History of the City of New York*, by Martha J. Lamb, New York, 1877; *New York*, by Theodore Roosevelt, New York, 1891; *Memorial History of the City of New York*, edited by James Grant Wilson, New York, 1892; *Philadelphia, A History of the City and Its People*, by Ellis Paxson Oberholtzer, Philadelphia, 1912; *A Topographical and Historical Description of Boston*, by Charles Shaw, Boston, 1817; *Boston*, by Henry Cabot Lodge, New York, 1891; *Journal of William Maclay*, edited by Edgar S. Maclay, New York, 1890; *Disunion Sentiment in Congress in 1794*, edited by Gaillard Hunt, Washington, 1905; *The Life of John C. Calhoun*, by Gaillard Hunt, Philadelphia, 1907; *The Bladensburg Races* (no place or date, but really New York, 1815); *A Statistical View of the Commerce of the United States*, by Timothy Pitkin, Hartford, 1816; *Treaties and Conventions of the United States*, Washington, 1873; *Charters and Constitutions of the United States*, Washington, 1878; *The U. S. Statutes at Large;* The Laws of the States (the Cession Laws; not the
281

general compiled statutes, which cannot be depended upon for historical purposes); *The Histories of the Religious Denominations* in the American Church History Series, New York; *Complete Works on Criminal Jurisprudence*, by Edward Livingston, New York, 1873.

For general descriptions:

An Historical View of the United States, by E. Mackenzie, New Castle upon Tyne, 1819; *Aperçu des Etats-Unis*, by Louis A. Felix, Baron de Beaujour, Paris, 1814; *Travels in America*, by Thomas Ashe, Newburyport, 1808; *A Summary View of America*, by Isaac Candler, London, 1824; *A Tour in America*, by Richard Parkinson, London, 1805; *A Short System of the Geography of the World*, by Nathaniel Dwight, Hartford, 1795; *Universal Geography*, by Mr. Malte-Brun, Philadelphia, 1827; *An American Universal Geography*, by Jedidiah Morse, Charlestown, 1819; *A New System of Modern Geography*, by Sidney E. Morse, Boston, 1822; *The World As It Is*, by Samuel Perkins, New Haven, 1837; *Elements of Geography*, by Benjamin Workman, Philadelphia, 1816.

For the Madisons, the White House, and the City of Washington:

The Court Circles of the Republic, by Mrs. E. F. Ellet, Hartford, 1869; *The First Forty Years of Washington Society*, by Margaret Bayard Smith, Gaillard Hunt, editor, New York, 1906; *The Life of James Madison*, by Gaillard Hunt, New York, 1902; *Dolly Madison*, by Maud Wilder Goodwin, New York, 1896; *Memoirs and Letters of Dolly Madison*, edited by her grandniece, Boston and New York, 1911.

Concerning women:

Letters on Female Character, by Mrs. Virginia Cary, Hartford, 1831; *The Discussion, or the Character, Education, &c., of Women*, Boston, 1837; *The Lady's Pocket Library*, Philadelphia, 1792; *The Female Friend, or the Duties of Christian Virgins*, by F—— L——, Baltimore, 1809; *Familiar Letters to Females*, by a Lady, Boston, 1834; *Vindication of the Rights of Women*, by Mary Wollstonecraft,

Philadelphia, 1794; *Nuptial Dialogues and Debates*, by Edward Ward, Philadelphia, 1811; *Sketches of the Fair Sex*, by a Friend of the Sex, Gettysburg, 1812; *Epistles on Women*, by Lucy Aiken, Boston, 1810; *Women in All Ages and Nations*, by Thomas L. Nichols, New York, 1854; *The American Lady*, Philadelphia, 1836; *The Excellency of the Female Character Vindicated*, by T. Branagan, Harrisburg, 1828; *Letters to a Young Lady in which the Duties, &c., of Women are Considered*, by Mrs. Jane West, New York, 1806; *The Young Woman's Guide to Excellence*, by William A. Alcott, Boston, 1840; *A Daughter's Own Book, or Practical Hints from a Father to His Daughter*, Philadelphia, 1836; *The Young Lady's Friend*, by a Lady, Boston, 1836; *A Practical Directory for Young Christian Females*, by Harvey Newcomb, Boston, 1833; *Parental Legacies, Consisting of Advice from a Lady of Quality to Her Children*, Boston, 1804; *A Mirror for the Female Sex*, by Mrs. Pilkington, Hartford, 1799.

On dress:

Costumes of Colonial Times, by Alice Morse Earle, New York, 1894; *Two Centuries of Costume in America*, by Alice Morse Earle, New York, 1903; *Modes and Manners of the Nineteenth Century*, by Max von Bohn, New York, 1909; *Costume of British Ladies from the Time of William I. to the Reign of Queen Victoria*, London, 1840; and the contemporaneous fashion-plates and illustrations in books.

On the laboring-men:

The Labor Problem, by William E. Barns, New York, 1886; *The Labor Movement in America*, by Richard T. Ely, New York, 1890; *The Labor Movement*, by George Edwin McNeill, New York, 1887.

On the theater and music:

History of the American Theatre, by William Dunlap, New York, 1832; *Early Concert Life in America*, by O. G. Sonneck, Leipzig, 1907; *The Star-spangled Banner, America, Yankee Doodle, Hail Columbia*, by O. G. Sonneck, Washington, 1909 (the chapter on *The Star-spangled Banner* issued separately in a much revised and enlarged version in 1914);

Plays and Players, by Laurence Hutton, New York, 1875; *The Democratic Songster*, Baltimore, 1794.

On literature:

Salamagundi, or the Whim-whams and Opinions of Launcelot Langstaff, New York, 1807; *Precaution* (James Fenimore Cooper), New York, 1820; *Old-time Schools and School-books*, by Clifton Johnson, New York, 1904; *James Fenimore Cooper*, by Thomas R. Lounsbury, Boston, 1883; *Washington Irving*, by Charles Dudley Warner, Boston, 1882; *Modern Chivalry*, by Hugh Henry Brackenridge, Richmond, 1815; *Contributions to American Educational History*, Vol. I (Herbert B. Adams), Washington, 1889; by Noah Webster: *American Selections of Lessons in Reading and Speaking*, Philadelphia, 1787, and later editions; *The American Spelling-book, Containing an Easy Standard of Pronunciation*, 1790 and other editions; *A Collection of Papers on Political, Literary, and Moral Subjects*, New York, 1843; *An American Dictionary of the English Language*, 1841 and other editions; *Dissertations on the English Language*, 1789; *The Elementary Primer*, 1831; *A Grammatical Institute of the English Language*, Hartford, 1784; *The Columbiad*, by Joel Barlow, London, 1809; *An Elegy on Titus Hosmer*, by Joel Barlow, Hartford (no date); *Noah Webster*, by Emily Ellsworth Fowler Ford and Emily Ellsworth Ford Skeil, New York, 1912 (privately printed); *Four Southern Magazines*, by Edward Reinhold Ropes, Richmond, 1902; *The Southern Literary Messenger*, by Benjamin Blake Minor, Washington, 1905.

On food and cookery:

Miss Beecher's Domestic Receipt Book, New York, 1846; *The Frugal Housewife, or Complete Woman Cook*, by Susannah Carter, New York, 1803; *The Art of Cookery made Plain and Easy*, by Mrs. Glasse, Alexandria, 1805; *The Art of Invigorating and Prolonging Life*, by the author of the *Cook's Oracle*, Philadelphia, 1823; *Apician Morsels*, by Dick Humbugius Secundus, New York, 1829; *The Young Housekeeper, or Thoughts on Food and Cookery*, by William A. Alcott, Boston, 1838; *Old Cookery Books and*

BIBLIOGRAPHY

Ancient Cuisine, by W. Carew-Hazlitt, New York, 1886; *The Housekeeper's Book*, by a Lady, Philadelphia, 1837; *Physiologie du Gout*, by Brillat-Savarin, Paris; *A History of the Oyster*, by T. C. Eyton, London, 1858; *Investigations on the Nutrition of Man in the United States*, by C. F. Langworthy and R. D. Milner, Washington, 1904; *The House Servant's Directory*, by Robert Roberts, Boston, 1828; *The Cook's Own Book*, by a Boston Housekeeper, Boston, 1837; *A New System of Domestic Cookery*, by a Lady, New York, 1817; *The Kentucky Housewife*, by Mrs. Lettice Bryan, Cincinnati, 1841; *The Experienced American Housekeeper*, Hartford, 1833; *A Short Treatise on the Habits and Character of the Oyster*, by John Gardener, Opener General at Le Count's United States Refectory, corner Fifth and Chestnut Streets, Philadelphia, 1837; *The Influence of Atmosphere on Human Health*, by Robley Dunglison, M.D., Philadelphia, 1835; "Ancient American Bread," article by Henry Chapman Mercer, 1894 (reprint); *The Food of Certain American Indians*, by Lucien Carr, Worcester, 1895 (American Antiquarian Society's Proceedings); *The New Mirror for Travellers*, by an Amateur (James Kirke Paulding), New York, 1828.

On communities:

Plan for a Free Community upon the Coast of Africa, London, 1789; *History of American Socialisms*, by John Humphrey Noyes, Philadelphia, 1870; *American Communities*, by William Alfred Hinds, Oneida, 1878; Second Edition, Chicago, 1908; *History of the Zoar Society*, by E. O. Randall, Columbus, 1900; *The Harmony Society*, by John Archibald Bole, Ph.D., Philadelphia, 1904; *The Communistic Societies of the United States*, by Charles Nordhoff, New York, 1875; *History of the Great American Fortunes*, by Gustavus Myers, Vol. I, Chicago, 1910; *Industrial History of the United States*, by Katharine Aman, Ph.D., New York, 1910; *The Economic History of the United States*, by Ernest Ludlow Bogart, Ph.D., New York, 1912; *Commercial Directory*, Philadelphia, 1823; *Robert Owen*, by Frank Podmore, London, 1906; *An Essay on*

Commonwealths, New York, 1822 (containing the constitution of the New York Society for Promoting Communities).

On sport, crimes, and vices:

The South Carolina Jockey Club, by John B. Irving, Charleston, 1857; *Game Fowls*, by J. W. Cooper, Media, Pa., 1859; *The Game Fowl, Its Origin and History*, by R. A. McIntyre, 1906; *History of the Temperance Reformation*, by Lebbens Armstrong, New York, 1853; *A Voice from the Washingtonian Home*, by David Harrison, Jr., Boston, 1860; *History of the First Inebriate Asylum*, by its Founder (J. Edward Turner), New York, 1888; *Political Truth* (Gaming Laws in Virginia), by Virginius, Richmond (no date); *Memoirs of Robert Bailey*, Richmond, 1822; *The Trail of Blood, Record of Crime*, New York, 1860; *United States Criminal History*, by P. R. Hamblin, Fayetteville, New York, 1836; *Lives of the Felons*, New York, 1846; *Lynch Law*, by James Elbert Cutler, New York, 1905; *The Record of Crimes in the United States*, Buffalo, 1833; *Murder in All Ages*, by Matthew Worth Pinkerton, Chicago, 1898; *The Exposition, Remonstrance, and Protest of Don Vincente Pazos*, Philadelphia, 1818; *Pirates' Own Book*, Philadelphia, 1841; *Narrative of a Voyage to the Spanish Main in the Ship "Two Friends,"* London, 1819; *The Sabbath in Puritan New England*, by Alice Morse Earle, New York, 1891; *Sunday Legislation*, by Abram Herbert Lewis, New York, 1902; *Proceedings of the Middlesex Convention*, Andover, 1814· *Sunday Laws*, by George E. Harris, Rochester, 1892; *American State Papers bearing on Sunday Legislation*, William Addison Blakely, editor, New York and Washington, 1890; *The American Turf*, New York, 1898.

On charitable institutions, hospitals, asylums, poorhouses, prisons:

Report of Secretary of State of New York, Returns of County Superintendents of the Poor, Albany, 1833; *Report of Delegate from Benevolent Societies of Boston*, Boston, 1834; *Report of the Examination of Poor-houses, Jails, &c., in the State of New York*, by Samuel Chipman, Albany, 1835; *Statement of the Provision for the Poor*, by Nessau W.

BIBLIOGRAPHY

Senior, London, 1835; *Remarks on Prisons and Prison Discipline*, from the *Christian Examiner*, Boston, 1826; *Directory of the Washington Benevolent Society*, Boston, 1813; *Charities in the District of Columbia* (Part III, historical), Washington, 1898; *History of Poor Relief Legislation in Pennsylvania*, by William Clinton Heffner, Cleona, Pa., 1913; *Private Charitable Institutions of the City of New York*, New York, 1904; *Report of William Crawford on the Penitentiaries of the United States*, 1834 (Parliamentary Report); *Penal and Charitable Institutions of Pennsylvania*, Harrisburg, 1897; *Thoughts on Penitentiaries and Prison Discipline*, by Mathew Carey, Philadelphia, 1831; *The Philanthropist*, by a Pennsylvanian, Philadelphia, 1813; *Report on the Penitentiary System in the United States*, New York, 1822; *Remarks on Prisons and Prison Discipline in the United States*, by D. L. Dix, Philadelphia, 1845; *Penal and Reformatory Institutions* (Russell Sage Foundation), Charles Richmond Henderson, editor, New York, 1910; *Hospitals, Their History, Organization, and Construction*, by W. Gill Wylie, New York, 1877; *The Charities of New York*, by Henry J. Cammann and Hugh N. Camp, New York, 1868; *American Charities*, by Amos G. Warner, New York, 1894 and 1908; *History of Philadelphia Almshouses and Hospitals*, by Charles Lawrence, Philadelphia, 1905; *Appeal to the Wealthy of the Land*, by Mathew Carey, Philadelphia, 1833; *The Overseers of the Poor of the City of Boston to Their Constituents*, Boston, 1822; *An Account of Bellevue Hospital*, Robert J. Carlisle, editor, New York, 1893; *Account of the Friends Asylum*, Philadelphia, 1814; *Memorial Soliciting a State Hospital for the Insane*, submitted to the legislature of Pennsylvania by Dorothea Lynde Dix, Philadelphia, 1845; *History of the Pennsylvania Hospital*, by Thomas G. Morton and Frank Woodbury, Philadelphia, 1895.

Miscellaneous:

Bioren's Pennsylvania Pocket Remembrancer, Philadelphia, 1816; *American Almanac*, Germantown, 1816; *The Farmer's Almanac*, Boston, 1831; *The New Haven Almanac*,

LIFE IN AMERICA ONE HUNDRED YEARS AGO

New Haven, 1825; *The Vermont Register and Almanac,*
Burlington, 1818; *Hagerstown Town and Country Almanac,*
Hagerstown, 1836; *Sam Slick of Slickville,* by Thomas C.
Haliburton, New York, 1878; *Old Town Folks,* by Mrs.
Harriet Beecher Stowe, Boston, 1869; *History of Yellow
Fever,* by George Augustin, New Orleans, 1909; *Century of
American Medicine,* New York, 1876; *A Treatise on Febrile
Diseases,* by A. P. Wilson, Philadelphia, 1816; *Introductory Discourse,* by David Hosack, New York, 1813;
Lectures, by David Hosack, Philadelphia, 1838; *Essays
on Various Subjects of Medical Science,* by David Hosack,
New York, 1824; *The American Rush - Light,* by Peter
Porcupine (William Cobbett), London, 1800; *Old Family
Letters Copied for Edward Biddle,* Philadelphia, 1892. The
following by Benjamin Rush: *An Account of the Causes
of Longevity,* Philadelphia, 1793; *Essays,* Philadelphia,
1806; *An Enquiry into the Effects of Ardent Spirits upon
the Human Body and Mind,* New York, 1811; *Medical
Enquiries and Observations,* Philadelphia, 1805; *Observations on the Origin of Malignant, Bilious or Yellow Fever
in Philadelphia,* Philadelphia, 1799.

INDEX

A

Actors and audiences, 88–89.
Adams, John, surviving signer, 8; on titles, 58; candidate for presidency, 74; appoints day of fasting, 115; diminished the power of the presidency, 260.
Adams, Mrs. John, 60.
Adultery, punishments for, 84.
Albany, travel to, 51.
Alien and Sedition Laws, 252.
Allen, Lieut. William H., U.S.N., 161.
Allston, Washington, portrait-painter, 85.
Amelia Island, headquarters for slave-smugglers, 164.
American Academy of Fine Arts, organized, 85.
American Colonization Society, 236–238.
American Whig Society, 261.
Analectic, The, 146.
Annapolis, society in, 71.
Anti-rent war, 231.
Appleton, James, report on temperance to Maine legislature, 174.
Apprentice system, 100.
Armstrong, John, Secretary of War, 9.
Art in America, 85.
Ashe, Thomas, writings on America, 28.
Astor, John Jacob, 230.
Augusta, mail route to, 52.
Aury, Louis de, Governor of Texas, 163–164.

B

Bache, Miss, granddaughter of Franklin, 89.
Bailey, "Major" Robert, gambler, 182.
Baker, Anthony St. John, 1.
Baltimore, population, 22; iron-works, 24; appearance of, 30; society in, 71; French opera in, 97; "Washingtonian movement" in, 174; yellow-fever epidemics, 208.
Banking, 231.
Baptists, disapproval of theater, 86; popularity of, 121.
Barbour, Senator James, 45.
Barker, James N., playwright, 92.
Barlow, Joel, of Connecticut, 114; author of "The Columbiad," 142–143.
Beaujour, Felix de, opinion of America, 30.
Bell Tavern, Richmond, 52.
Bellevue Hospital, New York, 197.
Benton, Senator Thomas H., 257.
Bigelow, Dr. Jacob, 205.
Billings, William, composer, 96.
Bingham, William, richest man in America, 230; enters Senate, 257.
Bladensburg, defeat at, 4.
Bladensburg Races, The, 268.
Blasphemy, laws against, 186.
Books in farm-houses, 104–105.
Boston, population, 22; glass-works, 24; appearance of, 30; stage at, 51; society of, 69–70; theaters, 87, 90; music in, 96; benevolent associations, 196–197.
Brashear, Dr. Walter, 213.

INDEX

D

Dallas, Alexander H., Secretary of the Treasury, 9.

Dallas, George M., U. S. Attorney at Philadelphia, 166.

Darley, Mr. and Mrs., actors, 89.

Dartmouth College founded, 128.

Deaf and dumb, schools for, 199.

Debts and debtors, 169–170.

Declaration of Independence, signers of, 8.

Delaware Indians, 21.

Delaware, slaves in, 21, 39; divorce in, 83; religious freedom in, 118; legal punishments in, 159; opposed Virginia and Kentucky Resolutions, 255.

Detroit, surrender at, 4.

Dickinson, Charles, 154.

District of Columbia, 21.

Divinity schools, 129–130.

Divorce in U. S., 83.

Doctors, 106; and medical treatment, 201–214.

Dow, Neal, law of, 174.

Dress, of women, 61; of men, 63.

Drinking, 32, 104, 171–175, 225–227.

Dueling, 154, 157.

Dunlap, William, playwright, 92.

Dutch in the U. S., 19–20, 32, 38.

E

Education, 124–138.

Elizabethtown, stage to, 50.

Ellery, William, signer, 8.

Ellsworth, Oliver, Senator, 250–251, 256; Chief Justice, 254.

Emerson, Rev. Joseph, girls' seminary of, 134.

England, American interest in and sympathy with, 10–12.

England, peace with United States, 4–5.

English in America, 32.

Entertainments and sports on farms, 103–104.

Episcopal Church lost state support, 119; new energy of, 121–122.

Episcopalians and the theater, 86.

Eppes, Mrs., 60.

Eustis, William, Secretary of War, 9.

Eye, The, published at Philadelphia, 144.

F

Factories and mills, 98–99.

Farm life, 103–104.

Federal Street Theater, Boston, 87.

Federalists, the, and Treaty of Ghent, 6.

Female Friend, The, 175.

Fitch, John, steamboat of, 56.

Floridas, 16–17.

Floyd, William, signer, 8.

Food, 216–223.

Foreign opinion of the United States, 27–33.

France, American interest in, 11–12.

Franklin, Benjamin, urges higher education, 124; on the folly of drinking, 173; investigated Mesmer, 214; on patriotism, 273.

Franklin House, Washington, 52.

French in the United States, 19–20.

Fulton, Robert, steamboat of, 56.

G

Gaillard, John, slaveholder, 43.

Gallatin, Albert, Secretary of Treasury, 9.

Gallaudet, Thomas H., 199.

Galveston Island, 163–164.

Gambling, 175–183.

Gaston, William, of North Carolina, 45.

Gehot, Joseph, musician, 97.

Genêt, Citizen, 92.

Georgetown College, opening of, 128.

Georgetown, Semmes Tavern at, 52; society in, 65.

Georgia, value of land in, 23; characteristics of people, 36; divorce in, 83; religious freedom in, 118; Methodists in, 121; criminal code of, 158.

291

INDEX

cination, 208; gives dinner to Alexander Hamilton, 223; opposition to large governmental powers, 260; friend of Madison, 266.

Jews, small number of, in United States, 123.

Jones, William, Secretary of the Navy, 9.

Joor, William, playwright, 92.

Journal of the Times, The, published at Baltimore, 144.

K

Kentucky, admission to Union, 17; population, 20; slaves, 21; characteristics of people, 38; divorce in, 83; religious freedom in, 118; Methodists in, 121; Shakers in, 239.

Key, Francis Scott, composer of "Star-spangled Banner," 94.

King, Rufus, Senator, 8–9, 250–251, 256.

King's Chapel in Boston, 96.

King's College (Columbia University) founded, 128.

Kissam, Dr. Richard S., 212.

L

Labor, conditions of, 98–103.

Lafitte, Jean, Pierre, and Dominique, outlaws, 162.

Land, value of, 23.

Languages used, 20.

Latrobe, Benjamin H., furnishes White House, 60.

Law, Andrew, composer, 96.

Law-schools, 130–131.

Law, Thomas, married Elizabeth Custis, 83.

Lear, Tobias, 201.

Lee, Ann, founder of Shakers, 239.

Lee, Richard Henry, Senator, 256.

Literary Magazine, The, 146.

Literary taste, 146–147.

Livingston, Edward, writer on prison reform, 191, 193; on poor relief, 195.

Livingston, Elizabeth Stevens, 76.

Livingston, Robert R., of Clermont, 76.

Local jealousies and misunderstandings, 34.

Louisiana, British evacuation of, 3; objections to acquiring, 15; admission, 17, 252; French population of, 19–20, 36; divorce laws in, 83; religious freedom in, 118; criminal code of, 159, 193.

Lowndes, Caleb, Quaker writer, 191.

Lowndes, William, 10; slaveholder, 43–45.

Lowndes, Mrs., 45.

M

McDonough, Commodore, toast to, 225.

McDowell, Dr. Ephraim, 204, 212.

Macaulay on parties, 11.

MacGregor, Gregor, freebooter, 163–164.

Mackenzie's opinions of Americans, 32.

Maclay, William, on titles, 58.

Macon, Nathaniel, of North Carolina, 45.

Madison, James, receives treaty, 3, 7; retirement from office, 9; slaveholder, 43; praised Portuguese minister, 64; inaugural suit of, 76; issues proclamation of thanks, 115; offers amendment to Virginia Bill of Rights, 116; owned interest in a racehorse, 177; Washington's criticism of, 201; listened to proposal to dissolve the Union, 251; preserved balance of power, 260; long public service, 261–262; scholarship, 263; break with Hamilton, 264; Clay's opinion of, 265; hatred of war, 266; appearance of, 267; private life, 269.

Madison, Mrs. Dolly, receives news of peace, 7–8; head of society, 60; clothes described, 61; exerted no political in-

293

INDEX

Noah, Mordecai M., journalist and playwright, 92.
Norfolk, appearance of, 30; yellow fever in, 208.
North American Review, 146.
North Carolina, population of, 20; value of land in, 23; characteristics of, 35–37; early marriages in, 77; excluded non-Christians from office, 118; Methodists in, 121; legal punishments in, 159; discusses disunion, 252.
Norwich University, 132.

O

"Octagon House" in Washington, 4.
Ohio, 17; admission to Union, 17; population, 20; characteristics of people, 38; Shakers in, 239.
Oldmixon, Mrs., actress, 89.
O'Neil's Tavern, Washington, 52.
Opera, 97.
Orchestra, 89.
Outlaws, 165.
Owen, Robert, 245–246.

P

Paine, Robert Treat, signer, 87.
Paine, Thomas, American writer, 87.
Paine, Tom, English writer, influence of writings in United States, 118–119.
Panama Canal proposed, 25.
Parkinson's writings on America, 28.
Parties, origin, 11.
Partridge, Capt. Alden, academy of, 132–133.
Paterson, Wm., in Senate, 256.
Patriotism, 273–279.
Patterson, Commander Daniel T., U.S.N., 162.
Paulding, James Kirke, author, 145.
Peace, news of, 2.
Peales, the, portrait-painters, 85.
Penn, William, does away with death-penalty, 189.

Pennsylvania, population, 19–20; manufactories, 24; characteristics of people, 38; abolished slavery, 39; labor in, 101; denies rights to atheists, 118; poor-law of, 195–196; hospital for the insane, 198; other hospitals, 200.
Pennsylvania Academy of Fine Arts, organized, 85.
Pennsylvania, University of, 129.
Periodicals, 144–146.
Perth Amboy, steamboat line to, 51.
Philadelphia, population of, 22; appearance, 30; trade, 38; stage line, 49; society, 68; orchestra and theater, 89–90; Jews in, 123; first almshouse, 196; Female Charitable Society, 197; doctors, 203; yellow fever in, 208–209.
Phile, Philip, composer, 94.
Physick, Dr. Philip S., 203, 213.
Piano-makers, 96.
Pickering, Timothy, of Massachusetts, 8.
Pinckney, Charles, influence of, 9.
Pinkney, William, Attorney-General, 9.
Piracy and pirates, 160–165.
Pise, Charles C., chaplain of Senate, 115.
Placide, actor-manager's benefit, 90–91.
Population of United States, 19; of different states, 20.
Porter, Commodore David, 161.
Portfolio, The, 146.
Postage, cost of, 54.
Post-roads, 52.
Poverty and methods of relief, 194–200.
Presbyterians, disapprobation of the theater, 86; growth of church, 122.
President, the, 259, 272.
Prices of food, 101–102.
Princeton College, 55.
Princeton University, 128–129.
Prisons, 188–193.

295

INDEX

Swedes in United States, 20.
Swiss in United States, 20.

T

Taxes, 101.
Tayloe, Col. John, places house at disposal of President Madison, 4.
Taylor, John, Senator, 250–251.
Teachers' salaries, 136.
Temperance societies, first, 173.
Tennessee, admission, 17; slave population, 21; characteristics of people, 38; restriction of religious freedom in, 118; Methodists in, 121.
Theater, the, in United States, 86–92.
Thorndike, Israel, Boston shipper, 230.
Thornton, William, and negro colonization, 234–235.
Thornton, Dr. William, architect, 4, 85; steamboat, 56; organized dancing assembly, 67.
Tingey, Capt. Thomas, organized dancing assembly, 67.
Titles, 58–59.
Toasts, 225–226.
Tobacco, use of, 32.
Transportation, 48–57.
Travel, difficulties, 48; expense of, 52–54.
Treaty of peace, arrival of, 1; terms of, 5.
Trenton, stage to, 49.
Trumbull, John, painter, 85.

U

Unitarianism, beginnings of, 122.
United States, boundaries of, in 1783, 15–16; divisions, 17; population, 19–22.

V

Value of land, 23.
Van Buren, Martin, in Senate, 257.
Van Ness, John Peter, organized dancing assemblies, 67.

Vermont, admission to Union, 17; favored revealed religion, 117.
Vice, 171–187.
Vining, John, in Senate, 257.
Virginia, population, 20–21; value of land in, 23; characteristics of people, 35; influence of Capital on, 48–49; punishments in, 84; religious freedom in, 118; religious revivals in, 120; Methodists in, 121; colleges in, 127; crimes in, 157; racing interests, 177; discusses disunion, 252.
Virginia and Kentucky Resolutions, 255.
Virginia Bill of Rights, the, 116.
Virginia, University of, 127, 129.

W

Waddell, Rev. Moses, academy of, 132.
Wages, 100–101.
War of 1812, causes of, 4.
Warren, Dr. John Collins, 204.
Warville, Brissot de, interested in negro colonization, 235.
Washington, reception of news of Treaty of Ghent, 3–7; appearance of, 30; stage at, 51–52; social life of, 64–67; servants in, 102; horse-racing at, 179; charitable institutions, 197–198.
Washington, Bushrod, 236.
Washington, George, proclamation of, 114; Farewell Address, 116; illness of, 201; artificial teeth, 212.
Washington and Lee University, 127.
Waterhouse, Dr. Benjamin, 207.
Waverley novels, 125.
Webster, Daniel, in Senate, 257.
Webster, Noah, educational campaign of, 139–142.
Weekly Magazine, The, Boston, 144–145.
Welsh in United States, 20.
White House, society in, 60.
Whitlock, Mrs., actress, 89.
Whitman, Walt, on slavery, 41.

297

THE END